Wisconsin
BED & BREAKFAST
Cookbook

Largest Collection of Recipes Ever from the Wisconsin Bed & Breakfast Association

trails books
AN IMPRINT OF BOWER HOUSE
DENVER

 Bower House books may be purchased with bulk discounts for educational, business, or sales promotional use. For information, contact Bower House P.O. Box 7459 Denver, CO 80207 or visit BowerHouseBooks.com.

Cover and text design: Rebecca Finkel
Composition: Kari Luraas
Editor: Mira Perrizo

Front Cover Photos: Port Washington Inn; fruit/French toast from Canyon Road Inn; Rum Baba from Old Rittenhouse Inn
Back Cover Photos: Innkeeper Chef Natalie Neddersen of Eagle Harbor Inn; Innkeeper Chef Ben Bruno of the St. Croix River Inn (photos by Paramount Pixels)

The Bed & Breakfast Cookbook Series was originated by Carol Faino and Doreen Hazledine of Peppermint Press in Denver, CO in 1999.

Library of Congress Cataloging-in-Publication Data Available Upon Request

ISBN 978-1-889593-29-6

10 9 8 7 6 5 4 3 2

Contents

Hello Wisconsin!

We've been called America's Dairyland, the Badger State, Sconnie Nation and, of course, the Cheese State. Travelers have been invited to "escape to Wisconsin," to "stay just a little bit longer" and reminded "you're among friends."

We're known for our environmental ethic and family farming heritage. We produce more cranberries than any state in the nation and our Door County peninsula is famous for cherries. Maple syruping is big here as are u-pick orchards. And independent butcher shops abound offering dozens of varieties of artisan brats.

Visit WisconsinBandB.com to map out a tour based on these "foodie" finds:

Artisan Cheese Map
Wisconsin's artisan cheesemakers are leading a resurgence of handmade, small-batch specialty cheeses, reintroducing recipes that many believed were lost in the United States.

Micro-Brewery Map
Truth be told, long before Wisconsin became America's Dairyland, we were a beer state, thanks to the brewing know-how of German immigrants. Modern-day micro-breweries still deliver "*Gemütlichkeit*" in a big way.

Winery Map
Yes, that's right, grape-growing and wineries in Wisconsin. Many of the vineyards here are family-owned, with the wines produced in small batches from traditional or hybrid varietals. Fun fact: The Wollersheim Winery in Prairie du Sac was named Winery of the Year at the 2012 San Diego International Wine Competition. Take that, Napa Valley!

While other places may have these same goodies, we happen to think they taste better here in Wisconsin.

Cookies, yes. Cookie-cutter, never. While you're a guest of our B&Bs, expect tips on local finds from our innkeepers. Take a page from their book. Eat and sleep the local flavor.

P.S. To burn off the calories, bike, golf, or go birding. Handy statewide maps covering each of these activities may also be accessed at WisconsinBandB.com.

U.S. Measurement Equivalents

pinch/dash	1/16 teaspoon
½ teaspoon	30 drops
1 teaspoon	1/3 tablespoon
3 teaspoons	1 tablespoon
½ tablespoon	1½ teaspoons
1 tablespoon	3 teaspoons; ½ fluid ounce
2 tablespoons	1/8 cup; 1 fluid ounce
3 tablespoons	1½ fluid ounces; 1 jigger
jigger	1½ fluid ounces; 3 tablespoons
4 tablespoons	¼ cup; 2 fluid ounces
5 1/3 tablespoons	1/3 cup; 5 tablespoons + 1 teaspoon
8 tablespoons	½ cup; 4 fluid ounces
10 2/3 tablespoons	2/3 cup; 10 tablespoons + 2 teaspoons
12 tablespoons	¾ cup; 6 fluid ounces
16 tablespoons	1 cup; 8 fluid ounces; ½ pint
1/8 cup	2 tablespoons; 1 fluid ounce
¼ cup	4 tablespoons; 2 fluid ounces
1/3 cup	5 tablespoons + 1 teaspoon
3/8 cup	¼ cup + 2 tablespoons
½ cup	8 tablespoons; 4 fluid ounces
2/3 cup	10 tablespoons + 2 teaspoons
5/8 cup	½ cup + 2 tablespoons
¾ cup	12 tablespoons; 6 fluid ounces
7/8 cup	¾ cup + 2 tablespoons
1 cup	16 tablespoons; ½ pint; 8 fluid ounces
2 cups	1 pint; 16 fluid ounces
3 cups	1½ pints; 24 fluid ounces
4 cups	1 quart; 32 fluid ounces
8 cups	2 quarts; 64 fluid ounces
1 pint	2 cups; 16 fluid ounces
2 pints	1 quart; 32 fluid ounces
1 quart	2 pints; 4 cups; 32 fluid ounces
4 quarts	1 gallon; 8 pints
1 gallon	4 quarts; 8 pints; 16 cups; 128 fluid ounces
8 quarts	1 peck
4 pecks	1 bushel

1	Appleton	Franklin Street Inn
2	Baileys Harbor	Inn at Windmill Farm
3	Baraboo	Pinehaven B&B
4	Bayfield	Artesian House, Pinehurst Inn Old Rittenhouse Inn
5	Belleville	Cameo Rose Victorian Country Inn
6	Blue River	Cream Pitcher B&B
7	Burlington	Hillcrest Inn & Carriage House
8	Cambridge	Lake Ripley Lodge B&B, Oscar H. Hanson House B&B
9	Camp Douglas	Sunnyfield Farm B&B
10	Cedarburg	Washington House Inn
11	Cross Plains	Enchanted Valley B&B
12	DePere	Sabamba Alpaca Ranch and B&B
13	Eagle	Eagle Centre House B&B
14	Eagle River	Inn at Pinewood, Inc.
15	Eau Claire	Otter Creek Inn
16	Egg Harbor	Bay Point Inn, Door County Lighthouse Inn
17	Elkhart Lake	Jay Lee Inn
18	Elkhorn	Ye Olde Manor House
19	Ephraim	Eagle Harbor Inn
20	Fond du Lac	Dobranoc Inn
21	Fort Atkinson	Lamp Post Inn
22	Green Lake	Angel Inn McConnell Inn Miller's Daughter B&B
23	Hartford	Westphal Mansion B&B
24	Hayward	Forest Moon B&B
25	Horicon	Honeybee Inn B&B
26	Hudson	Escape by the Lake Phipps Inn
27	Hustler	Fountain Chateau B&B
28	La Crosse	Four Gables B&B
29	Lake Geneva	Lazy Cloud B&B
30	Lake Mills	Fargo Mansion Inn Sweet Autumn Inn
31	Lodi	Victorian Dreams B&B
32	Madison	Annie's B&B Speckled Hen Inn Token Creek Eco-Inn
33	Manawa	Lindsay House B&B
34	Manitowoc	Westport B&B
35	Marinette	Riverside Manor B&B

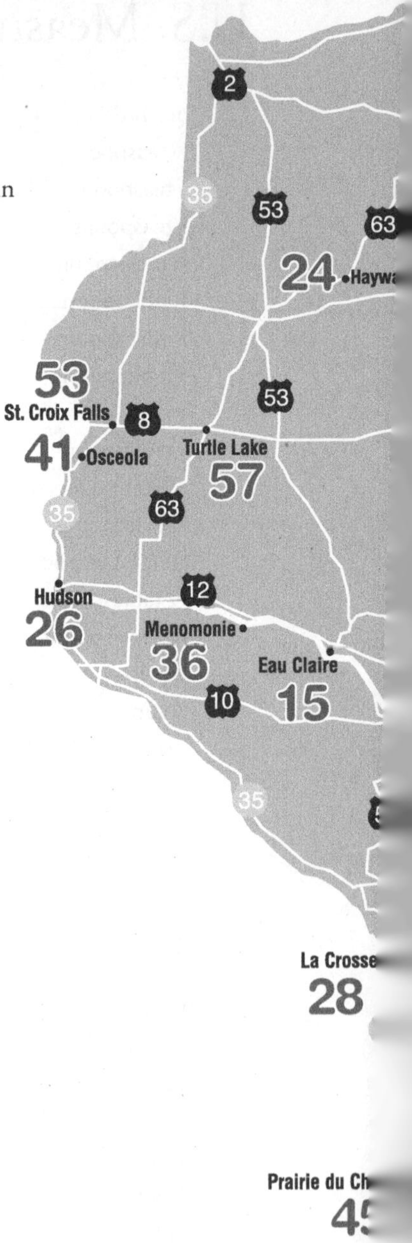

seek the unique

WisconsinInBandB.com

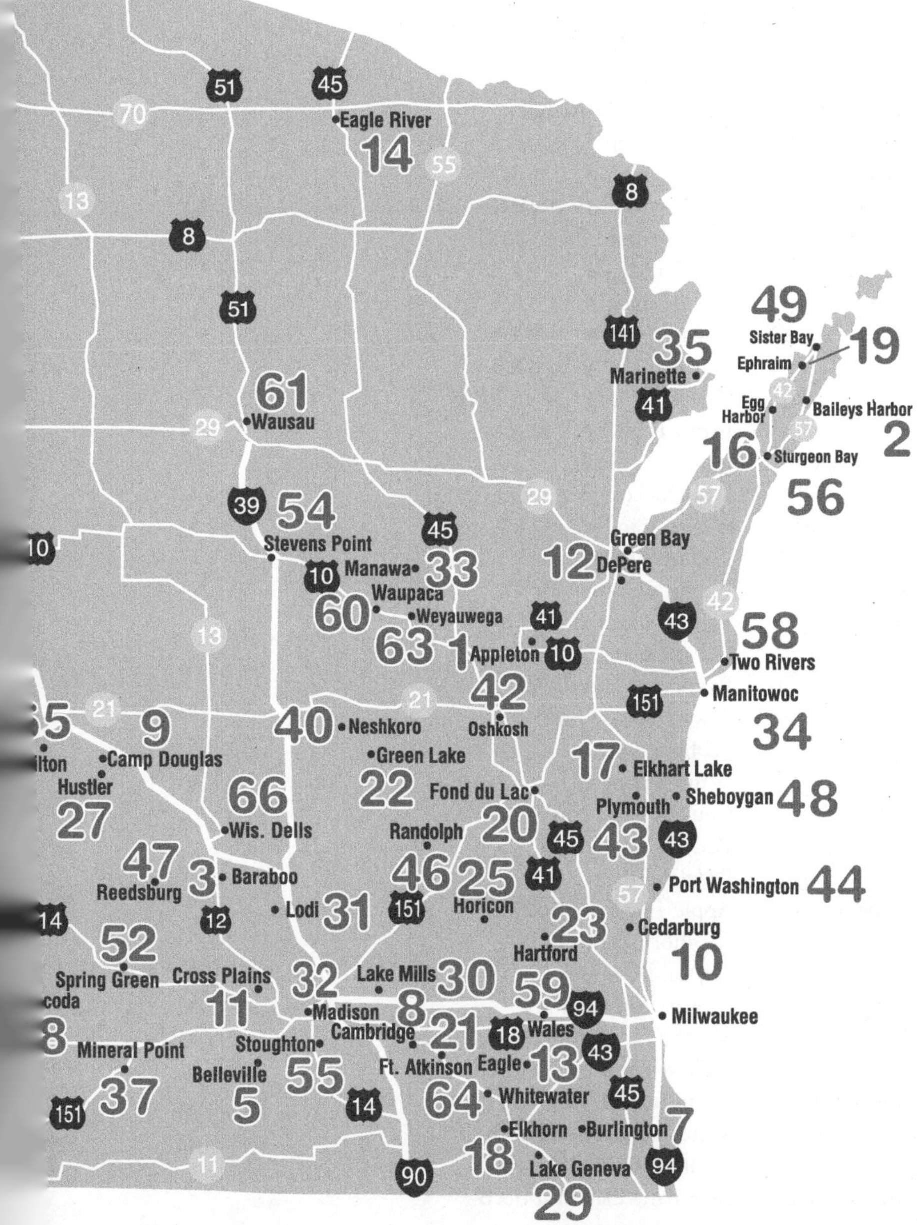

36	Menomonie	Country Comfort
37	Mineral Point	Brewery Creek Inn & Brewpub
38	Muscoda	Victorian Rose B&B
39	Neillsville	O'Neill Manor
		Tufts' Mansion
40	Neshkoro	Riverview B&B
41	Osceola	St. Croix River Inn
42	Oshkosh	Brayton B&B
43	Plymouth	Inn on Hillwind
44	Port Washington	Port Washington Inn
45	Prairie du Chien	Neumann House B&B
46	Randolph	Heaven Scent B&B
47	Reedsburg	Parkview B&B
		Pine Grove Park B&B
48	Sheboygan	Lake Orchard Farm B&B
49	Sister Bay	Inn On Maple
		Woodenheart Inn
50	Soldiers Grove	Inn at Lonesome Hollow
51	Sparta	Franklin Victorian B&B
		Grapevine Log Cabins B&B
		Justin Trails B&B Resort
52	Spring Green	Hill Street B&B
53	St. Croix Falls	Wissahickon Farms Country Inn
54	Stevens Point	A Victorian Swan On Water
		Dreams of Yesteryear
55	Stoughton	Altemus Corners B&B
56	Sturgeon Bay	Black Walnut Guest House
		Garden Gate B&B
		Reynolds House B&B
		Sawyer House B&B
		Scofield House
		White Lace Inn
57	Turtle Lake	Canyon Road Inn
58	Two Rivers	Red Forest B&B
59	Wales	Pedal'rs Inn
60	Waupaca	Apple Tree Lane B&B
		Cleghorn B&B
		Crystal River Inn
61	Wausau	Stewart Inn
62	Westby	Westby House Inn & Restaurant
63	Weyauwega	Willow Pond B,B & Events
64	Whitewater	Hamilton House B&B
		Victoria On Main B&B
65	Wilton	Amil's Inn B&B
66	Wisconsin Dells	Bowman's Oak Hill B&B

Wisconsin
BED & BREAKFAST

Establishments and their Signature Recipes

A Victorian Swan on Water

INNKEEPER Joan Ouellette
ADDRESS 1716 Water Street, Stevens Point, WI 54481
TELEPHONE (715) 345-0595 | (800) 454-9886
CONTACT victorianswan@charter.net | www.victorianswan.com
FEATURES 4 Rooms | Children age 3 and older welcome | Pet-free environment

"Last night we were two weary travelers and today we are surrounded by elegance, rested, pampered, and delighted in your warm companionship. Thanks for your most memorable hospitality."—Guest

A Victorian gem of a bed and breakfast welcomes you to Central Wisconsin where green means hiking and biking on the beautiful Green Circle Trail, or kayaking down the Plover or Wisconsin Rivers. Stroll our historic Main Street or walk along the Wisconsin River. Come back to a whirlpool, sauna, or massage, or just sit in front of a fireplace and read.

Our mission since 1986 has always been to provide our guests with a setting that is clean, comfortable, and beautiful, a setting with good food and great conversation.

Basic Egg Foo Yung

Yield: 5 servings

"This dish is a wonderful vehicle for using leftovers. I took a Chinese cooking class in the 1980s and Egg Foo Yung became one of our favorite supper dishes. I found that besides being easy, adding different vegetables, meats, or gravy could add variety to our mealtime."—Innkeeper

- ¼ cup diced or sliced green onions
- ½ cup fresh bean sprouts
- ¼ cup cooked meat (shrimp, beef, chicken, or pork)
- ½ tsp soy sauce
- Salt and pepper, to taste
- 2 extra large eggs
- canola cooking oil
- ½ tsp sugar
- ¼ tsp sesame oil (optional)

Brown Sauce

- 1 cup chicken broth
- 1 Tbsp cornstarch
- 2 Tbsp water
- ¼ tsp salt
- Pepper, to taste
- 2 tsp soy sauce
- 1 tsp sherry or vermouth

Before you begin, make sure that all of your vegetables are drained and dry. Combine all of the ingredients, except the eggs and oil, together in a bowl. Stir in the eggs but do not beat. Heat about ½-inch of oil in a fry pan or wok. Pour about ¼ cup of the mixture into the hot oil and let cook until slightly brown. Turn the egg patty over and cook for about 2 minutes longer. Remove from the pan and keep warm until all the patties are made. Serve hot over rice with brown sauce or gravy.

For the sauce: Simmer the chicken broth in a small kettle. Mix together the water and cornstarch. Combine the remaining ingredients and add, with cornstarch mixture, to the broth. Stir until it bubbles and is clear.

Altemus Corners B&B

INNKEEPER **Marge Stokstad**
ADDRESS **1345 Tower Drive, Stoughton, WI 53589**
TELEPHONE **(608) 695-0693**
CONTACT **margestokstad@hotmail.com | www.altemuscorners.com**
FEATURES **5 Rooms; Private & shared baths | Children age 12 and older welcome | Pet-free environment**

Altemus Corners B&B, located in Stoughton, Wisconsin—only 25 minutes from beautiful Madison—makes a perfect weekend getaway any time of year. This old-fashioned, 1870s farm home, situated in the heart of farm country, has been completely refurbished but still features the original woodwork, layout, and ambiance. Period antiques and handmade Victorian lampshades accent every room, and fresh flowers from the gardens can be found throughout the house.

The southern-style front porch with gazebo is an excellent place to eat breakfast and relax on warm summer days. A full breakfast is served each morning and dishes include all homemade quiche, tarts, Danish Kringle, whole grain waffles and pancakes, fruits, yogurt, and beverages. Desserts and alcohol-free beverages are served in the evening.

French Fruit Tart

Yield: 8–10 servings

Fresh fruit, such as strawberries, blueberries, pineapple, kiwi, citrus and raspberries

For Pastry:
- 1½ cups flour
- ½ tsp salt
- 1 Tbsp sugar
- 9 Tbsp butter, cut into small pieces
- 3–4 Tbsp ice water

Preheat oven to 400°F. Sift dry ingredients into a bowl. Cut (or rub with hands) butter into flour mixture until it resembles coarse crumbs. Sprinkle in ice water. Work dough in bowl until it just holds together. Form into a ball, wrap in plastic and refrigerate 30 minutes.

Roll out pastry dough to fit a 9-inch tart pan, taking care not to stretch the dough. Roll between waxed paper for ease. Roll the rolling pin across the top of tart pan to cut off excess pastry. Prick the bottom of pastry all over with a fork. Cover dough with foil and fill with dried beans. Bake for 15 minutes, then remove foil and beans and continue baking until shell is golden, 10–15 minutes. Allow to cool.

For Pastry Cream:
- 1 cup milk
- ½ vanilla bean, split lengthwise
- 4 egg yolks
- ¼ cup sugar
- 1 Tbsp flour

Place milk and vanilla bean in a medium heavy saucepan. Bring milk just to a boil over medium heat. Cool slightly, remove vanilla bean, scrape seeds into milk, then discard the pod. Whisk egg yolks and sugar together in a bowl until blended and then sprinkle in flour, continuing to whisk the mixture. Gradually whisk in milk, then return mixture to saucepan. Cook over low heat, stirring until thickened, about 10 minutes. Remove from heat and set aside to cool.

Assemble tart by spreading cooled pastry cream into cooled shell. Arrange fresh fruit on pastry cream. Four cups washed and hulled strawberries may be macerated with ¼ cup sugar for 30 minutes and then arranged upright atop mixture for a strawberry tart. Keep chilled.

Amil's Inn B&B

INNKEEPERS David & Anita Reeck
ADDRESS 27038 State Hwy 131, Wilton, WI 54670
TELEPHONE (608) 435-6640
CONTACT stay@amilsinn.com | www.amilsinn.com
FEATURES 4 Rooms | Children welcome/inquire | Pet-free environment | Will accommodate guests' special dietary needs

Amil's Inn B&B is nestled in the Kickapoo Valley in Wilton. This delightful country home was constructed by Amil Reeck and his wife, Whilhelmine "Minnie," in 1910, and has been fully remodeled by Amil's grandson, David Reeck. David and his wife Anita welcome you into their historic home, which captures the allure of times gone by, with all the comforts of today. The newly remodeled home has four gust rooms each with private bathes.

The B&B is just minutes from the Elroy-Sparta Bike Trail, Wildcat State Park, and the Kickapoo Valley Reserve. Wilton is a village in a small setting of farming and surrounding hills that is located mid-trail between tunnels no. 1 and no. 2 on State highways 71 and 131, 15 miles south of Tomah, the entrance to the Kickapoo River Recreation Area. Nearby you will also find horseback riding, canoeing, antique shopping, cranberry tours, Amish tours, biking, and so much more. The Reeck family invites you to join them for quality accommodations in the beautiful countryside of Wisconsin's Kickapoo Valley. Simple, comfortable, cozy.

Crantastic Quiche

Yield: 6 to 8 servings

- ½ lb. mild Italian sausage
- ¼ cup diced onion
- 1 clove garlic, minced
- ½–¾ cup dried cranberries
- 1 sheet frozen puff pastry, thawed
- 1 cup Monterey Jack cheese, shredded
- 1 cup frozen broccoli pieces
- 5 eggs, lightly beaten
- 1½ cups half & half
- ½ tsp salt
- ¼ tsp pepper
- ½ cup Swiss cheese, shredded
- fresh parsley and cranberries for garnish (optional)

Preheat oven to 375°F. In a medium skillet, brown the sausage, onion and garlic. Remove from heat, drain fat and add dried cranberries. Stir and set aside.

Spray bottom of a 9- or 10-inch deep pie pan with nonstick cooking spray. Roll out 1 sheet of puff pastry to fit inside pan, pressing pastry dough up the sides of the pan. Sprinkle the shredded Monterey Jack cheese over puff pastry. Spread the sausage and dried cranberry mixture on the top of the cheese. Next sprinkle the broccoli on top of the sausage mixture.

In a medium bowl, combine the eggs, half & half, salt and pepper; whisk to combine and then pour into the pie pan. Top with Swiss cheese. Bake for 40–50 minutes, or until a knife inserted near the center comes out clean. Let stand 10 minutes before cutting. If desired, garnish with fresh parsley and cranberries.

Angel Inn B&B

INNKEEPERS Kathy & Dave Greening
ADDRESS 372 S Lawson Drive, Green Lake, WI 54941
TELEPHONE (920) 294-3087
CONTACT info@angelinns.com | www.angelinns.com
FEATURES 5 Rooms | Children welcome/inquire | Pet-free environment

Angel Inn B&B is located directly on the picturesque shores of beautiful Green Lake. A circa 1910 Greek Revival lakefront B&B, we feature five tastefully appointed guest rooms, with all the amenities of today. Fall in love with the quiet pace, stunning natural beauty, spectacular sunrises, watch the moonlight shimmer across the lake, all from the porches and our boathouse deck! Experience the finest in Green Lake lodging.

Breakfast at Angel Inn is truly a unique experience. You'll awaken to the aroma of freshly brewed coffee and a generous gourmet breakfast that may be enjoyed either in our lakefront dining room, or outside on the veranda overlooking the water. An unforgettable dining experience!

Wild Blackberry Breakfast Parfait

Yield: 5 servings

2 cups old fashioned oats
4 cups vanilla yogurt
½ cup whipping cream
4 Tbsp brown sugar, packed
½ tsp cinnamon
¼ tsp nutmeg
1 Granny Smith apple, cored and diced (leave apple skins on)
1 banana, peeled and diced
½ cup chopped nuts (optional)
4 Tbsp half & half (or whipping cream)
½ cup dried cherries, or golden raisins not used in directions
4 cups fresh blackberries, rinsed and drained
4 Tbsp sugar
Mint leaves for garnish

Mix together in a medium bowl the old fashioned oats and yogurt. Add whipping cream. Stir in brown sugar, cinnamon and nutmeg. Stir in fruits and nuts. Cover and refrigerate overnight. In the morning, remove from refrigerator and add a little half & half (or whipping cream), to make it the consistency desired.

Rinse fresh blackberries and drain. Place in bowl and add sugar. Gently stir in sugar and let stand a few minutes for juice to come out of fruit.

In parfait glass layer oatmeal mixture, berries, and finish with a small dollop of oatmeal on top. Garnish with berries and a mint leaf!

Tips: Try strawberries, raspberries, or blueberries instead of blackberries.

Annie's B&B

INNKEEPERS	**Annie & Larry Stuart**
ADDRESS	**2117 Sheridan Drive, Madison, WI 53704**
TELEPHONE	**(608) 244-2224**
CONTACT	**innkeeper@anniesinmadison.com | www.anniesinmadison.com**
FEATURES	**1 Full suite | Children welcome/inquire | Resident pets only**

All to yourselves ... total seclusion ... You are the only guests at Annie's! Enjoy peace and seclusion at Madison's most uncommon lodging.

Surrounded by trees and lush gardens, Annie's is nestled alongside a beautiful wooded vista of south Warner Park, near the eastern shore of Lake Mendota. Stroll the lakeshore at sunset and explore the marshes and woods to catch a glimpse of deer, fox, and countless birds.

The rustic cedar shake house is a gem—owner-designed in the 1960s and chock-full of fascinating original art reflecting a deep appreciation of nature. The suite includes a pine-paneled library with lannon stone fireplace, a perfect place to read and listen to music. There is also a master bedroom, a smaller bedroom, and full bath. On the lower level, enjoy a double Jacuzzi or view movies from Annie's extensive collection in the DVD theater, complete with popcorn, all for you alone.

Annie's Breakfast Cookies

Yield: 2 Dozen

3½ cups milk
6 Tbsp vegetable oil
6 large eggs, beaten
1 cup raisins
4 cups old-fashioned oats
4 Tbsp brown sugar
1 Tbsp baking powder
½ tsp salt
1½ cups chopped fruit of choice (apples, cranberries, or bananas)
1 cup chopped nuts

In a large bowl, combine the milk, oil, beaten eggs, and raisins. Add the oats and soak for five minutes. Stir in the brown sugar, baking powder, and salt. Fold in the fruit and nuts. Spread ¼ cup of the batter on an oiled griddle set to no more than 325°F. Turn once, do not allow it to brown but rather to just cook through. Continue until all the batter has been used.

Tips: These pancakes will be thick and hearty. Serve with maple syrup, fresh fruit, a generous heap of country bacon or sausages, and a tall, frosty glass of fresh orange juice.

Apple Tree Lane B&B

INNKEEPERS Michael & Kerri Thiel

ADDRESS E3192 Apple Tree Lane, Waupaca, WI 54981

TELEPHONE (715) 258-3107 | (877) 277-5316

CONTACT thielkerri@aol.com | www.appletreelanebb.com

FEATURES 5 Rooms | Children age 10 and older welcome | Pet-free environment

Imagine escaping to a beautiful place rich in history, tradition, and comfortable elegance.

Let the Apple Tree Lane B&B welcome you to their 1880s Victorian farmhouse located on seven acres along the Crystal River. Inside this beautiful home you will enjoy the comforts of five large guest suites, each with private attached baths and luxury amenities.

A gourmet candlelit breakfast, often featuring the inn's signature apple creations, is served mornings in the formal dining room, set with crystal, china, and silver. Guests may also breakfast in their room or on the covered porch if they choose.

Apple Streusel Muffins

Yield: 16 Muffins

- 1½ cups quick oats
- 1 cup all-purpose flour
- ½ cup sugar
- ¾ tsp salt
- 2½ tsp baking powder
- ½ tsp baking soda
- 1 tsp cinnamon
- 1 egg, lightly beaten
- 1 cup milk
- 3 Tbsp butter
- 1½ cups cored, peeled, and diced apples of choice
- ½ cup powdered sugar

Streusel

- ½ cup oats, regular not quick
- 2 Tbsp firmly packed brown sugar
- 2 Tbsp butter

Caramel Drizzle

- ½ cup dark brown sugar
- 3 Tbsp butter
- 2 Tbsp cream
- ½ cup powdered sugar

Preheat oven to 400°F. Process the oats in a food processor for 2 minutes. In a bowl, combine the processed oats, flour, sugar, salt, baking powder, baking soda, and cinnamon. Make a well in the center and add the egg, milk, and butter. Stir just until moistened and fold in the apples. Fill greased muffin cups 2/3 full. In a small bowl, blend together all of the streusel ingredients using a fork. Sprinkle over the tops of the muffins and bake 15–20 minutes.

For the caramel drizzle: While the muffins bake, place all of the caramel drizzle ingredients, except the powdered sugar, together in a saucepan and bring to a boil over medium-high heat. Cook and stir 2 minutes. Remove from heat and blend in the powdered sugar. Remove the muffins and cool slightly before drizzling with caramel. Enjoy!

Artesian House

INNKEEPER Al Chechik
ADDRESS 84100 Hatchery Road, Bayfield, WI 54814
TELEPHONE (715) 779-3338
CONTACT artesian@ncis.net | www.artesianhouse.com
FEATURES 3 Rooms | Children welcome | Pet-free environment

The Artesian House, the vision of Margaret Rdzak and Al Chechik, opened in June 1996. Sadly, Margaret enjoyed the fulfillment of her dream only briefly, and succumbed to cancer that October. Today, the inn reflects a creative mix of the contemporary and the eclectic, and is comfortably secluded on 24 acres close to Bayfield and Lake Superior. Its walking trail features lupines in June and berries and apples in summer and fall. There are three individually themed guest rooms, a great room with floor-to-ceiling windows, a rain garden, and a newly added solar installation for hot water.

A wonderful experience with a most congenial host, gorgeous rooms, spectacular architecture, and sumptuous breakfasts."—Guest

Dutch Baby Oven Pancake

Yield: 6-8 servings

"Twin Cities guests recognize this as a panekuchen, still offered at a popular Minneapolis restaurant."—Innkeeper

3 large eggs
¾ cup milk
¾ cup flour
¼ cup butter

Preheat oven to 425°F. In a medium bowl, beat the eggs, add in the milk and gradually beat in the flour; mix well. Melt the butter in a 2–3 quart cast-iron skillet on the stovetop. Pour the batter into the skillet and place in the heated oven. Bake 28–30 minutes, until puffy and evenly browned.

To serve: Cut into wedges. For breakfast, serve with fresh fruit, yogurt, syrup, and powdered sugar. For dessert, serve with ice cream, whipped cream, chocolate sauce, and cherries. Use your imagination; it's great with everything!

Bay Point Inn

INNKEEPERS	Myles Dannhausen & Corrina Luedtke
ADDRESS	7933 State Highway 42, Egg Harbor, WI 54209
TELEPHONE	(800) 707-6660
CONTACT	stay@baypointinn.com | www.baypointinn.com
FEATURES	10 Rooms | Children welcome/inquire | Pet-free environment

At Bay Point Inn, guests will enjoy spectacular water views punctuated with the islands of Green Bay and framed by pristine woodlands. The inn offers spacious one-bedroom accommodations with luxurious interior décor. Outside, guests will find luscious gardens that mirror the magnificence of a European vacation villa.

Bay Point Inn is the ultimate vacation experience in Door County, complete with the designer furnishings, Italian porcelain tile baths, Gilchrist & Soames bath amenities, Hydro-Thermo massage whirlpools, a gourmet breakfast buffet, pools overlooking the shoreline, and many romantic enhancements.

Egg Strata

Yield: 1 serving

"This year Myles discovered Silicone muffin pans and now his egg concoctions pop right out of the pan. Use a donut cutter to make a puck the size of the bottom of the muffin cavity and cube the remaining bread and incorporate it into the egg mixture. (For some reason potato bread works best.)"—Innkeeper

- 1 Piece of potato bread cut into rounds (2 per), with remaining bread cubed
- 2 Tbsp precooked meat and/or vegetable
- 1 egg per serving
- 1½ tsp milk (approx. per egg)
- Salt & pepper to taste
- 2 Heaping Tbsp cheese (this is Wisconsin)

Cut two circles out of the potato bread with donut cutter. (The second circle is for an additional serving.) Place bread round in bottom of sprayed muffin cup. Add cubed cooked sausage or ham or vegetables. Beat egg and milk seasoned with salt & pepper. Incorporate cubed bread and cheese into egg mixture. (Or put the cheese(s) in each cup with the remaining ingredients.) Pour egg mixture into cavity. Top with more of ingredients if you wish. Bake in 350°F convection oven for 25 minutes.

Variations: Try different seasonings to enhance flavor profile. Season salts, garlic, onion, oregano, thyme, basil, chives. Also try zucchini & onion (precooked in microwave); asparagus, spinach & feta; shrimp, mushroom, carrot, peppers, chorizo. Try specialty cheeses that add tremendous flavor like: leek & morel, olive Cheddar, Chili-lime Cheddar, smoked Gouda, Asiago, or Munster.

Black Walnut Guest House

INNKEEPERS Geri Ballard & Mike Shatusky
ADDRESS 454 N 7th Avenue, Sturgeon Bay, WI 54235
TELEPHONE (920) 743-8892 | (877) 255-9568
CONTACT stay@blackwalnut-gh.com | www.blackwalnut-gh.com
FEATURES 4 Rooms | Children welcome/inquire | Resident pets only

Discover one of Door County's hidden treasures. The Black Walnut Guest House in Sturgeon Bay is a welcoming four-room B&B. Each room has been uniquely designed and tastefully decorated and includes a double whirlpool tub, fireplace, small refrigerator, and private bath. A warm continental breakfast consisting of homemade muffins, fresh fruit, hot and cold cereal, yogurt, homemade granola, juice, coffee, and tea is served to your door each morning.

The Black Walnut Guest House is situated in a quiet neighborhood one-half block from one-of-a- kind Jefferson Street shops, and just a short walk from Sturgeon Bay's Historic Downtown. Discover the Door County Historical, Maritime, and Fairfield museums, The Miller Art Museum, Third Avenue Playhouse, and both fine and casual dining.

Morning Glory Muffins

Yield: 12 Muffins

"This recipe was passed down from my mom, along with all of her other muffin recipes, when we bought my parents' B&B, The Barrington Inn on Block Island, in Rhode Island."—Innkeeper

- 3 eggs
- 1 cup vegetable oil
- ½ tsp vanilla extract
- 1¼ cups sugar
- 2 cups flour
- 2 tsp baking soda
- ½ tsp salt
- 2 tsp cinnamon
- 1½ cups shredded carrots
- 2 large apples, chopped
- ¾ cup shredded coconut
- ½ cup raisins (optional)
- ½ cup pecans

Preheat oven to 375°F. In a large bowl, cream together the eggs, oil, and vanilla. Beat until well blended. Add the sugar and mix to combine. In a separate bowl, sift together the flour, baking soda, salt, and cinnamon. Add the flour mixture to the batter and beat well. Fold in the carrots, apples, coconut, raisins, and pecans. Divide the batter evenly among greased or lined muffin cups and bake 18–25 minutes.

Bowman's Oak Hill B&B

INNKEEPERS	David & Nancy Bowman
ADDRESS	4169 State HWY 13, Wisconsin Dells, WI 53965
TELEPHONE	(888) 253-5631
CONTACT	bowmansoakhillbb@aol.com | www.bowmansoakhillbedandbreakfast.com
FEATURES	3 Rooms; 3 Cottages | Children welcome/inquire | Pet free environment, Resident pets only (outdoor cat and 2 dogs)

From the spacious romantic bedrooms, lovely bathrooms, and the yummy breakfast served in our dining area or on our large deck, to the eight acres of park-like setting and 25 acres of woods to wander, you will have the opportunity to rest, reflect, relax and be renewed both in body and spirit during your stay with us here at Oak Hill.

Bowman's Oak Hill is just a brief 5-minute drive from the center of the Wisconsin Dells River District. Innkeepers David and Nancy are happy to help guests with their plans for a memorable stay. Nearby attractions include the zip-line and kayaking tours available, Crystal Grand Music Theater, the Rick Wilcox Magic Theater, casual and fine dining, river boat tours, the Tommy Bartlet Water Ski show, both indoor and outdoor water parks, horseback riding, and golfing.

Southwest Frittata

Yield: 6 servings

"I received this recipe from a friend then put my own spin on it. Our guests love it and are also pleased with how simple it is to put together. A great perk for busy homes."—Innkeeper

7 large eggs
1 can creamed corn
1 4-oz. can sliced black olives, drained
1 4-oz. can diced green chilies
2 cups shredded Cheddar or Mexican mix cheese

Preheat oven to 350°F. Beat the eggs in a large bowl. Add remaining ingredients. Stir together and pour into 10-inch glass pie pan. Bake for 50–60 minutes. Bake until set.

I serve this dish with black bean and corn salsa, sour cream and fresh sliced avocado.

Variation: You may also use whole corn and ¼ cup half & half in place of the creamed corn. Fresh slices of tomatoes on the side are also nice, right out of our garden.

Brayton B&B

INNKEEPERS Nicole & Scott Brayton
ADDRESS 143 Church Avenue, Oshkosh, WI 54901
TELEPHONE (920) 267-0300
CONTACT stay@braytonbb.net | www.braytonbb.net
FEATURES 4 Rooms | Children welcome/inquire | Resident pets only

Brayton B&B is not your typical inn. You will not find any doilies, lace or country motif at the inn. You are greeted with casual elegance and deep rich hues that are present throughout the entire home. Original architecture is apparent inside and out. Modern day amenities and luxury products are proof positive that your accommodations are up to date and comfortable.

Each morning, we serve a complimentary full breakfast in our family dining room at the time that you choose. Two options are always presented, which consist of a sweet dish such as stuffed French toast and/or a savory dish such as asparagus quiche. Your dietary needs are important to us as well. We have a variety of lactose free, vegetarian and vegan recipes to please.

Banana Walnut Cinnamon Roll

Yield: 4 generous portions

"I am always looking for things to do with bananas that are getting too ripe and I get tired of making banana bread all the time. One day, my daughter left a package of refrigerated cinnamon rolls sitting out on the counter. They exploded. Instead of throwing them away, I threw them in a bowl, chopped them up and started adding ingredients. The Banana Walnut Cinnamon Roll was born."—Innkeeper

- 3 eggs
- 1 cup mashed ripe bananas (2–3 medium)
- 3 Tbsp sugar
- 1 can (17.5 oz.) Pillsbury Grands Refrigerated Cinnamon Rolls w/Cream Cheese Icing
- ½ cup flour
- ⅓ cup brown sugar
- ¼ cup butter, softened
- ¾ cup chopped walnuts
- ¼ cup maple syrup
- Banana slices

Preheat oven to 350°F. Spray an 8-inch square glass baking dish with nonstick spray.

Beat eggs, bananas and sugar with wire whisk until blended. Separate dough into 5 rolls; cut each roll into 8–9 pieces. Gently stir dough pieces into egg mixture until well coated. Spoon mixture into baking dish; spread evenly.

Mix flour and brown sugar. With a fork, cut in butter until mixture looks like coarse crumbs. Stir in walnuts. Sprinkle mixture over dough mixture in baking dish. Bake 35–40 minutes until center is puffed and edges are deep golden brown. Cool 10 minutes. Meanwhile, in a small bowl, mix icing and maple syrup until blended. When ready to serve, cut into squares and drizzle with maple syrup and icing mixture. Garnish with banana slices.

Brewery Creek Inn & Brewpub

INNKEEPERS Deb & Jeff Donaghue
ADDRESS 23 Commerce Street, Mineral Point, WI 53565
TELEPHONE (608) 987-3298
CONTACT info@brewerycreek.com | www.brewerycreek.com

FEATURES 5 Rooms; 2 Cottages | Children age 12 and older welcome | Resident pets only

The Brewery Creek Brewpub Restaurant (yes, we brew beer too!) has been serving lunch and dinner to inn guests and the general public since 1998. The restaurant is a small and intimate space that seats about 40 and is located in the same building as the main inn.

We believe that to make really good food you need to slow down, get involved, and follow two basic principles. First, use quality ingredients—there is no substitute and they are a cook's best friends. Use them whenever you can. Second, make your food from scratch, from basic ingredients. We do. So, if you are staying with us, or even if you're just in town for a few hours, stop by for a beer, a burger, a sandwich, steak, pasta, or an entrée salad. And save room for a great dessert.

Kentucky Bourbon Pecan Pie

Yield: 1 Pie

"This is a fairly traditional, restaurant-style pecan pie that we have adapted."—Innkeeper

- 1 unbaked pie shell
- 1¼ cups dark corn syrup
- 1 cup dark brown sugar
- 4 Tbsp butter
- 1 cup pecans, halves or pieces
- 4 eggs
- 1 tsp vanilla extract
- 2 Tbsp straight bourbon whiskey
- 2 Tbsp heavy cream

Preheat oven to 350°F and line a 9-inch pie dish with the unbaked crust. Melt the corn syrup and brown sugar together in a saucepan over medium-high heat. Stir frequently to prevent sticking and burning. When the mixture begins to boil, add the butter and nuts and remove from heat. In a medium bowl, beat the eggs until they are just mixed. Add the vanilla, whiskey, and cream to the sugar mixture and then temper the eggs—whisk a small amount of the hot sugar mixture into the eggs in order to heat them and prevent them from scrambling. Add the egg mixture to the sugar mixture, whisking to combine. Pour the mixture into the pie shell and place the pie plate on a cookie sheet to catch any batter that may boil over. Bake 45–60 minutes.

Variations: Substitute either brandy or rum for the whiskey. You can also use light brown sugar and light corn syrup, but the flavor is not as deep.

Cameo Rose Victorian Country Inn

INNKEEPERS	Dawn & Gary Bahr
ADDRESS	1090 Severson Road, Belleville, WI 53508
TELEPHONE	(608) 424-6340
CONTACT	innkeeper@cameorose.com | www.cameorose.com
FEATURES	4 Rooms; 1 Suite | Children age 12 and older welcome | Pet-free environment | Will accommodate guests' special dietary needs

Nestled amid 120 acres of rolling hills and scenic woodlands is the Cameo Rose, a peaceful retreat just minutes from Madison, New Glarus, and many charming historic communities.

Situated near four state bike trails, this park-like estate, enhanced with miles of meandering groomed hiking trails, is teeming with birds, deer, and other wildlife. Victorian gardens, gazebos, and pergolas display a profusion of roses and flowers surrounding the hanging swings, seating areas, and hammocks tucked inside. The pond with its three impressive waterfalls also features a 16-foot screened gazebo, strategically placed to offer a panoramic view of the rocky outcroppings on the majestic hillside beyond.

We proudly serve a four-course breakfast using the finest, fresh ingredients incorporating our organic herbs, edible flowers and local produce. It is our pleasure to accommodate guests' dietary restrictions or preferences to ensure that everyone will enjoy a delicious and satisfying meal to start their day.

Black Raspberry & Chambord Poached Pears

Yield: 8 servings

Black Raspberry Chambord Sauce (Can be prepared ahead—stores in fridge for weeks and can also be prepared without the alcohol)

- 2 cups fresh or frozen black raspberries
- 2/3 cup water + 1/4 cup water to mix with cornstarch
- 1/2 cup sugar
- 1 Tbsp fresh squeezed lemon juice
- 2 Tbsp Chambord (raspberry liqueur)
- 1 Tbsp cornstarch

Place raspberries in a blender with the water to purée and then strain mixture over a small saucepan to remove the seeds. Add remaining ingredients to saucepan, except for the cornstarch, and bring to a low boil over medium heat, stirring often to prevent sticking. Reduce heat to low and simmer for 30–40 min. Stir cornstarch into the 1/4 cup of water until completely dissolved and then add to the berry mixture. Cook and stir until the sauce thickens. Serve warm over cooked pears.

Poached Pears

- 8 fresh firm pears (I prefer Bosc)
- 2 Tbsp fresh squeezed lemon juice
- 1/2 cup sugar

Using a large kettle with the capacity of covering the pears with water while cooking, add water and place on the stove. Core pears using an apple corer and peel completely. Use a knife to trim the bottoms if necessary so that the pears will stand upright when served. Bring the water, sugar and lemon juice to a boil and then turn down to low until pears are fully cooked—slightly firm, but tender enough to cut with a butter knife—approximately 45 minutes, depending on how firm the pears are to begin with. Test pear texture with a toothpick. Remove from heat and rinse with cold water. Drain and place in bowls—one per guest. Ladle 2–3 tablespoons of the Black Raspberry Chambord Sauce over the top. Garnish with a dollop of whipped cream and shaved Ghirardelli Chocolate, using approximately 1 tablespoon per serving.

Canyon Road Inn

INNKEEPERS Patti Gilkey & Turner Reaney
ADDRESS 575 West Town Line Road, Turtle Lake, WI 54889
TELEPHONE (715) 986-2121 | (888) 251-5542
CONTACT info@canyonroadinn.com | www.canyonroadinn.com
FEATURES 6 Rooms | Children not allowed | Pet-Free Environment | Will accommodate guests' special dietary needs

Nestled in the beautiful Northwoods of western Wisconsin, Canyon Road Inn is the perfect getaway in all seasons. Situated on a quiet lake among 14 wooded acres, guests are surrounded by the serenity of nature. Enjoy casual elegance in one of our six spacious and recently renovated guest suites. Each feature a comfy king-size bed, private bathroom, relaxing double whirlpool or claw-foot soaking tub, a cozy fireplace and private patio or deck that overlooks the lake or woods.

Start your day with the aroma of freshly brewed coffee and a sumptuous breakfast. An abundant fare of sweet and savory entrées, fresh baked goods, seasonal fruits, meats, and juices are all served family style. We are happy to accommodate special dietary needs.

Eggchiladas

Yield: 2 servings

"Moving Back to Wisconsin from Arizona to enjoy the four seasons again, we brought some of our Southwest flavors with us. This recipe is easily adapted for as many servings as you need to prepare. Just increase the ingredients and pan size accordingly. Guests get a kick out of our Margarita Muffins (page 209) that are a great accompaniment to the Eggchiladas."—Innkeeper

1 link chorizo (or ¼ lb. spicy pork sausage)
6 eggs
1/8 tsp onion powder
1/8 tsp chili powder
3 Tbsp sour cream
1 Tbsp diced chili peppers
tortilla chips
Cheddar cheese
tomatoes (optional)
black olives (optional)

Preheat oven to 325°F. Lightly grease 2 individual Au Gratin style dishes. In a skillet, brown and drain the link of chorizo (or ¼ lb. of spicy pork sausage). Whisk together 6 eggs, seasoned with 1/8 teaspoon each of onion powder and chili powder. Scramble the eggs until firm but still moist. Fold in sour cream and a tablespoon of chili peppers.

Layer in each dish: crushed tortilla chips to cover bottom; shredded Cheddar cheese; chorizo; eggs; shredded Cheddar cheese. Bake for 20 minutes. Garnish with chopped tomatoes and black olives, serve and enjoy … ¡Olé!

Cleghorn B&B

INNKEEPERS Bob & Linda Yerkes
ADDRESS N2080 Cleghorn Road, Waupaca, WI 54981
TELEPHONE (715) 258-5235 | (800) 870-0737
CONTACT lyerkes@charter.net | www.cleghornbandb.com
FEATURES 4 Rooms | Children welcome/inquire | Resident pets only

Our guests say that Cleghorn B&B is so warm and friendly, it's like a "home away from home." Cleghorn is a romantic getaway and a safe, cozy place to stay while on business or pleasure.

Cleghorn is located on a wooded lot adjacent to Waupaca's beautiful Chain O' Lakes and the picturesque village of Rural, a beautiful area with lots of lakes, woods, rustic roads, and biking, hiking, and cross-country skiing paths. Each morning we serve gourmet breakfasts in a peaceful, country setting; you can enjoy the antics of the birds and wildlife right out the dining room window.

Viennese Cheese Puffs

Yield: 8–12 servings

"My sister-in-law said that this is a favorite recipe in her restaurant in Oregon. Now it has become a favorite here at our B&B."—Innkeeper

- 2 pkgs. large crescent rolls
- 2 (8-oz.) pkgs. cream cheese
- 1 egg, separated
- 1 cup sugar (or ½ cup sugar and ½ cup Splenda)
- 1 tsp vanilla extract
- 1/3 cup sugar
- 1 tsp cinnamon

Preheat oven to 350°F. Press one package of crescent rolls into the bottom of a 9x13-inch pan, closing all perforations. In a medium bowl, mix together the cream cheese, egg yolk, sugar, and vanilla. Spread the mixture over the crescent rolls. Place the second package of rolls on waxed paper cut to the size of the pan. Seal all seams. Place over the cheese mixture (removing the waxed paper). Brush with egg white and sprinkle with a mixture of 1/3 cup sugar and cinnamon. Bake 30 minutes.

Cobblestone B&B

INNKEEPER Mary Lou Campion
ADDRESS 319 S Main Street, Birchwood, WI 54817
TELEPHONE (715) 354-3494
CONTACT cobblestone@centurytel.net | www.cobblestonebb.com
FEATURES 5 Rooms; Private & shared baths | Children welcome | Pets welcome/inquire

Cobblestone B&B is designed around the concept of simple comfort and elegance. Take a step back in time as you sip tea and relax on the front porch swing. Enjoy an elegant breakfast next to a crackling fire on a wintry morn. Take a piece of the Northwoods home after browsing through ye old gift shoppe.

Much thought has been taken to keep the house in its original state while updating to add private baths, fireplaces, and other amenities. Cobblestone's most popular room is the English Garden Suite, which offers a king-size bed and whirlpool tub for two imported from France. A close second is the Love at First Site room with its copper and nickel soaking tub.

Cranberry Frappè Smoothie

Yield: 2 servings

"My Frappè was generated by my guests! I always serve a banana orange frappè. It was cranberry fest and my guests came back talking about cranberries, so I thought it would be memorable for them to have Banana Orange Cranberry Frappè."—Innkeeper

- 3 cups fresh squeezed orange juice
- 1 banana
- ½ cup fresh cranberries
- ½ cup shaved ice

Place ingredients together in a blender and mix to desired consistency.

COUNTRY COMFORT

INNKEEPERS Loren & Judy Gifford
ADDRESS N5126 410th Street (aka Paradise Valley Road), Menomonie, WI 54751
TELEPHONE (715) 233-0113
CONTACT info@staycountrycomfort.com | www.staycountrycomfort.com
FEATURES 3 Rooms; Private baths | Children over age 8 welcome | Pet-free environment | Will accommodate guests' special dietary needs

Country Comfort B&B, located an hour southeast of the Minneapolis and St. Paul area, is that special place created for your rest and relaxation—your home away from home! Whether you're looking for a weekend getaway from the city or a week of fun and adventure, Country Comfort will meet and exceed your lodging needs.

Enjoy a very comfortable night's sleep in one of our three spacious guest rooms, all with private baths. Wake up to the smell of great coffee and a scrumptious and plentiful breakfast, such as Pumpkin Pecan Pancakes with homemade caramel sauce, Menomonie Pancakes, or our Omega Scrambler, to name a few.

Our B&B is that special place where you can feel at home and have plenty of fun or solitude. Stay right on the Red Cedar Trail and have a great view of the Red Cedar River that will melt your cares away! Country Comfort is open year round for your relaxation and rest. We invite you to explore the beautiful countryside surrounding us. We hope to see you soon!

Menomonie Pancake
A Gluten-Free Wild and Black Rice Pancake

Yield: 8–10 servings

"Life, within doors, has few pleasanter prospects than a neatly arranged and well-provisioned breakfast table."—Nathaniel Hawthorne

Menomonie means wild rice in the Ojibwa language, so we wanted to create a recipe featuring wild rice. We added the cranberries to include awareness of Wisconsin's leading production of cranberries throughout the U.S.!

- ¾ cup cooked wild rice
- ¾ cup cooked Emperor's rice (sometimes called black rice)
- 1½ cups Pamela gluten free flour
- ¼ cup dried cranberries
- ¼ cup chopped walnuts
- ¼ cup raisins
- 3 eggs
- ¾ cup water or 1 cup coconut milk

Combine rice, flour and nut-fruit mixture. Beat eggs and combine with water or coconut milk. Mix the wet and dry ingredients until just combined.

Proceed like regular pancakes—cook until golden brown on both sides.

Cream Pitcher B&B

INNKEEPERS Diane & Vern Dalberg
ADDRESS 16334 Gault Hollow Road, Blue River, WI 53518
TELEPHONE (608) 536-3607
CONTACT crmptchr@mwt.net | www.mwt.net/~crmptchr
FEATURES 4 Rooms | Children not allowed/inquire | Pet-Free Environment | Will accommodate guests' special dietary needs

The Cream Pitcher B&B is situated among the hills in Richland County; this unglaciated area offers awesome beauty as well as outdoor activities in every season. There are more than 3 miles of hiking trails through the 100 acres of woodlands. Watch deer, turkeys and other wildlife; see and hear many species of birds; enjoy the creek that flows close by.

The innkeepers have a large collection of pitchers from the 1930s, 40s, and 50s. The home is embellished with antiques. The Cream Pitcher was meticulously handcrafted to ensure the proper blend between modern amenities and old-fashioned quality and comfort.

Guests of the Cream Pitcher experience a retreat in nature. Sports enthusiasts can enjoy hiking, biking, cross-country skiing, snow shoeing, fishing, or just relaxing. Everyone who visits enjoys the quiet … and a breakfast to remember!

Eggs Taos

Yield: 8 servings

1 large clove garlic, minced
½ onion, chopped
¼ cup butter
¼ cup flour
2 cups milk, heated
1 7-oz. can chopped green chilies
½ tsp salt
¼ tsp pepper
10 eggs, whisked
2 avocados
8 flour tortillas
3 cups grated Monterey Jack cheese (and/or Cheddar)
1 cup sour cream
1 tomato, chopped or 1 cup salsa

Preheat oven to 350°F. In a large skillet, sauté garlic and onion in butter over high heat. Stir in flour. Add heated milk and whisk constantly until thick. Add green chilies, salt and pepper. Remove sauce from heat and set aside.

In a large skillet, scramble eggs, set aside. In a small bowl mash or slice avocados. Spoon 2 tablespoons sauce, 1/8 of the eggs, and 1/8 of the avocado on each tortilla. Sprinkle with cheese. Roll up and place seam down in a 9x13-inch baking dish. Spoon remaining sauce over tortillas and sprinkle with cheese. Bake for 20 minutes or until hot.

To serve, top with sour cream and tomato or salsa.

Crystal River Inn B&B

INNKEEPERS Deb & Robert Benada
ADDRESS E1369 Rural Road, Waupaca, WI 54981
TELEPHONE (715) 258-5333
CONTACT cri@crystalriverbb.com | www.crystalriver-inn.com
FEATURES 7 Rooms; 2 Cabins/Cottages| Children welcome/inquire | Resident pets only | Will accommodate guests' special dietary needs

Our Crystal River Inn B&B is the heart of the 1853 Andrew Potts farmstead. In keeping with this heritage, breakfast is a full, hot, delicious meal prepared with down-home flavor in our homemade bread and our own jellies of native fruit like wild grapes, plums and high bush cranberry. Robert sometimes adds Southern flair from his native Louisiana (biscuits, sausage gravy, cornbread …). In our effort to be "green," we use local fruit and produce, and vegetables from our own garden when available, along with serving pure Wisconsin maple syrup. We also brew only fair trade, organic coffee. We delight in fixing meals for special diets, such as gluten-free and vegetarian. We serve your breakfast in a bright, airy room overlooking the Crystal River and our woods.

Helen's Breakfast Soufflé

Yield: 8 servings

Adapted from Helen Potts Robinson in the Parfreyville UMC Anniversary Cookbook *by Robert Benada.*

- 8 slices white or wheat bread, torn or cubed
- 2 Tbsp dried onion
- 2 cups Cheddar cheese, grated
- 8 eggs
- 4 cups milk
- 1 tsp salt*
- ¼ tsp pepper
- 2 dashes Tabasco Sauce, to taste
- Chives

Plan ahead, this dish needs to be refrigerated overnight.

Place the bread cubes in a greased 9x13-inch baking dish and sprinkle the dried onion over the top. Spread the cheese over the bread cubes. In a medium bowl, beat together the eggs, milk, salt, pepper, and Tabasco sauce. Pour the egg mixture over the bread and cheese layer, sprinkle on chives, cover, and refrigerate overnight.

The following morning: Preheat oven to 350°F and bake 1 hour. To prepare individual servings, place 1/8 of the mixture into a greased shallow ovenproof dish and bake 35–40 minutes.

Tips and Variations: In place of salt, use ¼ teaspoon of Penzey's Fox Point Seasoning per egg. Green Jalapeño Tabasco is also great on this dish and is far less hot than standard Tabasco. Try adding ½–1 cup chopped turkey, ham, or for a meatless version, add 2 Portobello Veggie Burgers.

Dobranoc Inn

INNKEEPER **Jamie Drohman**
ADDRESS **109 South Park Avenue, Fond du Lac, WI 54935**
TELEPHONE **(920) 322-1120**
CONTACT **stay@dobranocinn.com | dobranocinn.com**
FEATURES **4 Rooms; 1 Suite | Children not allowed | Pets welcome/inquire | Will accommodate guests' special dietary needs**

Where European elegance meets Midwestern charm, the Dobranoc Inn offers you all the finest amenities found in the best B&B's and the comforts of home. Each room is its own distinct experience. Our goal is to make each visit unique and memorable. Pick the room that fits your needs and you're sure to have a getaway fit for a king … or queen.

In addition to each room's features, we offer Wi-Fi throughout the inn, LED televisions in each guest room, computer for guest use, small butler's pantry offering coffee, tea, and a small refrigerator for guest use, hair dryers in each bath, individual use travel-sized toiletries, clothes steamer and irons are all available for guest use. The inn is pet-friendly inside and out with a large fenced in area. The Dobranoc Inn combines elegance and comfort with an exclusive atmosphere that will have you longing to return.

Christine's Crème Brûlé French Toast

Yield: 4 servings

½ stick unsalted butter
1 cup brown sugar
2 Tbsp corn syrup
1 loaf French bread in 1-inch slices (to equal 14 slices)
5 eggs
1½ cups half & half (or milk)
1 tsp vanilla
1 tsp Grand Marnier (or orange zest and brandy, but you don't have to add this)
¼ tsp salt

Plan ahead—dish needs 8-hour refrigeration.

Melt butter, brown sugar, and corn syrup in saucepan over medium heat. Stir until smooth. Grease a 13x9x2-inch baking dish. Pour brown sugar mixture in dish. Tightly fit cut bread into dish. Do not use the butts of the bread. Wisk eggs, half & half, vanilla, Grand Marnier, and salt until well combined. Pour mixture over the bread slices. Cover dish and chill 8 hours or up to 1 day. Preheat oven to 350°F and bring dish to room temperature. Bake uncovered on middle rack 35–40 minutes until edges are puffy and golden. Prep time 20 minutes.

Door County Lighthouse Inn

INNKEEPERS Claire & Frank Murphy
ADDRESS 4639 Orchard Road, Egg Harbor, WI 54209
TELEPHONE (920) 868-9088 | (866) 868-9088
CONTACT info@dclighthouseinn.com | www.dclighthouseinn.com
FEATURES 5 Rooms | Children welcome/inquire | Pet-free environment

Travel to beautiful Door County and experience our rich maritime history while visiting the ten lighthouses that dot the 300 miles of shoreline. Our B&B makes you feel like you are staying in the eleventh lighthouse of Door County.

Delight in the warm homey atmosphere filled with lighthouse décor. Start each day's adventure with a full breakfast and great conversation with fellow lighthouse and Door County enthusiasts.

Winter in Door County includes sleigh rides, wineries, fireside lunch, the Door County Progressive Dinner, and our Romance Packages. In summer and fall we offer packages such as the Self Guided Lighthouse Tour, Trolley Lighthouse Package, Trolley Ghost Adventures, and a day trip to Rock Island's Pottawatomie Lighthouse.

First Assistant Citrus Fruit Cup

Yield: 6 servings

"This recipe was adapted from the Williams Sonoma Kitchen Library."—Innkeeper

- 1 1/3 cups water
- 2/3 cup sugar
- 1 vanilla bean, split in half lengthwise
- 4 large naval oranges
- 2 large grapefruits
- Fresh mint sprigs

Combine the water, sugar, and vanilla bean together in a saucepan over medium-high heat. Cook, stirring constantly, to make a syrup. Peel and segment the oranges and grapefruits and place the citrus pieces in a serving bowl. Take the saucepan off the heat and remove the vanilla bean. Pour the syrup over the citrus pieces and toss to coat. Garnish with mint sprigs and serve.

Tips and Variations: For an extra treat, serve this citrus cup with a scoop of vanilla ice cream on the side. Also, because fresh fruit tastes best when it is in season, try substituting other citruses throughout the year. Tangerines, tangelos, and clementines (small mandarin oranges) are just a few alternatives to oranges. Grapefruit is available year-round because it is grown in so many different regions.

Dreams of Yesteryear B&B

INNKEEPERS Bonnie & Bill Maher
ADDRESS 1100 Brawley Street, Stevens Point, WI 54481
TELEPHONE (715) 341-4525
CONTACT bonnie@dreamsofyesteryear.com | www.dreamsofyesteryear.com
FEATURES 6 Rooms; Private & shared baths | Children welcome/inquire | Pet-free environment

Dreams of Yesteryear B&B is an antique embellished, National Historic Register Queen Anne Victorian. It's also the only B&B within the designated Historic Downtown Main Street Business District of Stevens Point. The inn is conveniently located in a quiet residential neighborhood amid other architectural beauties and has been featured in *Victorian Homes* magazine. Dreams is situated just one block from the Green Circle trails and the Wisconsin River, and is conveniently located near the university, Sentry Insurance Golf Course, restaurants, and shops.

Enjoy historic ambiance with today's comforts while you experience the history and stories that make the Victorian era come alive. Owners Bonnie and Bill are both from Stevens Point and they invite you to share in their Victorian dream. As a guest once said, "Dreams of Yesteryear is truly the kind of place Victorian dreams are made of."

Dreams Sausage Strata

Yield: 8 servings

"A photo of this delightful dish is featured on my website. Guests tell me that it tastes as good as it looks."—Innkeeper

- 12 slices white bread, crusts removed
- ¾ cup grated sharp Cheddar cheese
- 1 lb. Italian sausage, browned
- 8 large eggs
- 3 cups milk
- ½ tsp salt
- 1 tsp garlic powder
- 1 tsp dry mustard

Plan ahead, this dish needs to be refrigerated overnight.

Grease or spray a 9x12-inch cake pan. Line the bottom of the dish with bread. Sprinkle the cheese then the sausage over the top. In a large bowl, combine the milk, eggs, and spices. Pour the mixture over the bread, cover with plastic wrap, and refrigerate overnight.

The following morning: Preheat oven to 350°F and bake 45 minutes.

Eagle Centre House B&B

INNKEEPERS Riene Wells Herriges & Dean Herriges
ADDRESS W370 S9590 State Road 67, Eagle, WI 53119
TELEPHONE (262) 363-4700
CONTACT info@eagle-house.com | www.eagle-house.com
FEATURES 5 Rooms | Children age 12 and older welcome | Pet-free environment

Let's pretend the year is 1846 and you're a weary traveler approaching an inn. Today's traveler seeks respite, too! So, relax and enjoy the best life had to offer over 160 years ago, enhanced with today's finest amenities. Eagle Centre is a replica of an 1846 Greek Revival stagecoach inn furnished in authentic period antiques and situated on 20 scenic acres. Wood-burning stoves, fireplaces, and double whirlpools add comfort. A full breakfast is included with any stay and is served on antique Tea-Leaf china.

Eagle Centre is located in the Southern Kettle Moraine Forest, a location that offers hiking, biking, skiing, and horse trails. Chicago is just two hours away, Milwaukee just under an hour. Other nearby attractions include Lake Geneva, Madison, Ten Chimneys, and Old World Wisconsin.

Pumpkin Bread

Yield: 1 Loaf

½ cup salad oil
½ cup water
1½ cups sugar
2 eggs
1 cup pumpkin
1⅔ cups flour
½ tsp cloves
½ tsp cinnamon
½ tsp nutmeg
1 tsp baking soda
1 tsp baking powder
1 cup raisins (optional)
½ cup nuts (optional)

Preheat oven to 350°F. Grease and flour a 9x5-inch loaf pan. In a small bowl, whisk together the oil and water. In a large bowl, combine the sugar, eggs, and pumpkin. Sift together the flour, cloves, cinnamon, nutmeg, baking soda, and baking powder. Add the flour mixture to the pumpkin mixture and mix to combine. Add the oil/water mixture and stir to incorporate. Fold in the raisins and nuts and pour into the prepared pan. Bake 1 hour, or until a knife inserted in the center comes away clean.

Eagle Harbor Inn

INNKEEPERS Nedd & Natalie Neddersen
ADDRESS 9914 Water Street, Ephraim, WI 54211
TELEPHONE (920) 854-2121 | (800) 324-5427
CONTACT nedd@eagleharbor.com | www.EagleHarborInn.com
FEATURES 9 Rooms | Children welcome/Inquire | Resident pets only

Eagle Harbor Inn is a traditional B&B with nine rooms named for women innkeepers of Ephraim's past. The romantic Great Room features an open-beam ceiling and other amenities include double whirlpool with robes, custom soaps & loofah, fireside wingchairs, and private balcony—perfect for honeymoons and anniversaries.

A wonderful homemade breakfast is served each morning and homemade afternoon treats are available each day around mid-afternoon.

The inn features an indoor pool, sauna, Wi-Fi, and workout room. Golf and honeymoon packages are available to make your stay extra special.

Herbed Lavosh
(An Unleavened Cracker)

Yield: 4 sheet pans

"Lavosh is a wonderfully versatile cracker which can be made savory or sweet, such as with cardamom or cinnamon and sugar. It also freezes very well for up to two months. And it can be put in oblong clear bags tied up with a ribbon to give as a healthy gift! I just taught a Wellness Cooking Class with this recipe and it was a hit!"—Innkeeper

2½ cups flour
1 tsp sugar
1 tsp salt
2/3 cup water
1 egg white
2 Tbsp melted butter

Topping:

2 beaten egg whites
All types of herbs: oregano, thyme, basil, chives: fresh or dried; sea salt & pepper; cajun seasoning, sesame & poppy seeds; garlic powder, etc.

To make sweet lavosh: Cinnamon & sugar, cardamom & sugar, etc.

Preheat oven to 400°F. Mix flour, sugar, salt and sift. Add water, egg white and melted butter. Mix well to make a stiff dough. Knead until smooth. Divide into fours and roll paper thin. Place in greased half-sheet pan or cookie sheet, pulling edges out as far as you can as dough will be springy. Brush with egg whites and sprinkle whatever topping combinations you want your crackers to taste like. Bake for 10–12 minutes until golden. Turn in oven half way through if oven has hot spots.

Will make 4 half-sheet pans of large crackers: Break up into midsize pieces and serve as large shards to be broken up by guests. Enjoy!

Enchanted Valley B&B

INNKEEPERS Kenneth & Marcia Helgerson
ADDRESS 5554 Enchanted Valley Road, Cross Plains, WI 53528
TELEPHONE (608) 798-4554
CONTACT kmhelgerson@enchantedvalley.com | www.enchantedvalley.com
FEATURES 2 Rooms | Children welcome/inquire | Pet-free environment

A Piece of Heaven … The secluded Enchanted Valley B&B, nestled in the beautiful rolling hills and valleys of rural Cross Plains, lies on five acres of lush woods and open fields. Our home is a soothing, yet energizing, certified Feng Shui space. Window walls and a cathedral ceiling incorporate structure with nature, and likewise, body with soul. Heavenly feather queen beds, a wood burning stove or bonfire for cool nights, a bountiful garden, gourmet vegan breakfasts, and decks to enjoy breathtaking panoramic views ensure reveling "in the moment."

A concert of singing birds beckons you each morning from the patio door in your bedroom to your private deck. As you stroll through Ken and Marcia's numerous organically grown vegetable, herb, and flower gardens, listen to the many species of birds they attract to their paradise. The Jacuzzi, therapeutic massage, Reiki master teaching, outside cedar sauna, labyrinth and naturopathy, iridology, and "mindfulness" (i.e. Thich Nhat Hanh) conversations make your stay an everlasting one.

Salmon Loaf

Yield: 4 servings

- ½ cup salad dressing
- 1 can cream of celery soup
- 2 eggs, beaten
- ½ cup chopped onion
- ½ cup chopped green pepper
- 1 tsp lemon juice
- 16 oz. salmon
- 1 cup bread crumbs, plain

Preheat oven to 350°F. In a large bowl, combine the dressing, soup, and eggs. Add in the onion, peppers, and lemon juice and mix well. Toss the salmon lightly in the bread crumbs and combine with the other ingredients. Place the mixture in a greased loaf pan and bake 1 hour.

Tip: Use canned, boneless and skinless salmon in this dish for a quick timesaver.

Escape by the Lake

INNKEEPER Karen Langfeldt
ADDRESS 922 Sally's Alley N, Hudson, WI 54016
TELEPHONE (715) 381-2871
CONTACT relax@escapebythelake.com | www.escapebythelake.com
FEATURES 2 Rooms | Children welcome/inquire | Pet-free environment

Nestled among mature pines, Escape by the Lake spans 100 feet of beautiful Lake Mallalieu shoreline along the scenic lower St. Croix River. Located on the former site of the North Shore Resort, serenity still abounds. Our lakeshore retreat hosts the best of nature—from majestic eagles to vigorous walleye. Let Escape by the Lake's calm surroundings nurture you and soothe your soul. Bird watch from the deck, fish from the dock, escape on the paddleboat, or simply bask in the year-round pleasures of the lake. Sparkling summers ease into autumn's brilliant show of changing leaves along the lakeshore followed by a peaceful blanket of white. Winter is perfect for cross-country skiing, ice fishing, or simply enjoying the view.

With just two guest rooms, you are assured VIP treatment. Choose from the Garden Room overlooking the lake and featuring Euro-lake cottage décor, or the Grand View Suite with its breathtaking view, traditional furnishings, and wood-burning fireplace: It's your choice. So whenever your travels bring you to the area, or you simply crave a retreat, come be our guests, and escape.

Easy Cheese Danish

Yield: 8 servings

"I often serve this for my bread course when I only have one room of guests—I cut the recipe in half and bake only 18–20 minutes. Guests always rave about how wonderful and tasty this simple recipe is. It is adapted from California Sizzles: Easy and Distinctive Recipes for a Vibrant Lifestyle. "—Innkeeper

- 8 oz. cream cheese, softened
- 1½ tsp vanilla extract
- ¼ cup sugar
- 2 pkgs. crescent roll dough
- 1 egg, beaten
- 4 oz. sliced almonds

Preheat oven to 350°F. In a medium bowl, mix together the cream cheese, vanilla, and sugar to make the filling. Unroll 1 can of crescents on a cookie sheet, sealing perforations. Spread the filling on the dough, leaving a ¼-inch border around the edge. Unroll the second can of crescent rolls and lay on top of the first layer. Seal the edges with a fork. Brush the top with the beaten egg and sprinkle with almonds. Bake 30 minutes, or until golden.

Fargo Mansion Inn

INNKEEPERS Barry Luce & Tom Boycks
ADDRESS 406 Mulberry Street, Lake Mills, WI 53551
TELEPHONE (920) 648-3654
CONTACT fargo@charter.net | www.fargomansion.com
FEATURES 5 Rooms | Children not allowed | Resident pets only

The Fargo Mansion Inn is an elegant Queen Anne Victorian mansion listed on the National Historic Registry. The inn is the perfect romantic getaway. Each of the inn's private baths features hand-laid Italian marble and double whirlpool baths. A full breakfast is served each morning and you can sit and enjoy a complimentary beverage while you relax on the inn's great wrap-around porch.

Fargo Mansion is conveniently located just two blocks from the Lake Mills Town Square and a short drive from Madison, Milwaukee, and Chicago. Also nearby are the Aztalan State Park, Rock Lake, and Glacial Drumlin bike trail. So as Barry and Tom say, come and relax and make yourself at home!

Barry's Very Berry Muffins

Yield: 1 Dozen

"We have used this recipe for over 20 years. We wanted something simple to make breakfast preparation easier. We came up with this basic white muffin recipe that could be easily adapted for seasonal fruits. Repeat guests often want to know if we are making our "Very Berry" muffins—they are not afraid to ask for the leftovers."—Innkeeper

1½ cups flour
½ cup sugar
2 tsp baking powder
½ tsp salt
1 egg
½ cup milk
½ stick butter, melted
1½ cups berries of choice, or combination

Preheat oven to 375°F and grease the cups of a muffin tin. In a large mixing bowl, sift together the dry ingredients. Add the milk, egg, and butter; mix. Fold in berries of choice. Scoop the batter into the muffin cups, filling each about ½ full. Sprinkle a bit of sugar over the top of each muffin before baking for a crispy top. Bake 20–25 minutes, or until done.

Variation: For fall, add ½ can pumpkin pie filling, 1 teaspoon cinnamon, and 1 teaspoon nutmeg in place of the berries for Pumpkin Muffins.

Forest Moon B&B

INNKEEPERS Leonard & Carol Anderson

ADDRESS 12546 W. County Highway OO, Hayward, WI 54843

TELEPHONE (715) 638-2529

CONTACT forestmoon1@centurytel.net | www.forestmoonbb.com

FEATURES 4 Rooms | Children age 12 and over welcome | Resident Pets only | Will accommodate guests' dietary needs

Forest Moon B&B is a rustic two-story log home that was built by hand by the original owner, who cut down all the trees and gathered the rocks for the large fireplace. The house is located in a clearing in the hills between Hayward and Cable near several hiking, biking, and ski trails, and the Chequamegon National Forest. There are also many lakes and golf courses nearby.

The B&B, which was described by a guest as being "rustic in the best possible way," has four bedrooms decorated in Northwoods style. Guests can relax in the three season room, in the second floor loft, or in the great room in front of the fire. A full breakfast is served each morning that usually includes muffins, fruit, an egg dish, meat, juice and coffee.

Havarti Baked Eggs

Yield: 1 serving

Adapted from *The American Country Inn and Bed & Breakfast Cookbook*. It was submitted by the Chanticleer Bed and Breakfast Inn in Ashland, Oregon for that cookbook.

"This is my favorite egg dish—our guests love it and it's so easy!"—Innkeeper

- 1 tsp butter
- 2 Tbsp cream
- 2 eggs
- salt and pepper
- Havarti cheese, grated

Preheat oven to 425°F. Melt the butter in a 6 oz. ramekin to coat the sides and bottom. Add the cream, then the eggs (gently to not break the yolks). Season with salt and pepper. Sprinkle with enough Havarti cheese to cover the top of the eggs. Bake for 18 minutes to have eggs thoroughly set.

Tip: Bake for less time if you want the yolks to be a little runny.

Fountain Chateau B&B

INNKEEPER Susanne Soltvedt
ADDRESS 202 E. Main Street, Hustler WI 54637
TELEPHONE (608) 427-3787
CONTACT innkeeper@fountainchateau.com | www.fountainchateau.com
FEATURES 8 Rooms | Children welcome/inquire | Pet-Free Environment | Will accommodate guests' special dietary needs

The Fountain Chateau B&B is a restored historic hotel built in 1922. It is handicap accessible with an elevator, outside ramp and a first floor bathroom with a wheelchair-in shower. The Harmony Bistro Restaurant located inside the Fountain Chateau is open Wednesday through Saturday from 7:00–2:00 and a Sunday Buffet from 10:30–2:00. The facility is appropriate for small weddings, bridal showers, birthday parties, family reunions and business meetings. The Fountain Chateau is located one block from the Omaha Bike Trail, which connects to the Elroy/Sparta Trail.

Cranberry-Apple Casserole

Yield: 8–10 servings

"This recipe is so quick and easy and so delicious. Sure to bring positive comments from guests."—Innkeeper

- 2 cups fresh cranberries
- 3 cups unpeeled apples, chopped
- 1 cup sugar
- ½ cup brown sugar
- 1 cup oatmeal
- ½ cup melted butter

Preheat oven to 350°F. Mix cranberries, apples and sugar together and place in a 9-inch casserole dish. Then mix brown sugar, oatmeal, and melted butter together and place on top of cranberry mixture. Bake for approximately 40 minutes.

Four Gables B&B

INNKEEPERS Gerald & Nancy Jorgensen
ADDRESS W5648 US Highway 14-61, La Crosse, WI 54601
TELEPHONE (608) 788-7958
CONTACT forgables@juno.com | www.wbba.org/inns/FourGablesBedandBreakfast_LaCrosse_WI.html
FEATURES 3 Rooms; Private & shared baths | Children not allowed | Pet-free environment

Our 1906 Queen Anne historical home has survived straight-line winds, hail, snow, and torrents of rain. We purchased the home in 1982. Unfortunately, it was deteriorating after years of neglect, but we saw the potential in this gem and embarked on a painstaking restoration. In 1997 we opened the B&B and began pampering our guests, a practice that continues today and ultimately brings them back for more. Our guests use two words to describe our home and our four-course breakfast: "romantic elegance."

Our back fields offer deer and wild turkey sightings on an almost daily basis and we are located within five miles of historic downtown La Crosse, the Mississippi and its sightseeing cruises. Other area attractions include local festivals, skiing, and historic sites.

Coq au Vin

Yield: 6 servings

"This is a quick gourmet recipe without all the fuss."—Innkeeper

- 6 boneless skinless chicken breasts
- Salt and pepper
- 1 Tbsp flour
- ¼ cup butter
- Brandy
- 8 shallots, peeled
- 1¼ cups good white wine
- ½ pound morel mushrooms, or a combination of wild mushrooms
- ½ tsp herbes de Provence
- ¼ cup heavy cream

Season the chicken pieces with salt and pepper; dust with flour. Melt the butter carefully in a large sauté pan or flameproof casserole, watch carefully so that is doesn't burn. Quickly brown the chicken on both sides. Remove from pan and keep warm. Pour a splash of brandy into the pot and set alight. When the flames have died down, add the shallots, wine, and mushrooms. Return the chicken to the pan and season with herbes de Provence. Cover and simmer for approximately 30–35 minutes, or until done. Remove the chicken and arrange on a serving platter.

Bring the juices to a rolling boil and allow to reduce just a bit. Lower the heat and add the cream, stirring to make a smooth sauce. Adjust the seasonings and pour the sauce over the chicken breasts to serve.

Franklin Street Inn

INNKEEPERS Judy & Ron Halma
ADDRESS 318 East Franklin Street, Appleton, WI 54911
TELEPHONE (920) 209-9711 | (888) 993-1711
CONTACT info@franklinstreetinn.com | www.franklinstreetinn.com
FEATURES 4 Rooms | Children age 5 and older welcome | Pet-free environment | Will accommodate guests' special dietary needs.

"Every bite of Judy's breakfast brought an explosion to our taste buds, what a treat!"—Guest

"Judy has collected many recipes to offer guests with special dietary needs."—Guest

The award-winning 1897 Victorian Franklin Street Inn, located in the downtown historical district of Appleton, begins its eighteenth year. We aim to go beyond your expectations to guarantee a pleasurable stay, and we want to thank our guests for voting the inn Best B&B in the Fox Valley for 2011.

Each of our four rooms/suites has been decorated with great attention to detail. Whatever amenities you value most in your bed and breakfast experiences, just look for it here because we have it: on-site massage, whirlpools, fireplaces, and your reservation includes a full, scrumptious breakfast served in our formal dining room or in your suite. Enjoy the antique décor throughout the house; it combines the elegance of the nineteenth century with the amenities of the twenty-first. Open our door for charm and hospitality!

Apricot-Orange Cream Scones

Yield: 8 scones

"I have been told numerous times, 'Your scones are the best that I have ever sampled.' "—Innkeeper

- 2 cups flour
- 3 Tbsp sugar
- 3 tsp baking powder
- 2 tsp orange peel, grated
- ½ tsp salt
- ½ cup dried apricots, chopped
- ½ cup white vanilla chips
- 1⅓ cups whipping cream

Frosting:

- 2–3 Tbsp orange juice
- Zest from 1 orange
- 1 cup powdered sugar

Preheat oven to 400°F. Grease a cookie sheet lightly. Combine first seven ingredients in a large bowl. Mix well. Add whipping cream all at once. Stir just until dry ingredients are moistened. (I have had to use more cream, usually by about ¼ cup) Knead dough 6–7 times until smooth on a lightly floured surface.

Divide in half and pat into two 6 inch rounds. Cut into 4 wedges. Place rounds 2 inches apart on cookie sheet.

Frosting:

Grate orange for zest and then juice the orange. Mix orange juice, zest and powdered sugar, then drizzle over scones. Bake for 10–13 minutes till golden brown. Cool 5 minutes. Serve warm for best quality.

Tip: You can combine first seven ingredients and store in airtight bowl. Then in the morning add the cream and follow recipe from there. Refrigerate orange zest and juice. Add powdered sugar to make the frosting in the morning.

Franklin Victorian B&B

INNKEEPERS Jennifer & Steve Dunn
ADDRESS 220 East Franklin Street, Sparta, WI 54656
TELEPHONE (608) 366-1427
CONTACT innkeeper@franklinvictorianbb.com | www.FranklinVictorianBB.com
FEATURES 2 Rooms; 2 Suites | Children age 12 and older welcome | Pet-Free Environment | Will accommodate guests' special dietary needs

Breakfast consisting of fresh fruits (in season), homemade muffins, breads, coffeecake, and scones, breakfast meat, as well as a hot entrée, homemade sorbets, juices, fresh roasted coffee, chai, or tea, and good conversation (we accommodate special dietary needs when made known at time of reservation or arrival). Early morning coffee, chai, and teas are available, and throughout the day the beverage area is available with cocoas, tea, cider, and water (hot & cold) and snacks.

Breakfast is served in the dining room, or if you prefer a little more privacy or special occasion, our guest rooms have Room Service available. We serve a variety of dishes, and hope to make each meal during your stay different and memorable.

Wild Rice Quiche

Yield: 6–8 servings

6 eggs, well-beaten
1 can regular cream of mushroom soup
1½ cups shredded sharp Cheddar cheese
1 cup cooked wild rice
½–1 cup ham or bacon bits or sausage
¼ cup onion, finely chopped
salt and pepper and any seasoning you wish

Preheat oven to 375°F. With mixer, beat eggs, then add soup, cheese, rice, meat, and onion. Add salt and pepper. Mix well with mixer. Pour into quiche dish or 9–10-inch pie plate sprayed with cooking spray. Bake for 35–45 minutes or until a knife inserted in center comes out clean. Let stand a few minutes before serving. Can be prepared the night before and baked the next morning.

Variation: Can be a vegetation dish by leaving out the bacon bits.

Garden Gate B&B

INNKEEPER Robin Vallow
ADDRESS 434 N. 3rd Ave., Sturgeon Bay, WI 54235
TELEPHONE (920) 217-3093
CONTACT stay@doorcountybb.com | www.doorcountybb.com
FEATURES 4 Rooms; 1 Suite | Children welcome/inquire | Pet-Free Environment | Will accommodate guests' special dietary needs

At the Garden Gate B&B, truly "Breakfast is our Signature." Each morning is a new dining experience as the multiple place settings transform into elegance. You are greeted with soft music and a lavish meal. Our breakfast cannot be beat as we offer beverages, fruit, a main dish, and bread or muffins. Each meal may include items such as a quiche dish, French toast, stratas, meat in or on the side, fresh fruit, scrumptious muffins, or fresh strawberry yogurt. The innkeeper works for local farmers so you can expect strawberries or raspberries with your breakfast. Most of the ingredients come from the local farmers' market. We do cater to your dietary needs, so please do not hesitate to ask. And remember "Breakfast is our Signature."

Brunch Strata

Yield: 8 servings

"This recipe is filled with wonderful ingredients bought from the local farmers' market. Guests love it!"—Innkeeper

- 3 cups sliced mushrooms
- 3 cups chopped zucchini
- 2 cups fully cooked ham, cubed
- 1½ cups chopped onions
- 1½ cups chopped green peppers
- 2 garlic cloves, minced
- ⅓ cup vegetable oil
- 3 8 oz. pkgs. cream cheese, softened
- ½ cup half & half cream
- 12 eggs
- 4 cups day old bread, cubed
- 3 cups (12 oz.) shredded Cheddar cheese
- 1 tsp salt
- ½ tsp pepper

Sauté mushrooms, zucchini, ham, onions, green peppers and garlic in oil until vegetables are tender. Drain, pat dry and set aside.

In mixing bowl, beat cream cheese and cream until smooth. Beat in eggs and stir in the bread, cheese, salt, pepper and vegetable mixture.

Pour into 8 individual ramekin dishes. Bake uncovered at 350°F for 35–40 minutes or until knife inserted near the center comes out clean. Let stand for 10 minutes before serving.

Grapevine Log Cabins B&B

INNKEEPERS Ole & Janice Knutson
ADDRESS 19149 Jade Road, Sparta, WI 54656
TELEPHONE (608) 269-3619
CONTACT okgrapevine@centurytel.net | www.grapevinelogcabins.com
FEATURES 3 Cabins | Children welcome | Pets Welcome/inquire

Our bed and breakfast consists of three log cabins that each comfortably accommodate up to four people. Grapevine is a quiet romantic getaway for guests looking to relax for a weekend or longer.

Breakfast is served each morning in the main house. Small groups will enjoy a sit-down, family-style breakfast and larger parties are served buffet-style. Our guests are always surprised by the great selection and we always get compliments. After breakfast enjoy a walk on our mile-long hiking trail through the woods. We are also located just a mile and a half from the world famous Elroy-Sparta bike trail.

Swedish Pears

Yield: 4–6 servings

"This is a very popular breakfast recipe. We always get good comments about it."—Innkeeper

- 2 cans pears
- 1 lemon or use 1 Tbsp of lemon juice in the bottle, for fresh pears.
- 6 Tbsp butter or margarine
- 6–8 Tbsp sugar
- 1½ Tbsp flour
- 2 Tbsp half & half
- ½ cup slivered almonds
- nutmeg

Preheat oven to 350°F. Put pears in a buttered 9x9-inch glass cake dish. Melt butter and sugar and flour in a pan until thick and smooth. Stir in cream and almonds. Pour over pears and bake for 30 minutes. Top with nutmeg.

Tips & variations: If using fresh pears, squeeze a tablespoon of lemon juice on them to keep them from browning. Recipe can also be made with granny smiths apples, and can be refrigerated the night before and baked in the morning.

HAMILTON HOUSE B&B

INNKEEPERS Jim & Kathleen Fleming

ADDRESS 328 W Main Street, Whitewater, WI 53190

TELEPHONE (262) 473 1900

CONTACT kathie@bandbhamiltonhouse.com | www.BandBHamiltonHouse.com

FEATURES 8 Rooms | Children welcome/inquire; age 15+ or any age with whole house rental | Pet-Free Environment | Will accommodate guests' special dietary needs.

Your personal Memory Artisans at the Hamilton House are dedicated to providing contemporary comfort with traditional hospitality, while preserving the privacy you need to make the most of your time away.

A well-rounded hot breakfast is prepared with a touch of indulgence, satisfying your need for "just a little something." You can choose to enjoy breakfast by firelight in the formal dining room or indulge in a private breakfast delivered to your guest room. Diet restrictions are a welcome opportunity to create something out of the ordinary.

Spacious guest rooms feature inviting beds, jetted tubs and/or fireplaces. Sun-filled parlors provide a tranquil haven for reading, games, or quiet conversation. Stroll to shops, restaurants, lake, and parks.

Breakfast Meatloaf

Yield: 8 servings

"This was created as a result of looking for something interesting, but lighter, to serve guests who do not eat pork or red meat. Guests are surprised by the delicate tartness that the apple gives this breakfast meatloaf. Best prepared the day before allowing flavors to blend."—Innkeeper

1 lb. ground chicken
1 medium Granny Smith apple, grated
1 medium onion, grated
2 cups plain stuffing croutons (I like Pepperidge Farm)
2 large eggs
Parsley, thyme, and rosemary

Preheat oven to 350°F. Spray pie pan or loaf pan with cooking oil. Mix all ingredients in a large bowl. Press evenly into pan. Sprinkle top with parsley, thyme, and rosemary.

Bake for 50–60 minutes until browned. Cut into wedges and serve—good warm or cold.

Variation: Can be made with any combination of ground chicken, pork, or veal.

Heaven Scent B&B

INNKEEPERS Todd & Beth Ehlenfeldt
ADDRESS 425 Grove Street, Randolph, WI 53956
TELEPHONE (920) 763-2170
CONTACT heavenscentbb@centurytel.net | www.heavenscentbb.com
FEATURES 2 Rooms | Children welcome/inquire | Resident pets only

Heaven Scent B&B, a former Catholic Church, is located in the village of Randolph, Wisconsin. As you enter the former sanctuary, you will stand in awe of the beautiful handcrafted woodwork, 21-foot-high ceilings, and original stained-glass windows.

Start your day with coffee, tea, or juice before getting ready for a delicious home-cooked breakfast. Enjoy your meal in the common area in front of the gas fireplace. After breakfast, enjoy our gardens and deck, or watch the large-screen TV. Antique shopping, fishing, hiking, sightseeing, and fine dining are just a short drive away.

Whether you are visiting family and friends or enjoying a much-needed getaway, stay with us at Heaven Scent B&B and relax.

Lemon Wisconsin Ricotta Pancakes with Warm Blueberry Compote

Yield: 6 servings (3 pancakes each)

4 cups (2 pints) blueberries, fresh or frozen
2 tsp cornstarch
1 cup sugar
½ cup water
¼ cup prepared lemon curd (from 10- to 12-oz. jar)
1 Tbsp fresh orange juice
Pinch of salt
1 Tbsp butter
½ tsp pure vanilla extract

2 cups all-purpose flour
2 tsp baking powder
½ tsp salt
2 Tbsp sugar
Grated zest of 1 lemon
2 eggs, separated
1 cup (8 oz.) Wisconsin ricotta cheese
1½ cups milk, preferably whole milk
Confectioners' sugar

Blueberry Compote: In sauté pan, combine blueberries, cornstarch, sugar, water, lemon curd, orange juice, and pinch of salt. Gently cook over medium heat until blueberries are tender but not broken down, and mixture simmers and thickens. Remove from heat; stir in butter and vanilla. Set aside to cool slightly.

Pancakes: In medium bowl, sift flour, baking powder, salt and sugar. Stir in lemon zest. Set aside. In large bowl mix 2 egg yolks and ricotta cheese. Fold in dry ingredients, alternately, with milk. In a separate bowl, whip 2 egg whites until medium-stiff peaks form. Fold into batter.

Final Preparation: Heat buttered nonstick skillet or griddle over medium high heat or to 350°F (water drops on skillet should skitter or sizzle when hot). For each pancake, pour ¼ to ⅓ cup batter and cook until bubbles form on top. Turn and cook until bottom is golden brown and pancake is cooked through. To serve, stack 3 pancakes on each plate with a dollop of the remaining prepared lemon curd between pancakes. Sprinkle with confectioners' sugar and pour compote over pancakes.

Hill Street B&B

INNKEEPERS Jay & Kelly Phelps

ADDRESS 353 W Hill Street, Spring Green, WI 53588

TELEPHONE (608) 588-7751

CONTACT hillstbb@frontier.com | www.hillstreetbb.com

FEATURES 7 Rooms; Private & shared baths | Children welcome/inquire | Resident pets only

We welcome you to our home and invite you to relax in one of our two living rooms filled with handcrafted woodwork, or on our front porch. We start your day with a full breakfast and always have homemade cookies and tea in the afternoon and evening.

We are conveniently located within walking distance of downtown Spring Green where you can browse through a variety of shops and art galleries. We are also close to many area attractions such as Frank Lloyd Wright's Taliesin, the American Players Theatre, and the House on the Rock. Recreational activities include championship golf, canoeing on the Wisconsin River, bicycling the county roads and trails, and hiking in the state parks.

Almond Date Scones

Yield: 1 Dozen

1 cup all-purpose flour
1 cup whole wheat pastry flour
¼ cup brown sugar
1 Tbsp baking powder
¼ tsp salt
6 Tbsp unsalted butter
⅓ cup almond paste, cut into small pieces
½ cup chopped dates
1 beaten egg
½ cup half & half
½ tsp almond extract
¼ cup raw, coarse sugar

Preheat oven to 375°F. In a large bowl, combine the flours, brown sugar, baking powder, and salt. Cut in the butter until the mixture resembles coarse crumbs, then cut in the almond paste. Add the chopped dates and mix to combine. In a separate bowl, whisk together the egg, half & half, and almond extract, then combine with the dry ingredients. When just combined, use a medium scoop to drop the scones onto a sheet pan lined with parchment paper or a nonstick baking sheet. Sprinkle with coarse sugar and bake 15 minutes, until golden brown. Turn the pan halfway through cooking. Serve warm with your favorite butter or jam.

Hillcrest Inn & Carriage House

INNKEEPERS Gayle & Mike Hohner
ADDRESS 540 Storle Avenue, Burlington, WI 53105
TELEPHONE (262) 763-4706 | (800) 313-9030
CONTACT hillcrest@thehillcrestinn.com | www.thehillcrestinn.com
FEATURES 6 Rooms | Children welcome/inquire | Pet-free environment

Tranquility awaits visitors at The Hillcrest Inn & Carriage House. Guests enter through the gates of the original stone pillars before approaching the 1908 Edwardian estate. A panoramic seven-mile view of waterways is framed by the foliage and flower gardens that abound on this four-acre property. Relaxing on the porches or taking a quiet stroll to the ornate gazebo nestled in the woods are experiences to be treasured.

The main house has been meticulously restored to its original splendor, offering guests warmth, serenity, and beauty. Turn-of-the-century furnishings take guests back in time to a more peaceful and elegant era. Lace curtains on the windows, down comforters on the beds, classical music drifting up the staircase, and the aroma of cinnamon wafting from the oven are sure to please the weary traveler. A formal four-course breakfast, which always includes a taste of chocolate, is served on fine china and stemware in the dining room each morning.

Individual Raspberry Cheesecakes with Chocolate Ganache

Yield: 12 ramekins

"The visual WOW factor does not disappoint on taste either—a guest favorite."—Innkeeper

Crust:

20 oreo cookies (smashed into small pieces)
2 Tbsp butter

Filling:

1 (8 oz.) tub Cool Whip (thawed)
1 (8 oz.) pkg. cream cheese
¾ cup raspberry preserves
½ cup sugar
1 Tbsp sea salt

Topping:

1 (12-oz.) pkg. semisweet chocolate chips
¼ cup half & half
2 (6-oz.) pkgs. fresh raspberries

Crust: Preheat oven to 350°F. Mix cookie crumbs and butter in a small glass bowl. Microwave 1 minute. Pat into 12 ramekins. Bake for 10 minutes.

Filling: Combine all ingredients in bowl of mixer and beat. Place in ramekins on top of crust.

Topping: Microwave chocolate chips and half & half in small glass bowl for one minute. Stir till smooth. Spread on the filling in the ramekins when cool. Stand up fresh raspberries in the chocolate topping.

Honeybee Inn B&B

INNKEEPERS Barbara & Fred Ruka

ADDRESS 611 E. Walnut Street, Horicon, WI 53032

TELEPHONE (920) 485-4855

CONTACT Innkeeper@honeybeeinn.com | www.honeybeeinn.com

FEATURES 4 Rooms | Children over age 12 welcome | Resident pet only | Will accommodate guests' special dietary needs

Established as a bed and breakfast in 2003 by Barbara and Fred Ruka, the Honeybee Inn is a Queen Anne/Craftsmen–style home built in 1902, with 5,000 square feet. Four individually decorated guest rooms have gorgeous fireplaces, whirlpools, feather beds, and shower spas. Delectable gourmet, multi-course breakfasts are served every morning. In 2011 and 2012, it was one of *Midwest Living Magazine's* top B&B's in the Midwest. Honeybee Inn is located a few blocks from the Horicon Marsh National Wildlife Refuge, the largest freshwater cattail marsh in the U.S. People come from all over the country to birdwatch, canoe, bike, and hike in this natural wonderland.

Waffle of Insane Greatness

Yield: 3 large waffles

"An easy, crispy, light, tasty waffle that my guests go nuts over!"—Innkeeper

- ¾ cup flour
- ¼ cup cornstarch
- ½ tsp baking powder
- ¼ tsp baking soda
- ½ tsp salt
- 1 Tbsp sugar
- 1 cup buttermilk
- ⅓ cup vegetable oil
- 1 large egg, beaten
- ¾ tsp vanilla

In a medium bowl, combine flour, cornstarch, baking powder, baking soda, salt and sugar. Mix well. Add buttermilk, oil, beaten egg and vanilla. Mix well and let batter sit for 30 minutes. Preheat waffle iron. Fill and cook according to manufacturer's instructions, until crisp and golden.

Inn at Lonesome Hollow

INNKEEPERS	Nora & Pete Knapik
ADDRESS	15415 Vance Road, Soldiers Grove, WI 54655
TELEPHONE	(608) 624-3429
CONTACT	info@lonesomehollow.com | www.lonesomehollow.com
FEATURES	3 Rooms; 2 Suites; 1 Cabin | Children welcome/inquire | Pets welcome/inquire

Our Inn is situated on 160 acres of mostly wooded rural land near Soldiers Grove, in the Driftless Area of southwest Wisconsin. Our Kickapoo Valley B&B lies between La Crosse and Prairie du Chien. We offer four miles of private hiking trails, and our skies are completely free of light pollution so the stargazing is superb.

We have three deluxe rooms in the main house, a two-bedroom cabin, and a separate house with two very private suites. Full country breakfasts using organic and locally grown ingredients are served family-style each morning. Breakfasts are complemented by raspberry and wild blackberry jams, prepared using berries picked from our gardens and woods, and maple syrup produced from our own trees.

Berry Good Baked French Toast

Yield: 6–8 servings

"This recipe was clipped out of a magazine and stuck into one of Pete's retirement cards, since he told everyone we were opening a B&B. This is the most often requested recipe by our guests."—Innkeeper

- ½ cup flour
- 1½ cups milk
- 1 Tbsp sugar
- ½ tsp vanilla
- ¼ tsp salt
- 1 tsp cinnamon
- ½ tsp nutmeg
- 6 eggs
- 10 slices (1-inch thick) French bread cut into ½-inch cubes
- 3 oz. cream cheese cut into ½-inch cubes
- 1 cup fresh or frozen blueberries, raspberries, or blackberries
- ½ cup chopped pecans

Plan ahead—dish needs overnight refrigeration.

Grease a 9x13-inch baking dish. Place flour, milk, sugar, vanilla, salt, cinnamon, nutmeg, and eggs in a large bowl, and beat with a hand mixer until smooth. Add bread cubes and stir until coated. Pour bread mixture into pan. Top evenly with cream cheese, berries, and pecans. Cover and refrigerate overnight up to 24 hours. The next day, remove bread mixture from refrigerator at least 30 minutes before baking. Bake, uncovered, at 350°F for 30 minutes or until golden brown. Cut into serving size pieces. Sprinkle with powdered sugar. Serve with maple syrup.

Inn at Pinewood

INNKEEPERS Jane & Bill Weber
ADDRESS 1820 Silver Forest Lane, Eagle River, WI 54521
TELEPHONE (715) 477-2377
CONTACT pinewood@nnex.net | www.inn-at-pinewood.com
FEATURES 4 Rooms; 4 Suites | Children over age 6 welcome | Resident pets only | Will accommodate guests' special dietary needs.

The Inn at Pinewood is a former classic 1934 log hunting and fishing lodge. The original sienna log walls remain and the hulking fieldstone fireplace has no doubt heard its share of fish tales. Sit by the fire to chat, read, or just relax. The large common area is filled with antiques and is a great place to hold a meeting, family reunion, or small wedding, yet is still cozy enough for two.

Enjoy breakfast in the sunlit garden room and you may get the chance to see Northwoods wildlife. After breakfast take advantage of the watercraft available for rent, join the loons on private Carpenter Lake, and watch the eagles perch in the trees. At night, sit around the fire pit to count stars and enjoy the peace and quiet that our guests say is abundant.

"Wacky" Cake

Yield: 9x13 cake

"This recipe was handed down to me by a relative. I'm not sure where this cake got its name, but all I can say is that this is one of the most moist chocolate cakes I have ever eaten. It's so good, you don't even need to frost it. Just serve with some delicious vanilla ice cream. This cake is as easy as a box mix but so much better."—Innkeeper

- 3 cups flour
- 2 cups sugar
- 6 Tbsp cocoa
- 2 tsp baking soda
- 1 tsp salt
- 2 tsp vinegar
- ¾ cup canola oil
- 2 tsp vanilla
- 2 cups cold water

Grease and flour a 9x13-inch cake pan. Measure flour, sugar, cocoa, baking soda, and salt and put in medium size bowl. Mix the dry ingredients well then make three holes in the dry ingredients with a spoon. Next, in first hole add the vinegar, second hole add the oil, and the third hole add the vanilla. Over all, pour 2 cups cold water. Beat well with a mixer. Batter will be soupy and delicious. Place in the 9x13 cake pan. Bake at 350°F for 35 to 40 minutes or until a toothpick comes clean when inserted in the middle of the cake. Do not over bake.

Delicious Fudge Frosting:

- 1 cup sugar
- ¼ cup margarine
- ¼ cup milk
- dash of salt

Bring these ingredients to a boil in medium saucepan. Once it starts boiling, remove from heat and stir in ½ cup chocolate chips and 1 teaspoon vanilla. Stir until melted. Frosts a 9x13-inch cake.

Inn at Windmill Farm

INNKEEPERS Ed Fenendael & Frank Villigan
ADDRESS 3829 Fairview Road, Baileys Harbor, WI 54202
TELEPHONE (920) 868-9282
CONTACT windmillfarmwi@aol.com | www.1900windmillfarm.com
FEATURES 3 Rooms | No children | Pet-free environment

Relax in the quiet intimacy of an early 1900 restored farmhouse located in a pastoral setting in the central part of the Door County Peninsula. The Inn at Windmill Farm, featured in *Door County Magazine* and the *Wisconsin Trails* magazine, is situated on ten acres along with the original barn, well house, windmill, and orchard.

The award-winning Inn at Windmill Farm provides you with a step back to a gentler time. The rooms are all air-conditioned and a guest telephone is available in the library, keeping with the quiet atmosphere of the inn, and to make your visit relaxing and peaceful. Windmill Farm is located within easy reach of all that Door County has to offer and our goal is to make your stay one of your best experiences ever.

Crispy Cookies

Yield: about 4 Dozen

- 1 cup sugar
- 1 cup brown sugar
- 1 cup butter
- 1 cup vegetable oil
- 1 egg
- 1 tsp vanilla extract
- 3½ cups flour
- 1 tsp baking soda
- 1 tsp salt
- 1 tsp cream of tartar
- 1 cup oatmeal
- 1 cup Rice Crispies
- 1 cup flaked coconut
- ½ cup chopped pecans

Preheat oven to 350°F. In a large bowl, cream together the sugar, brown sugar, butter, and vegetable oil. Add in the egg and vanilla and mix to combine. In a separate bowl, sift together the flour, baking soda, salt, and cream of tartar. Add to the creamed mixture and blend well. Stir in the oatmeal, Rice Crispies, coconut, and pecans and drop by teaspoonfuls onto a cookie sheet. Press each cookie with a fork and bake 15 minutes.

Variation: To make a chocolate version, add in ¾ cup cocoa, 1 extra egg white, ½ cup brown sugar, ½ cup granulated sugar, and 1/3 cup butter or oil. Follow instructions as above and sprinkle with powdered sugar once the cookies are cool.

Inn on Hillwind

INNKEEPERS John & Jean Hayes

ADDRESS N4922 Hillwind Road, Plymouth, WI 53073

TELEPHONE (920) 892-2199

CONTACT hillwind@execpc.com | www.innonhillwind.com

FEATURES 3 Rooms; 2 Suites | Children welcome depending on age/inquire | Some pets welcome/inquire | Will accommodate guests with special dietary needs

Country comfort awaits you in this 1848 Victorian farmhouse set on six picturesque acres. The inn features five romantic rooms, all with private baths (most with double whirlpools), and queen or king–size beds, dressed in luxurious linens. All rooms have fireplaces—just the spot for curling up with a good book and cup of hot cocoa—and all have private porches that are perfect for birdwatching or stargazing. Savor a home-cooked breakfast served in the dining room or delivered to your room. Enjoy hiking, biking, swimming, canoeing, or skiing in nearby Kettle Moraine State Forest or browse the shops in Kohler and Plymouth. A perfect blend of privacy and pampering will make your stay at Inn on Hillwind a truly memorable experience.

Blueberry French Toast

Yield: 8–10 servings

"This recipe was shared with us by one of our guests and has become a frequently requested favorite."—Innkeeper

1 large loaf French bread
6 eggs
3 cups milk
2 tsp vanilla
1 cup brown sugar
1 cup pecans or walnuts, chopped
2 cups fresh or frozen blueberries

Plan ahead, dish needs overnight refrigeration.

Spray 9x13-inch pan with cooking spray. Slice bread into 1-inch slices and layer in pan. Combine eggs, milk and vanilla and pour over bread in pan. Cover and refrigerate overnight. Next morning, spread brown sugar, nuts and berries on top of bread. Bake at 350°F for about 50 minutes. Sprinkle with powdered sugar and serve with syrup on the side.

Variation: Although we've only made this with blueberries, one could try other berries/fruits for a change of pace.

Inn on Maple

INNKEEPERS Louise & Bill Robbins
ADDRESS 2378 Maple Drive, Sister Bay, WI 54234
TELEPHONE (920) 854-5107
CONTACT innonmaple@dcwis.com | www.innonmaple.com
FEATURES 6 Rooms | No Children | Resident pets only | Will accommodate guests' special dietary needs

Inn on Maple is a charming Historic Register home with six upstairs guest rooms, each featuring antique armoires and queen-sized beds with wonderful fresh linens. The inn also has a separate room with two twin beds, great for visiting families. Watch a movie, play a game, or curl up with a book by the fire in the comfortable Gathering Room. Spend the afternoon relaxing on the backyard deck as you watch the birds fly by.

Each morning you'll enjoy a delightful full breakfast that includes fresh fruit, homemade muffins or bread, a daily entrée, juice, coffee, and tea. Breakfast is served on the enclosed front porch, or outdoors on the deck, weather permitting. Afternoon cookies and beverages are also served daily.

Blueberry Croissant Puff

Yield: 10 ramekins

- 4 large croissants, cut into pieces
- 1½ cups fresh or frozen blueberries or thawed frozen cherries
- 1 8-oz. pkg. cream cheese warmed to room temperature
- ⅔ cup sugar
- 2 eggs
- 1 tsp vanilla
- 1¼ cups milk
- Powdered sugar
- Maple syrup

Preheat oven to 350°F. Place croissant pieces evenly in 10 ramekins (½ cup size) or across bottom of 9-inch baking dish. Sprinkle with blueberries.

Beat cream cheese, sugar, eggs and vanilla in a blender until well blended. Gradually add milk, blending until smooth. Pour evenly over croissant pieces. Let stand for 20 minutes. Bake at 350°F for 20–25 minutes or until set in the centers and golden brown. (Using oval ramekins, bake 20 minutes in convection oven. Adjust your time accordingly.

Serve warm, sprinkled with powdered sugar and maple syrup.

Jay Lee Inn

INNKEEPERS Monica & Leo Lettow
ADDRESS 444 S Lake Street, Elkhart Lake, WI 53020
TELEPHONE (920) 876-2910
CONTACT mlettow@jayleeinn.com | www.jayleeinn.com
FEATURES 7 Rooms; Private & shared baths | Children welcome/inquire | Pets welcome/inquire

This Victorian Federal home, located on one acre of lake-view property, was built in 1902 by William and Carolyn Krueger. The inn is situated along the original historic path of the Elkhart Lake racetrack. Throughout the years, the property has been used as a boarding house, an inn, and even as additional guest rooms for area resorts and hotels. The home has been completely renovated to reveal its original charm, and owners Leo and Monica thought it appropriate to re-name the home "Jay Lee Inn," the name given by Jacob and Leitha Stein back when the inn was affiliated with Pine Point Resort.

Today the inn offers a total of seven spacious guest rooms. Five of the rooms are located on the second floor and offer private baths, while the two rooms located on the third floor have a shared bath. A large dining room and sitting room with piano are available for guests to enjoy during their stay. Each morning a hot gourmet breakfast is served.

Swedish Flop

Yield: 8-10 servings

"This is a family recipe that has been a super favorite for birthdays and any other special occasion."—Innkeeper

1 cup butter, divided
2 cups flour, divided
1 cup plus 2 Tbsp water
1 tsp vanilla
3 eggs
Chopped nuts and/or shredded coconut

Confectioners' Sugar Frosting
¾ cup powdered sugar
1 heaping Tbsp butter
1 heaping Tbsp Crisco
½ tsp vanilla extract
2 Tbsp milk

Preheat oven to 350°F. Cut ½ cup of the butter into 1 cup of flour and mix to make coarse crumbs. Sprinkle 2 tablespoons water over the flour mixture and blend quickly with a fork. Roll or pat out dough into two long strips (about 10–12 inches) on an ungreased cookie sheet. Combine 1 cup water and the remaining ½ cup butter in a saucepan and bring to a boil. Add the vanilla. Remove from heat and beat in the remaining 1 cup flour, stirring by hand with a wooden spoon. Add the eggs one at a time, beating well after each addition. Spread the dough over the pastry strips and bake 55–60 minutes, or until lightly browned. (It will flop at this point.) Allow to cool slightly before drizzling with frosting. Sprinkle with your choice of nuts, coconut, or sprinkles.

For the frosting: Mix together all ingredients, adding just 1 tablespoon of milk at first. Add additional milk to make frosting of desired consistency.

Justin Trails B&B Resort

INNKEEPERS Don & Donna Justin
ADDRESS 7452 Kathryn Ave., Sparta, WI 54656
TELEPHONE (608) 269-4522
CONTACT info@justintrails.com | www.justintrails.com
FEATURES 3 Suites; 3 Cabins/Cottages | Children welcome/inquire | Pets welcome/inquire | Will accommodate guests' special dietary needs

A certified green inn set on a boutique organic farm with flower and vegetable gardens, row crop corn, alfalfa, prairie grasses and small grains, 150-acre woodlot, with 10 miles of hiking/cross country ski trails, and two disc golf courses to keep you entertained.

No diet too complicated—vegan, gluten free—I'll cook something tasty for you. Justin Trails granola, fresh fruit or fruit sauce, yogurt, choice of scrambled eggs, French toast or pancakes, bacon on the side, if you like. We're pet and child friendly with log cabins, a cottage, and 3 suites in our foursquare house. Breakfast served in the Lodge at booths between 7:30 and 10:00 a.m. Justin Trails Resort is the perfect place for a wedding ceremony and reception, or anniversary/birthday/shower party.

Donna's Fabulous Brownies

Yield: 24 servings

"The fruit gives a moist tartness that prevents this from being a 'too sweet' brownie."—Innkeeper

- 2¼ cups white sugar
- ¾ cup soft butter
- 4 large eggs
- 1 cup plain yogurt
- 3 cups fresh or frozen cranberries
- ½ cup cocoa powder
- 2 tsp almond extract
- 3 cups whole wheat flour
- 1 tsp baking soda
- ¾ tsp salt
- 1 cup milk chocolate chips
- 1 cup craisins (dried cranberries)

In a food processor, blend together sugar and butter; add eggs and blend; add yogurt and blend; add cranberries, cocoa powder and almond extract and blend.

In a large mixing bowl, add flour, baking soda, salt, chocolate chips and craisins. Pour liquid mixture into dry ingredients and blend until all dry ingredients are incorporated. Pour into 10x15-inch brownie pan and bake at 350°F for 25–30 minutes until it tests done in the middle.

Frosting:

- 4 oz. lite cream cheese
- 1 stick butter
- 2 lb. powdered sugar
- 3 Tbsp blackberry jelly

Blend all ingredients in a food processor until blended, and spread on cooled brownies. Cut into 24 squares and serve.

Lake Orchard Farm B&B

INNKEEPERS Nate & Mary Calkins

ADDRESS N9214 County Road LS, Sheboygan, WI 53083

TELEPHONE (920) 693-8336

CONTACT mary@lakeorchardretreat.com | www.lakeorchardretreat.com

FEATURES 5 Rooms; 1 cottage | Children welcome in the cottage | Pet-Free Environment | Will accommodate guests' special dietary needs

Our sixth generation farm is the perfect location for your romantic couple's retreat or group crafting retreat. Our historical, picturesque setting will put your mind and body at ease. Located near Sheboygan, Wisconsin, our operating farm has an on-site 9-hole golf course, rolling fields, natural woods with walking and skiing trails, fruit orchards, and access to Lake Michigan.

A full breakfast including a homemade dessert is served daily. Guests may choose to eat in the dining room or in their own rooms. We take pride in using our own farm fresh eggs in every breakfast as well as fruit, vegetables, herbs, and apple cider from our own orchards and gardens. We are happy to accommodate any special dietary needs you may have.

Italian Sausage Casserole

Yield: 8 servings

"A hearty breakfast option for our guests! We always get compliments on this breakfast and have received many requests for this recipe. Served with basil potatoes (pg. 249), fresh fruit, and a cream cheese bar for dessert."—Innkeeper

- 1 lb. bulk pork sausage
- 1 lb. bulk Italian sausage
- 1 medium green pepper, chopped
- 1 cup sliced fresh mushrooms
- ½ cup chopped onion
- 2½ cups garlic and onion croutons
- 8 eggs
- 1½ cups milk
- 1 cup (4 oz.) shredded mozzarella cheese
- 1 cup (4 oz.) shredded Cheddar cheese
- 3–4 plum tomatoes, thinly sliced
- ½ cup shredded Parmesan cheese

Plan ahead, this dish needs overnight refrigeration.

Preheat oven to 350°F. Grease a 9x13 inch baking dish. Cook sausage, green pepper, mushrooms, and onions in a large skillet until meat is browned and vegetables are tender; drain. Place croutons in the greased baking dish; top with sausage mixture. Beat eggs and milk; pour over sausage mixture. Cover and chill for 8 hours or overnight. Remove from the refrigerator 30 minutes before baking. Bake, uncovered, at 350°F for 45 minutes. Sprinkle with mozzarella and Cheddar cheeses. Place tomato slices over the top; sprinkle with Parmesan cheese. Bake 15 minutes more or until a knife inserted in the center comes out clean. Let stand 5 minutes before cutting.

Lake Ripley Lodge B&B

INNKEEPERS Janice & Jim Hoiby

ADDRESS N4376 Friedel Avenue, Cambridge, WI 53523

TELEPHONE (877) 210-6195

CONTACT information@lakeripley.com | www.lakeripley.com

FEATURES 6 Rooms | Children welcome/inquire | Pet-free environment

Experience the tranquility of a glistening lake with towering pine trees and the romance of a sunset at this historic, charming inn at Lake Ripley Lodge Bed and Breakfast. In Cambridge, Wisconsin, just ten miles southeast of Madison and fifty miles from Milwaukee, the inn is conveniently located near bike/hike/ski trails, golf, pottery shops, and a microbrewery. Drift into a bygone era on our grand porch swing and enjoy lakefront luxuries, whirlpools, fireplaces, boats, and a lingering lakefront breakfast. We provide a guest refrigerator, popcorn, and snacks.

Relax on the lakefront lawn glider and enjoy s'mores over the patio fireplace. Whether you sunbathe on the swim pier or fish with the canoe, you will enjoy the history of the lake with its background on Ole Evinrude and the Harley-Davidson families. Lake Ripley Lodge B&B is a member of Wisconsin Travel Green Lodging and has recently completed four rain gardens incorporating Wisconsin native flowers and grasses.

Enjoy coffee on the porch swing as we prepare a delicious breakfast for you using locally grown produce. We will do our best to make your stay a memorable one!

Caramelized Onion Spinach Quiche

Yield: 1 quiche

- 1 pie pastry shell
- 1 medium white onion
- 3–4 Roma tomatoes
- 5 eggs
- 1 cup heavy cream
- 1 Tbsp ground fresh rosemary
- 1 tsp salt
- 1 tsp pepper
- 2 cups fresh spinach leaves

Preheat oven to 250°F and lightly bake the pastry shell. Slice the onion in half and then julienne (thinly slice). Sauté in a medium skillet or saucepan over low heat, or in the 250°F oven until brown. Thinly slice the tomato and set aside. In a medium bowl, combine the eggs, heavy cream, and spices and mix well. Remove the pie shell from the oven and increase oven temperature to 350°F.

Place the caramelized onion in the bottom of the pie shell. Place the spinach over the top of the onion. Pour the egg mixture over the onion and spinach and top with tomato slices. Bake 30–35 minutes, or until golden brown.

Lamp Post Inn

INNKEEPERS Debbie & Mike Rusch
ADDRESS 408 South Main Street, Fort Atkinson, WI 53538
TELEPHONE (920) 563-6561
CONTACT thelamppostinn@att.net | www.thelamppostinn.com
FEATURES 3 Rooms | Children welcome/inquire | Pet-free environment

Welcome to our 1874 Victorian home packed with antiques and adventure. You can soak in the claw foot tub filled with bubbles or relax in our over-sized Jacuzzi. Feel free to dress up in our antique clothes and jewelry for pictures or a night out on the town. There are antique victrolas in all of the rooms and hundreds of board games to play.

We are located just six blocks from the famous Fireside Dinner Theatre and four blocks from the newly developed river walk and bike trail. People from Chicago come to shop in our historic downtown shops such as I Love Funky's, Soap n Pepper, and Ravenwood. Whether you are a first time B&B-er or a seasoned one, you'll find our inn intriguing and cozy. Many of our guests return every year to reminisce and enjoy "the best breakfast they ever had."

Perfect Raspberry Pie

Yield: 1 Pie

"The people I cook for said they didn't want the recipe for this pie, they just wanted me to bake them more!"—Innkeeper

1 10-inch baked pie crust
4 cups fresh raspberries, divided
1 cup water, divided
3 Tbsp cornstarch
1 cup sugar

Place 3 cups of the raspberries in the baked pie shell. Mix 2/3 cup of water with the remaining 1 cup of raspberries in a saucepan and cook over medium-high heat for 3 minutes; set aside. In a small bowl, combine the remaining 1/3 cup water with the cornstarch and sugar. Add the sugar mixture to the cooked raspberry mixture and simmer together until clear. Cool and then pour over the fresh berries in the pie shell. Serve with whipped cream.

Did you know that raspberries are high in fiber, vitamins A and C, calcium, and a cancer-preventing substance called ellagic acid? This super fruit is traditionally harvested in summer and fall. Some raspberry tips: Don't wash your berries until you are ready to use them, refrigerate immediately after purchasing, and eat within 1–2 days. Frozen raspberries will keep best in vacuum-sealed packages.

Lazy Cloud B&B

INNKEEPERS Keith & Carol Tiffany
ADDRESS W4033 State Road 50, Lake Geneva, WI 53147
TELEPHONE (262) 275-3322
CONTACT love@lazycloud.com | www.lazycloud.com
FEATURES 10 Rooms | No children | Pet-free environment

Relax at the Lazy Cloud in the beautiful Lake Geneva, Wisconsin, area. All of our accommodations are done in our signature romantic style: Each accommodation has a luxurious double whirlpool tub and a blazing fireplace, and each is decorated in an individual theme with a daybed, couch, or loveseat for lounging, and a small dining area for two. Additionally, they all have candles, fluffy bathrobes, bubble bath, and bath pillows for your convenience. The game Enchanted Evening (a romantic couple's game) is also in each room and chocolates are placed on your bedside table.

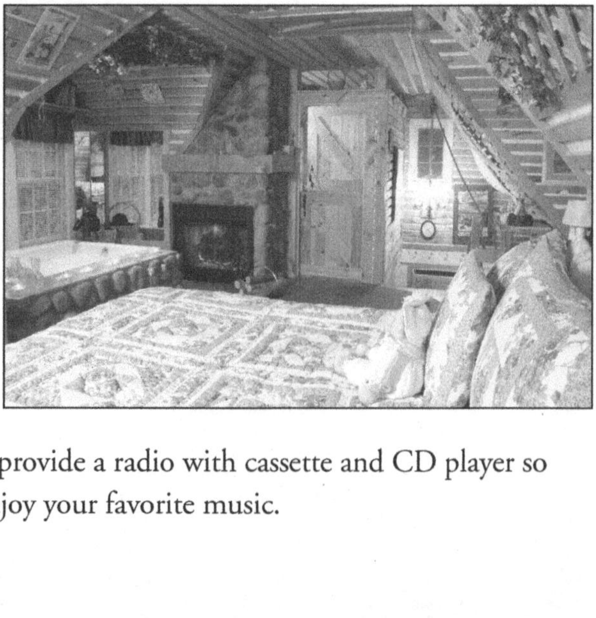

Each room has a small refrigerator and microwave for your convenience, and you'll receive a bottle of wine and a complimentary basket with microwave popcorn and flavored gourmet hot chocolate and cappuccino. We also provide a radio with cassette and CD player so you may relax and enjoy your favorite music.

Apple Crisp

Yield: 9 servings

"This is always a hit for the guests, especially in the cold winter months."—Innkeeper

5–6 apples, peeled and sliced
2 tsp cinnamon
½ cup soft butter
¾ cup flour
1 cup brown sugar

Preheat oven to 350°F. Place the apples in a 9x9-inch pan or deep-dish pie plate. Sprinkle cinnamon over the apples. In a small bowl, mix together the butter, flour, and sugar, being careful not to over mix. Crumble the mixture over the apples and bake 45 minutes.

Tip: For a shortcut, you may use peeled, sliced frozen apples. Put the apples in the pan the night before and let them thaw in the refrigerator overnight. Drain before topping.

Lindsay House B&B

INNKEEPERS Judy & Tim Trull
ADDRESS 539 Depot Street, Manawa, WI 54949
TELEPHONE (920) 596-3643
CONTACT lhousebb@wolfnet.net | www.lindsayhouse.com
FEATURES 4 Rooms | Will accommodate guests' special dietary needs

Lindsay House B&B is located in the center of Waupaca County, in the town of Manawa. This 1892 Victorian home has charm to spare while still offering modern amenities. Guest rooms feature handcrafted queen-sized beds, private baths, in-room TV's, and WiFi. Our distinctive packages make it easy to enjoy a romantic retreat or a relaxing getaway. Your stay includes morning refreshment at our coffee bar located just outside your door and a delicious full breakfast served in our elegant and inviting dining room.

We're surrounded by lakes, walking and biking trails, bird watching and plenty of seasonal adventures. Enjoy riding a snowmobile on 165 miles of scenic trails, dining, and shopping. Enjoy all of the year-round activities here in Waupaca County or just enjoy relaxing and finding rest here at Lindsay House B&B, anytime of year. We look forward to your visit.

Sunrise Potato Frittata

Yield: 46 servings

8 Tbsp unsalted butter, divided
2 cups peeled and (½-inch) diced potatoes
8 extra-large eggs
15 oz. ricotta cheese
¾ lb. Gruyère cheese, grated
½ tsp freshly ground black pepper
1 cup meat (I have used ham, breakfast sausage, sausage links, bacon, all chopped into bite-size pieces)
Penzeys Fox Point Seasoning or Penzeys Sunny Paris

Preheat the oven to 350°F. Melt 3 tablespoons of the butter in a 10-inch ovenproof omelet pan over medium-low heat. Add the potatoes and fry them until cooked through, turning often, 10 to 15 minutes. Melt the remaining 5 Tbsp of butter in a small dish in the microwave.

Meanwhile, whisk the eggs in a large bowl, then stir in the ricotta, Gruyère, melted butter, and pepper. Pour the egg mixture over the potatoes and add the meat and seasoning. Place the pan in the center of the oven and bake the frittata until it is browned and puffed, 50 minutes to an hour. It will be rounded and firm in the middle and a knife inserted in the frittata should come out clean. Serve hot.

Variation: When I bake this in individual ramekins or gratin dishes, I usually cook 1 small potato, diced small, in a bit of butter until fork tender. Sometimes I will add onion and bell pepper in with the potato. Then split between the 2 ramekins. Use 3 to 4 eggs for 2 people, mix cheeses, meat (such as leftover bacon or sausage or diced ham or even cooked chicken) and a bit of milk or even sour cream, canned evaporated milk, or half & half. Then bake them at 350°F for 25–30 minutes, until puffed and browned and they don't jiggle when you move them.

McConnell Inn

INNKEEPERS	Scott & Mary-Jo Johnson
ADDRESS	497 S Lawson Drive, Green Lake, WI 54941
TELEPHONE	(920) 294-6430 | (888) 238-8625
CONTACT	info@mcconnellinn.com | www.mcconnellinn.com
FEATURES	5 Rooms | 1 Suite | Children over age 15 welcome | Resident pets only | Will accommodate guests' special dietary needs

The McConnell Inn is named for its original owner, John McConnell, who built the home as his family residence in 1900. Through the years, the home was passed down to family members. The property was for sale for the first time in 1971. By 1979, five students from Ripon College owned the house and dubbed it "The Men's Club." Because of this history, we were fortunate that the building was left in its original state; no one had done any remodeling in the 1950s or 60s. We purchased the home in 1985 and opened within six months, but we are always making improvements to meet the changing needs of our guests.

McConnell Inn is conveniently located just a short walk to dining, shopping, the beach, parks and boat landings. There are three golf courses, with a total of 81 holes, within less than five miles. Backcountry roads are perfect for biking, and with views of geese, sandhill cranes, blue heron, many types of duck, red-tailed hawks, and eagles, we are a birder's paradise. Green Lake also has many celebrations throughout the year including Summer Solstice, Chalk Art Festival, Wisconsin State Chili Cook-Off, Concerts in the Park summer series, Harvest Festival, and Christmas by the Lake.

We have stayed in over 30 B&B's,
McConnell Inn is in our top three.—Guest

Almond Crescent Rolls

Yield: 20 rolls

"This has been a favorite at McConnell Inn for over 25 years. In our family, we started calling them Kyle's Favorite Rolls because our oldest son loves them. He now makes them and has created his own twist on my version."—Innkeeper

- 8 oz. small curd low-fat cottage cheese
- 8 oz. butter
- 2 cups flour
- 2 Tbsp butter, softened
- ½ cup brown sugar
- ½ cup sliced almonds

In a bowl, blend cottage cheese and butter together. Add in flour and mix until well blended. Divide dough in half, and roll to ¼-inch thick. Spread with 1 tablespoon softened butter and sprinkle with ¼ cup brown sugar and ¼ cup sliced almonds. Cut into wedges and roll into crescent shapes and place on parchment-lined baking sheet. Repeat with other half of dough. Bake at 375°F for 12–15 minutes till just golden.

Miller's Daughter B&B

INNKEEPERS Kris & Larry Herrell
ADDRESS 453 North Street, Green Lake, WI 54941
TELEPHONE (920) 294-0717
CONTACT info@millersdaughter.com | www.millersdaughter.com
FEATURES 5 Rooms | No children | Pet-free environment | Will accommodate guests' special dietary needs

Relax and unwind at the Miller's Daughter in Green Lake, Wisconsin. Our celebrated lake, tranquil hiking/biking trails, and friendly small-town atmosphere combine to make Green Lake the ideal place to get away.

The Miller's Daughter, built in 1905 as a parsonage, was renovated in 2003 with up-to-date amenities to provide you a comfortable stay. Our guest rooms are decorated in current contemporary styles. They include full private baths, 3 with large whirlpool tubs and fireplaces. We pride ourselves in making our guests' stay comfortable and relaxing. Enjoy the wraparound porch overlooking the perennial gardens. And don't forget the full gourmet breakfast served daily.

Stuffed French Toast with Mixed Berry Sauce

Yield: 10 servings

Filling:

- 8 oz. cream cheese, softened
- 2 Tbsp vanilla extract
- 2 Tbsp half & half
- 1 tsp cinnamon

- 1 loaf sour dough bread, sliced
- 1 loaf cinnamon bread, sliced
- 1 cup blueberries, frozen or fresh
- 10 eggs
- 1 cup milk
- 1 cup maple syrup
- Zest from one lemon

Mix the filling ingredients on medium speed until soft and smooth. Set aside. Cut the crusts off the loaves of bread. Starting with the sour dough bread, spread the cream cheese mixture on one side of each slice of bread. Take two slices and form a "sandwich" with cream cheese inside. Cube the sandwiches into 1-inch cubes and layer the cubes in the bottom of a greased 9x13-inch baking dish. Sprinkle blueberries over the first layer. Repeat the same process with the cinnamon bread. Spread these cubes on top of the first layer.

In a large mixing bowl, mix eggs, milk, maple syrup and lemon zest. Pour over bread layers and press down bread with the back of a spoon. Cover and refrigerate overnight or for several hours. In the morning, bake covered with foil for 45 minutes at 350°F. Uncover and bake an additional 15 minutes. Let rest 15 minutes before slicing. Serve with the following mixed fruit sauce ladled over the top.

Mixed fruit sauce:

- ½ cup sugar
- 4 Tbsp cornstarch
- 2 cup water
- 2+ cups of mixed frozen berries
- 10 whole strawberries

Blend sugar and cornstarch in a medium saucepan. Add water and stir to dissolve. Boil over medium heat, stirring frequently until bubbly. Add all fruit and reduce heat to medium/low. Simmer until the berries burst, about 15 minutes. Reduce to lowest heat setting and keep warm until ready to serve. Sauce will thicken more as it cools.

Neumann House B&B

INNKEEPER Luanne Neumann
ADDRESS 121 N Michigan St. Prairie du Chien, WI 53821
TELEPHONE (608) 326-8104
CONTACT theneumann09@centurytel.net | www.prairie-du-chien.com
FEATURES 3 Rooms | 1 Suite | Children over age 8 welcome | Resident pets only | Will accommodate guests' special dietary needs

Luanne will celebrate her Silver Anniversary of innkeeping in January 2013. When she started up the Neumann House B&B in Prairie du Chien, she was the extension home economist for Crawford County and brought to the career two university degrees in home economics education. Twenty-five years later, she still loves to cook breakfast and figures she has prepped over 20,000 of them.

During all those years of innkeeping, Luanne has had the opportunity to partner closely with the Villa Louis Historic Site located in Prairie du Chien. "I would dress up as the home's cook and prepare food on the antique wood stove." She refined her knowledge of Victorian foodways and table service.

Luanne has also become enthusiastic about the local foods movement. Dairy products, eggs and breakfast meats are purchased from local farmers. Fruits and vegetables are secured at the local farmers markets or grown in her own plot in the community garden. An herb garden is located in the back yard of the Neumann House.

Spring Mountain Eggs

Yield: 4 servings

2 Tbsp Butter
½ cup chopped fresh asparagus
½ cup thinly sliced celery
¼ cup minced onion
8 large eggs
½ cup water
1 cup grated Swiss cheese

In a small skillet, melt butter and add asparagus, celery, and onion, cooking until onion is translucent. Set aside. Beat eggs and water in mixing bowl. In a large skillet coated with nonstick spray and heated over medium temperature, cook eggs until just set up. Add cooked vegetables and grated cheese. Stir until eggs are thoroughly cooked.

Tip: Delicious served with whole grain toast. May substitute other spring vegetables such as morel mushrooms, in place of asparagus.

Old Rittenhouse Inn

INNKEEPERS The Phillips Family: Jerry & Mary, Mark & Wendy
ADDRESS 301 Rittenhouse Avenue, P.O. Box 584, Bayfield, WI 54814
TELEPHONE (715) 779-5111; (888) 611-4667
CONTACT frontdsk@rittenhouseinn.com | www.rittenhouseinn.com
FEATURES 16 Rooms; 3 Suites; 1 Cottage | Children welcome/inquire | Pet-free environment | Will accommodate guests' special dietary needs

The Rittenhouse Inn is a Country Inn B&B offering 20 guest rooms in three historic Bayfield homes with fireplaces, whirlpool tubs, and Lake Superior views. The inn was created in 1975 by Jerry and Mary Phillips, former music teachers from Madison, who used their life savings to purchase the Queen Anne Victorian and turn it into the state's first B&B. Today, the inn is operated by their son, Mark, and his wife, Wendy.

The Rittenhouse Inn's Landmark Restaurant serves a 5-course dinner showcasing the region's seasonal harvest from 5 to 9 p.m. nightly, with lighter dining options available. The restaurant is open for breakfast year-round, and brunch on summer Saturdays and Sundays. The Inn also hosts a variety of weddings and special events throughout the year.

Poached Pear Crème Brûlé

Yield: 6 servings

- 2 cups simple syrup
- 2 cups Chardonnay
- 1 vanilla bean, split and scraped
- 1 Tbsp lemon juice
- 3 pears, halved and cored

Créme Brûlé

- 2 large egg yolks, slightly beaten
- 2 large eggs, slightly beaten
- ¼ cup vanilla sugar, divided
- ½ vanilla bean, split and scraped
- ⅛ tsp salt
- 2 cups heavy cream, very hot

Port Wine Caramel Sauce

- 1 bottle Port wine
- ½ lb. butter
- 1 lb. brown sugar
- 1 tsp vanilla
- ¼ cup cream

Start with making the simple syrup by adding 2 cups sugar to 2 cups water and boil for 2 minutes. Add remaining ingredients except pears. Bring liquid to just under a boil. Add pears and poach until tender when pierced with a knife tip. Poaching time will depend on ripeness of pears.

For the Brûlé: Mix yolks and eggs, half the sugar, the vanilla bean and salt together in mixing bowl. Add hot cream slowly, beating constantly. Pour into 10x6-inch baking dish about 2-inches deep. Bake at 300°F in a water bath for 25–30 minutes or until knife inserted in center comes out clean. Scoop portions into serving dishes on top of poached pear halves and sprinkle with reserved vanilla sugar. Use a kitchen torch to lightly brown top, and serve with Port Wine Caramel Sauce.

For the Sauce: Reduce port slowly in a heavy bottom pot (do NOT let boil) until reduced to about ½ cup and let cool. In separate heavy bottom pan, melt butter. Add brown sugar and mix. Add vanilla and cream, and heat on mid-low heat until smooth and all sugar crystals have dissolved.

O'Neill Manor

INNKEEPER Julie Counsell
ADDRESS 824 Hewett St, Neillsville, WI 54456
TELEPHONE (715) 937-4360
CONTACT stay@oneillmanor.com | www.oneillmanor.com
FEATURES 4 Rooms | No children | Pet-Free Environment | Will accommodate guests' special dietary needs

O'Neill Manor is a 120-year-old Victorian home that still retains all the charm and richness of that era. Enjoy your breakfast in our dining room under its wood fretwork scrolls. One of the early "electric" houses in the area, we still showcase many of the original "electric outlets." (Neillsville was the second city in Wisconsin to have electricity.) Located on a three acre lot with almost 600 feet of river/creek frontage, the gently falling water invites guests to relax on the riverbank with a glass of our local wine and a good book.

All of our rooms are decorated to compliment the age of the home, retaining the original woodwork and hardwood floors, but with careful updating to ensure guests have all the modern conveniences. Luxury linens, memory foam mattresses, and whirlpool tubs invite our guests to relax and forget about the busy world outside.

Outdoor activities abound in this area. Hike, mountain bike, cross country ski, canoe or bring your horses. Trails are just steps away from the house. Feel like taking it easy? There is antique shopping, Amish nurseries, farmers' markets, wineries and specialty cheese factories within a short drive. Or just stay in town and do a self-guided walking tour of the many historic homes and structures in our community—you're staying in one!

Italian Mushroom Quiche

Yield: 2 pies

- 3 Tbsp butter
- ⅔ cup chopped shallots
- 1 8 oz. box portabella mushrooms, finely diced
- 1 8 oz. box button mushrooms, finely diced
- 8 large eggs
- 1½ cups half & half
- ⅔ cup milk
- ½ tsp salt
- ½ tsp pepper
- ½ tsp ground nutmeg
- 8 oz. shredded Italian six cheese blend
- 1 cup freshly grated Parmesan cheese

Preheat oven to 450°F. Spray/grease two 9-inch pie pans. We use pre-made pie crusts. Press them firmly into the bottom and sides of pans. Bake them until light golden brown, about 15 minutes. Reduce oven temperature to 325°F.

In a large skillet, melt butter over medium-high heat. Add shallots and sauté until beginning to soften, about 2 minutes. Add mushrooms, sprinkle with salt and pepper and sauté until the mushrooms are tender and beginning to brown, about 10 minutes. Transfer to a plate, spread out and cool.

Whisk eggs, half & half, milk, salt, pepper, and nutmeg in large bowl to blend. Stir in the shredded Italian six cheese blend (usually a blend of shredded mozzarella, provolone, Parmesan, romano, fontina and Asiago cheeses), and the sautéed mushroom/shallot mix. Pour filling into crusts. Sprinkle ½ cup of freshly grated Parmesan cheese over the top of each quiche.

Bake quiche until puffed, golden brown and set in center, about 45 minutes. Cool 15 minutes and cut into wedges to serve. This quiche also reheats wonderfully.

OSCAR H. HANSON HOUSE B&B

INNKEEPERS Duke & Mary Jane Mihajlovic
ADDRESS 303 E North Street, Cambridge, WI 53523
TELEPHONE (608) 423-4379 | (888) 706-7227
CONTACT info@ohhanson.com | www.ohhanson.com
FEATURES 4 Rooms | Children over age 12 welcome | Pet-free environment | Will accommodate guests' special dietary needs

In our 1883 Victorian, breakfast is half of the B&B experience and it's why our guests are treated to breakfast in their room and special attention is given to special dietary needs. On one occasion, two of our guests stayed to celebrate their 50th wedding anniversary. They were interested in our in-room breakfast service. After breakfast, we chatted with them before they left. The Mrs. had tears in her eyes. In 50 years, they had never had breakfast in their room and this was a special occasion they would fondly remember. The blueberry coffee cake is a guest favorite. It has a crunchy cinnamon-sugar topping and a tender crumb. It can be made gluten-free by using a light gluten-free flour blend and egg-free with an egg replacer.

Our spacious porch, comfortable parlor, beautiful gardens, and fountains invite you to stay and bask in the quiet of our inn. Experience the romantic personality of our rooms with in-room breakfast service, fireplaces, stained glass, spacious showers, and claw-foot soaking or Jacuzzi tubs. Feel the passion in your surroundings and recall your commitment to your heart and to that of another. We look forward to your stay and invite you to enjoy the pleasures of our home.

Blueberry Coffee Cake

Yield: 12 servings

Cake

- ½ cup butter, softened
- 8 oz. cream cheese, softened
- 1¼ cup sugar
- 2 eggs, room temperature
- 1 tsp vanilla
- ⅓ cup milk
- 2 cups sifted flour
- 1 tsp baking powder
- ½ tsp baking soda
- ¼ tsp salt
- 2 cups fresh blueberries

Topping

- ½ cup brown sugar
- ½ cup sifted flour
- 1 tsp cinnamon
- 3 Tbsp butter

Glaze

- 1 cup powder sugar, sifted
- 2 Tbsp milk
- ½ tsp vanilla

Preheat oven to 350°F. Cream together butter, cream cheese, and sugar for 4 minutes. Add eggs and cream together for 2 minutes. In a prep cup, mix together vanilla and milk. In a separate bowl, combine dry ingredients: flour, baking powder, baking soda, and salt. Add the flour mixture alternately with the vanilla-milk to the creamed ingredients. Stir in fresh blueberries. Spread in a 13x9-inch pan sprayed with cooking spray.

Combine topping ingredients and sprinkle top of cake with mixture. Bake for 30 minutes.

Allow to cool for at least 15 minutes. Mix glaze ingredients and drizzle on cake.

Tip: When serving a crowd, cut cake into slices with a serrated knife and then drizzle glaze.

Otter Creek Inn

INNKEEPERS	Shelley & Randy Hansen
ADDRESS	2536 HWY 12, Eau Claire, WI 54702
TELEPHONE	(715) 832-2945 | (866) 832-2945
CONTACT	info@ottercreekinn.com | www.ottercreekinn.com
FEATURES	6 Rooms | No children | Pet-free environment

When you spy this Wisconsin inn from the roadside, you'll be impressed by the charm of its unique setting. Tucked in among huge trees on a wooded hill, the Otter Creek Inn B&B, one of the longest operating Wisconsin B&Bs, beckons with a warm welcome. The one-acre wooded lot abounds with flowers in the summer, provides a panorama of colored leaves in the fall, and glistens under a snow-covered blanket during the Wisconsin winter.

This spacious English Tudor three-story inn is decorated in an inviting romantic country Victorian theme. It will enfold you in an aura of yesteryear but will provide you with all the lodging comforts of today. We serve full breakfasts every day of the week. Our breakfast menu allows a choice of entrées, serving times, and location to dine. You might enjoy your breakfasts in bed, in the privacy of your room, or in the common area.

Easy Blonde Brownies

Yield: 12 servings

"These are easy to make, just one saucepan and one baking pan, but are a favorite of young and old."—Innkeeper

- 2/3 cup margarine
- 2 cups brown sugar
- 3 eggs
- 1 tsp vanilla
- 2 cups flour
- 1 tsp baking powder
- 1 tsp salt
- 1–1½ cups semi-sweet chocolate chips

Preheat oven to 350°F and grease a 9x13-inch baking dish. Melt the margarine in a saucepan over low heat. Add the brown sugar and stir until melted. Beat in the eggs, vanilla, flour, baking powder, and salt. Spread the batter into the prepared pan and top with chocolate chips. Bake 25 minutes.

Blondies/butterscotch are said to have been invented long before the traditional chocolate brownie. Brownies were made popular when the mass production and distribution made chocolate more affordable, but blondies in various forms probably date back to the days of the traditional gingerbread cake.

January 22 is National Blonde Brownie Day!

Parkview B&B

INNKEEPERS Tom & Donna Hofmann
ADDRESS 211 N Park Street, Reedsburg, WI 53959
TELEPHONE (608) 524-4333
CONTACT info@parkviewbb.com | www.parkviewbb.com
FEATURES 4 Rooms; Private & shared baths | Children welcome/inquire | Pet-free environment | Will accommodate guests' special dietary needs

Parkview B&B, an 1895 Queen Anne Victorian, opened in 1989 in the Park Street Historic District of Reedsburg, Wisconsin, one block off of Main Street across from City Park. Wake-up coffee or tea is available prior to a full, homemade breakfast. Donna, a home economist, prepares breakfasts, including special diets, using local products as much as possible. Strawberry French Toast is the signature entrée during strawberry season. Rhubarb, strawberries, asparagus, and if you are really lucky, Tom may have found morel mushrooms that may be included in the spring breakfast menus. Summer menus use the abundance of local foods. Cherry Muffins using cherries from our own tree, and raspberries, blueberries, blackberries, and vegetables from local sources are common ingredients. Fall breakfasts may include Cranberry Scones, Apple Pancakes, and Pumpkin Waffles. Guests often comment on the great breakfasts.

Strawberry French Toast

Yield: 4–6 servings

"This recipe is the very best if one can use local strawberries during the season. Guests often comment that it is too pretty to eat!"—Innkeeper

- 5 eggs
- 1½ cups milk (may use some half & half in place of some of the milk if desired)
- ¼ cup strawberry jam
- 8–12 slices French bread, sliced ½- to ¾-inch thick
- 1 quart strawberries, cleaned and sliced
- ¼ cup sugar
- Whipped cream (if desired)
- Powdered sugar

Strawberry Butter

- ¼ cup strawberry jam
- ¼ cup butter, softened

Plan ahead, dish needs overnight refrigeration.

In a bowl, combine and beat eggs, milk and strawberry jam until well blended. Dip slices of French bread into egg mixture. Place slices in a 9x13-inch baking dish. Pour any remaining milk mixture over the French bread slices. Cover the dish and refrigerate overnight.

In the morning: Combine sliced strawberries with the sugar and let sit while preparing the French toast. To prepare French toast, heat griddle to 300°F and butter lightly. Place French toast slices on griddle, turning when golden brown, about 10–15 minutes on a side. Serve two pieces of French toast on each plate, spreading some strawberry butter on each piece. Top with sliced strawberries. If desired, place a dollop of whipped cream in the center and place a strawberry on top. Dust with powdered sugar.

Tips: If I have extra pieces of French toast, I freeze the slices before cooking and put them in zip-lock freezer bags. Then I can take out the number of slices desired, thaw them and cook them on the griddle.

PEDAL'RS INN

INNKEEPER	Dee Nierzwicki
ADDRESS	101 James Street, Wales, WI 53182
TELEPHONE	(262) 968-4700
CONTACT	info@pedalrsinn.com | www.pedalrsinn.com
FEATURES	4 Rooms

The Glacial Drumlin State Trail, on which Pedal'rs Inn is located, and its cyclists, inspired the name for this Christian inn. In the mid-1800s, the railway moved across the U.S. and the Elias family took that opportunity to put the town of Wales on the map. The Elias family built their home after signing a deal with the Chicago NW Railway. Travelers and ministers stayed at their home and nearby hotel. They sold it to Milwaukee's iconic George Webb, where he began his restaurants.

Guests experience all the area attractions including Ten Chimneys, Kettle Moraine State Forest and lakes, state trails, many local festivals and art fairs, and fabulous dining. It's the amazing four course breakfasts that turn novice inn goers into devoted ones.

Lemon Soufflé Pancakes

Yield: 4 servings

¾ cup buttermilk
2 farm eggs, separated
2 Tbsp fresh lemon juice
3 tsp lemon zest
1½ tsp pure vanilla extract
1½ Tbsp butter, melted
¾ cup all-purpose flour
1 tsp baking powder
3 Tbsp baker's sugar
1/8 tsp salt
1/8 tsp cream of tartar
2 Tbsp butter for cooking
Additional lemon zest strips for garnish

In small mixing bowl, whisk together buttermilk, egg yolks, lemon juice, zest, extract and melted butter. In medium bowl, whisk together flour, baking powder, sugar and salt. Preheat griddle on stovetop with medium-low heat. Pour buttermilk mixture into flour. Mix until combined but don't over mix. In mixer, whip egg whites until foamy. Add cream of tartar and continue whipping until peaks form. Transfer egg whites into batter. Fold in egg whites gently.

Lightly butter cooking surface. When butter forms bubbles, ladle out batter to form 3–4 inch wide cakes, Cook 3 minutes on each side. Top with lemon zest strips and serve with fresh fruit and marscapone on the side. Drizzle with honey.

Phipps Inn B&B

INNKEEPERS	Mary Ellen & Rich Cox
ADDRESS	1005 3rd Street, Hudson, WI 54016
TELEPHONE	(715) 386-0800
CONTACT	info@phippsinn.com | www.phippsinn.com
FEATURES	6 Rooms | Children welcome/inquire | Pet-free environment | Will accommodate guests' special dietary needs

We're close to home, yet a hundred years away. Let the Phipps Inn become your favorite escape!

The Phipps Inn is the premier Queen Anne Victorian B&B in Wisconsin's St. Croix River Valley. It is located on Historic Third Street in the beautiful city of Hudson, a short walk from downtown restaurants, shops, and the river.

We offer many common areas including three parlors, two porches, and a billiards room. We are known for our four-course gourmet breakfasts and our friendly yet unobtrusive hospitality. All Phipps Inn guest rooms have fireplaces, whirlpool tubs, and private baths. We specialize in the three Rs: romance, relax, and refresh.

Phipps Inn Country Casserole

Yield: 12 servings

"This is one of the first recipes we served at the Phipps Inn. It's easy, delicious, and a favorite with guests. Our gluten-free guests love it. We often reserve a single serving and bake in a small ramekin for vegetarian guests. The salsa is an optional addition that wakes up those who haven't had enough coffee!"—Innkeeper

16 oz. bulk breakfast sausage
2 lbs. Southern-style frozen hash browns
8 oz. shredded Mexican blend cheese
8 oz. shredded Cheddar cheese
6 large eggs
2 cups milk
½ tsp seasoning salt, such as Lawry's
½ tsp dry mustard
Paprika
Salsa

Plan ahead, this dish needs overnight refrigeration.

Brown sausage and drain. In a very large bowl, combine sausage, hash browns (do not have to be thawed), the Mexican cheese, and half of the Cheddar cheese. Beat eggs, milk, and seasonings for about a minute with a hand mixer, then combine with the sausage and egg mixture. Pour into a greased 9x13-inch glass baking dish, top with remaining Cheddar cheese, sprinkle with paprika, cover and refrigerate overnight. Remove from refrigerator about 2 hours before serving to come to room temperature. Bake for 55–60 minutes at 350°F. Let stand 10 minutes. Serve with salsa.

Pine Grove Park B&B Guest House

INNKEEPERS Jean & Kurt Johansen
ADDRESS S2720 County Road V, Reedsburg, WI 53959
TELEPHONE (608) 524-0071 | (866) 524-0071
CONTACT info@pinegroveparkbb.com | www.pinegroveparkbb.com
FEATURES 4 Guest houses | No children | Resident pets only

Pine Grove Park B&B is a Wisconsin Dells B&B tucked in the middle of 55 beautiful acres near Reedsburg, Wisconsin. We are located in the southwestern part of the state and are central to many beautiful state parks and other area attractions.

Each guest house has a private entrance, covered porch, and large window overlooking our varying landscapes and pond. The relaxing extra-large whirlpool tub, romantic gas-stove fireplace, scrumptious country gourmet breakfast, and warm hospitality will make you wish you had discovered our prime accommodations sooner!

Our charming Wisconsin Dells lodging is surrounded with lush greenery and set among sandstone outcroppings on a diverse landscape including woodlands, wetlands, oak savannahs, and native wildflower gardens. Enjoy our picturesque landscape and wildlife with a relaxing walk on our trails or just sit and reflect on a bench by the pond.

Breakfast Torte with Pancetta & Parmesan Cheese

Yield: 4 servings

- 1 puff pastry
- 3–4 oz. sliced pancetta
- 3 large eggs
- 2/3 cup heavy cream
- ½ cup whole milk
- 3 Tbsp chopped fresh Italian Parsley
- 1/3–½ cup shredded Parmesan cheese
- Salt & pepper to taste

Preheat oven to 400°F. Roll out thawed puff pastry and place in a 9-inch round tart pan. Refrigerate while assembling the remaining ingredients. Dice the pancetta and brown it in a fry pan until crisp, drain. Whisk the eggs, heavy cream, milk, parsley and salt and pepper in a bowl until blended. Add the diced pancetta and Parmesan cheese. Mix to blend and pour into prepared tart pan. Bake for approximately 20 minutes or until crust is slightly browned.

Pinehaven B&B

INNKEEPERS Lyle & Marge Getschman
ADDRESS E13083 State Highway 33, Baraboo, WI 53913
TELEPHONE (608) 356-3489
CONTACT pinehavenbnb@centurytel.net | www.pinehavenbnb.com
FEATURES 4 Rooms; 1 Cottage | Children welcome/inquire | Pet-free environment

At Pinehaven B&B you will find a serene, scenic setting. The tree-lined drive leads you to a view of our small spring-fed lake that flows into the Baraboo River, with the Baraboo Bluffs in the background.

We have the best of both worlds: A quiet country vacation spot within fifteen miles of all the great tourist attractions for Baraboo and Wisconsin Dells. Our guests can use the rowboat, fish (catch and release), relax in the gazebo, and enjoy the flower gardens. Many of our guests ask Lyle for a tour to see the horses as well.

Chicken Cordon Bleu Strata

Yield: 8–10 servings

"Chicken for breakfast? Why not! Our guests love it. One of our regular guests proclaimed it a 'keeper' for our collection of breakfast entrées."—Innkeeper

- 6 cups toasted bread, cubed
- ¾ cup chicken broth
- ½ cup finely chopped celery
- ½ cup chopped broccoli
- ¼ cup chopped onion
- ¼ cup diced green bell pepper
- ¼ cup chopped carrots
- 2 cups diced cooked chicken
- ¾ cup cubed ham
- ¾ cup grated Swiss cheese
- ¾ cup mayonnaise
- 1 tsp salt
- ¼ tsp pepper
- 4 eggs
- 1½ cups milk
- 1 cup cubed Cheddar cheese

Preheat oven to 325°F and grease a 13x9-inch baking dish. Place the bread cubes in the bottom of the dish and pour the chicken broth evenly over the top. Gently sauté or steam the celery, broccoli, onion, bell pepper, and carrots until crisp-tender. In a medium bowl combine the chicken, ham, Swiss cheese, and vegetables. Add the mayonnaise and season with salt and pepper. Mix well and spread over the bread cubes. In a medium bowl, slightly beat the eggs. Mix in the milk and pour over the mixture. Bake 50 minutes and remove from oven and sprinkle with Cheddar cheese cubes. Return to oven for 10 minutes. Remove when the cheese is hot and bubbly and let stand 10 minutes before slicing.

Pinehurst Inn

INNKEEPERS Nancy & Steve Sandstrom
ADDRESS 83645 State HWY 13, Bayfield, WI 54814
TELEPHONE (715) 779-3676 | (877) 499-7651
CONTACT innkeeper@pinehurstinn.com | www.pinehurstinn.com
FEATURES 8 Rooms | Children welcome/inquire | Resident pets only

Pinehurst Inn, an 8-room B&B located south of Bayfield, merges the elements of the ideal lodging experience: serene location, activities for mind and body, and soothing amenities to rejuvenate.

The historic main house, built in 1886, features five guest rooms, all designed with guests' comfort in mind. Pinehurst Inn Garden House, our "green building," complements the main inn in both design and spirit. Here you'll enjoy three guest rooms, each with whirlpool bath and fireplace, and private decks. Each stay includes our heart and soul-warming breakfast.

"Eco Friendly Elegance"—National Geographic Traveler

Pinehurst Apple Lavender Scones

Yield: 1 dozen

"This recipe pulls together a mix of items from our own gardens and fruit from our local Bayfield orchards. We adapted this recipe from a basic scone recipe given to us by a friend."—Innkeeper

- 2 cups organic whole wheat pastry flour
- ¼ cup organic sugar
- 1 Tbsp baking powder
- ¼ tsp cinnamon
- ¼ tsp salt
- 2 tsp chopped lavender leaves
- ⅓ cup cold butter
- 1 cup buttermilk
- 1 tsp lemon juice
- 2 tsp lemon zest
- 1½ cups peeled cubed apples, or Bosc pears

Preheat oven to 375°F. Combine the flour, sugar, baking powder, cinnamon, salt, and lavender in a medium bowl. Using a pastry blender cut the cold butter (divided into 6–7 pieces) until the consistency is coarse and crumbly. Add the buttermilk, lemon juice, lemon zest, and cubed apples and stir with a fork until just moistened. If the mixture is too dry, you can add a drop or two of additional buttermilk.

Knead the dough 5–6 times on a floured surface. Roll out to ¾-inch thickness and cut into preferred shapes. We use a greased scone pan to create consistent sizes. You can also drop the batter onto a greased cookie sheet lined with parchment paper. Brush the tops of the scones with egg white and sprinkle with a mixture of sugar and cinnamon. Bake 15–18 minutes, or until golden brown.

Port Washington Inn

INNKEEPERS Rita & Dave Nelson
ADDRESS 308 W Washington Street, Port Washington, WI 53074
TELEPHONE (262) 284-5583
CONTACT stay@portwashingtoninn.com | www.portwashingtoninn.com
FEATURES 3 Rooms; 2 Suites | No children | Pet-free environment | Will accommodate guests' special dietary needs

We invite you to visit the Port Washington Inn for inspiration for the fare you share with your family. We share a full made-from-scratch breakfast with our guests, and each morning of their stay they can look forward to sampling something that wasn't on the previous day's menu. That is important because so many of our guests are here several nights to truly enjoy the peaceful privacy and generous hospitality that are the hallmarks of the inn. Lake Michigan is just four blocks from the inn, with views of the lake from the Top of the World Suite and Grace's Suite. Walk the beach, visit the lighthouse and the marina, or navigate the bike trail. Enjoy Tall Ships at the Maritime Festival!

Granola

Yield: 24 servings

- 3 cups oats (we use thick rolled organic oats)
- 1½ cups wheat flakes
- 1½ cups rye flakes
- ½ cup wheat germ
- 1 cup millet (optional)

- ¾ Tbsp cinnamon
- ¼ cup sugar
- 1 tsp kosher salt
- 5/8 cup apple juice
- ½ tsp vanilla extract
- ¼ cup canola oil

- ½ cup almonds, chopped
- ½ cup pecans, chopped
- ½ cup raisins
- ½ cup dried cranberries
- ½ cup dried apricots, chopped

Preheat oven to 325°F. In a bowl, combine the oats, wheat flakes, rye flakes, wheat germ, and millet. In a separate bowl, combine the cinnamon, sugar, salt, apple juice, vanilla, and canola oil. Add the wet mixture to the grains and mix thoroughly. Spread out on baking sheets and bake for 14 minutes, stirring halfway through. Remove and cool thoroughly then add nuts and fruit to the cooled baked mixture and place in sealed container.

Tip: This granola freezes well.

Red Forest B&B

INNKEEPERS Kay & Alan Rodewald
ADDRESS 1421 25th Street, Two Rivers, WI 54241
TELEPHONE (920) 793-1794 | (888) 250-2272
CONTACT info@redforestbb.com | www.redforestbb.com
FEATURES 4 Rooms | Children welcome/inquire | Pet-free environment | Will accommodate guests' special dietary needs

Welcome to Two Rivers and the Red Forest B&B. Two Rivers is a quaint little fishing port with two meandering rivers and one Great Lake, located 35 minutes south of Green Bay.

Relax and catch a cool lake breeze at our 1907 historic B&B. Four beautifully appointed guest rooms await your arrival. We offer a full breakfast, and the aroma of early morning coffee and tea to awaken your senses.

Baked German Apple Pancake

Yield: 4 servings

"Before opening our B&B 22 years ago, I tried several different breakfast recipes. I tried this recipe for our family Easter Brunch. It was an instant favorite, and a favorite of our guests ever since. As Two Rivers is the home of the 'Ice Cream Sundae' of course I serve it with the best vanilla ice cream made in Manitowoc, Wisconsin—Cedar Crest French Vanilla."—Innkeeper

- 3 eggs, separated
- 3 Tbsp flour
- 3 Tbsp milk
- Dash of salt
- 3 large Granny Smith apples, peeled, cored, and sliced ¼-inch thick
- ½ cup sugar
- 2 Tbsp butter
- 1 tsp cinnamon (Penzeys is the best)

Preheat oven to 350°F. Place a 9-inch ovenproof glass pie dish with deep sides in preheated oven. Beat egg whites until stiff. Mix flour, milk, salt and egg yolks in separate bowl with hand mixer. Then gently fold egg white mixture in.

Sauté apples, sugar, butter and cinnamon in a skillet for 2–3 minutes until apples are well coated. Pour apples into heated glass pie dish sprayed with nonstick cooking spray. Pour the batter over apples slices. Bake for 20 minutes at 305°F until the pancake is brown and puffy. Remove from oven and loosen sides. Place a round plate over glass pie dish and flip over. Cut the pancake in wedges and serve with maple syrup and a scoop of vanilla ice cream.

Reynolds House B&B

INNKEEPER Heather Hull
ADDRESS 111 S 7th Avenue, Sturgeon Bay, WI 54235
TELEPHONE (920) 746-9771 | (877) 269-7401
CONTACT hahull@reynoldshousebandb.com | www.reynoldshousebandb.com
FEATURES 5 Rooms | Children age 12 and over welcome | Pet-free environment

Reynolds House, a local landmark near downtown Sturgeon Bay, is a stately Queen Anne Victorian that has been beautifully restored to its circa 1900 grandeur. The home still features the original woodwork and leaded windows.

I serve my guests a two-course gourmet breakfast, voted "Best Breakfast" by *Arrington's Bed & Breakfast Journal's Inn Traveler*. This mouthwatering meal is served in our bright, plant-filled, circular solarium or the oak-paneled dining room. I am often asked to adapt my recipes to special diets. A recent guest dined gluten-free for almost a week, and she had the same breakfast as everyone else, even the blueberry streusel French toast! I love what I do, and it shows.

"The breakfast here is absolutely fabulous ... you can run all day to see the sights and shops in the area."—Guest

Door County Cherry Ham Strata

Yield: 6 servings

"Reynolds House was built by William Reynolds, whose family gained their wealth and prominence by growing and canning Door County cherries."—Innkeeper

- 1 loaf French bread, sliced ¼–½-inch thick
- 1 cup dried Door County cherries
- 1½ cups finely diced ham
- 8 oz. Swiss cheese, finely shredded
- ½ cup cherry syrup
- 10 large eggs
- 2¼ cups milk
- 1 tsp vanilla or cherry extract

Plan ahead, this dish needs to be refrigerated overnight.

Remove the crusts from the bread slices and grease 6 small soufflé dishes. Cover the bottom of each dish with bread. Layer cherries, ham, and cheese over the bread. Cube the remaining bread slices and sprinkle over the top of each dish. In a large bowl, combine the cherry syrup, eggs, milk, and vanilla; mix well. Divide the egg mixture evenly between the soufflé dishes. Arrange the filled dishes on a baking sheet, cover, and refrigerate overnight.

The following morning: Preheat oven to 350°F. Uncover the baking sheet and place in the oven. Bake 55–60 minutes, or until a knife inserted in the center comes away clean. Transfer the soufflés to individual plates and serve immediately. Enjoy!

Riverside Manor B&B

INNKEEPER Becky DeWitt
ADDRESS 1863 Riverside Ave, Marinette, WI 54143
TELEPHONE (715) 735-5600
CONTACT innkeeper@riversidemanor.net | www.riversidemanor.net
FEATURES 1 Room; 2 Suites | Children welcome/inquire | Resident pets only | Will accommodate guests' special dietary needs

Riverside Manor was built in 1881 by one of the city's founding fathers, Addison Fairchild. I began renovating the home in 2008 and opened the B&B in 2009. The Fairchild family all had important roles in the formation and direction of Marinette.

Riverside Manor sits along the historic Menominee River where it enters the bay of Green Bay across from Stephenson Island. You can walk the block to the foot bridge from the inn and cross over to this island. Here you will find a public boat launch, historical museum, and facilities available for picnics, music and even outdoor movies.

Each 4-course breakfast starts with coffee or tea and juice, served with homemade fresh baked goods. The selection may be homemade traditional English scones, Welsh cakes, muffins or pastry. There is always a choice of at least two. These are followed by yogurt parfait, the main entrée and dessert.

Strawberry Stuffed French Toast

Yield: 6 servings

"Guests love this particular dish and have often asked for it when making reservations."—Innkeeper

1	loaf uncut French bread
1	pkg. softened cream cheese
¼–½	cup confectioners' sugar
1/3	cup milk
1	qt. fresh strawberries, cleaned and sliced
2–3	eggs
½	cup milk
1	tsp vanilla flavoring
¼	tsp cinnamon (optional)

Slice French bread by making the first cut approximately ½ inch wide, going only about 2/3 down. Make the second cut about ½ inch from the first cut so you end up with a slice of bread about 1 inch wide with a "pocket" in the middle.

Mix cream cheese with the sugar and about 1/3 cup milk, until it reaches a spreading consistency. Spread a layer of cream cheese in the "pocket" of the bread. Place several slices of strawberries into the "pocket" of bread with the cream cheese.

In a bowl, mix eggs and about ½ cup of milk. Add the vanilla flavoring and cinnamon if desired. Whisk until frothy. Dip the prepared strawberry and cream cheese stuffed slice into batter, covering both sides. Place on hot griddle or frying pan prepared with a nonstick spray. Turn slice over when golden brown to cook other side. I typically serve three slices garnished with additional strawberry slices over the French toast and topped with a dusting of powdered sugar and whipping cream.

Riverview B&B

INNKEEPER Marilyn Brockopp
ADDRESS 219 W Wall Street, Neshkoro, WI 54960
TELEPHONE (920) 293-4423
CONTACT rivervu_marilyn@charter.net | www.theriverviewbnb.com
FEATURES 3 Rooms | Children welcome/inquire | Pet-free environment

Riverview is located by the White River in Neshkoro, a quiet little fishing village that offers the joys of solitude and the jollity of nearby attractions. Visit the area bison farm, Prairie Nursery farm and flea markets, Ice Age and Rustic Road trails. In the summer, tube the White River, and visit the beach. In the winter enjoy cross-country skiing, and snowmobile trails. You can also drive to the EAA Museum, Wisconsin Dells, or even Lambeau Field, then return here to rest.

"As I am sitting in my favorite rocking chair and looking onto the lovely porch, I do not have the words to describe the emotions I have felt staying in your home. My first B&B experience was perfect. Your touch was warm, your home was cozy and your windows glowed with the light from your soul. Thank you for everything and more."—Guest

Blueberry French Toast Bake

Yield: 10–12 servings

"Adapted from Serve It Up With Love *(cookbook from a tennis benefit for the Child Advocacy Center of Mobile, AL)"*—Innkeeper

- 1 large loaf French bread
- 5 eggs, slightly beaten
- 1 tsp vanilla
- ¾ cup milk
- ¼ cup sugar
- ¼ tsp baking powder
- 4½ cups blueberries
- ½ cup sugar
- 2 tsp cornstarch
- 4 Tbsp melted butter

Trim all crust and slice bread lengthwise in ¾-inch thick slices and fit as a single layer into the bottom of 3-quart casserole dish (or large cake baking pan). Mix next 5 ingredients and pour over bread until absorbed. This may be refrigerated overnight. Place next 4 ingredients (sweetened fruit mixture—I also put together the night before, coating the fruit with the sugar and cornstarch, then stirring the melted butter in gently) into the bottom of another buttered 3-quart casserole and transfer soaked bread slices to the top of fruit. Sprinkle with 2 tablespoons of sugar, maybe a little cinnamon, and bake for 30 minutes at 375°F or until lightly browned. Serve with whipped cream if desired.

Variation: Dish is also excellent using peaches in place of blueberries.

Sabamba Alpaca Ranch and B&B

INNKEEPERS Tom & Sally Schmidt
ADDRESS 2338 Hickory Road, De Pere, WI 54115
TELEPHONE (920) 371-0003
CONTACT sschmidt@sabambaalpaca.com | www.sabambaalpaca.com
FEATURES 2 Rooms | Children welcome | Resident pets only | Will accommodate guests' special dietary needs

Our 1890 remodeled farmstead home is a family-friendly B&B that welcomes all visitors. The home is filled with maple and hickory wood floors, and the antique mantel in the guest living space is breathtaking.

Each guest room comes with comfy robes. Rosie's Room has a wonderful whirlpool tub and pillow-top bed that you won't want to leave and Lori's Room has a cozy fireplace. Enjoy breakfast in your room or in the dining room and watch the alpaca in the pasture. After, you can help with the daily care of the alpaca, or relax on the wrap-around porch and read a book or listen to music.

Here at Sabamba Alpaca Ranch and B&B, we are always ready for a new adventure. We especially enjoyed some guests in summer of 2011 who were vegan. We hadn't had much experience with vegan food and had a great time experimenting with recipes. Our guests enjoyed the meals and we enjoyed eating healthily for that week. Some of the recipes are now signature breakfasts for all our guests!

Vegan Berry and Nut Compote

Yield: 4–6 servings

"This has become a favorite with our B&B guests. We love that it features Wisconsin produce—cranberries and maple syrup."—Innkeeper

1 cup cashews
¾ cup dried pineapple
¾ cup dried cranberries
1 cup fresh blueberries
2 cups fresh strawberries, cut in fourths
1 cup fresh raspberries or blackberries
maple syrup or agave nectar

Grind cashews, pineapple and cranberries in a food processor until they are in small chunks. Press cashew/pineapple/cranberry mix into the bottom of individual ramekins, making a "crust." Top each crust with a handful of fresh berries. Drizzle with maple syrup or agave nectar. Serve and enjoy!

Tips: Try different berries and nuts. Top with a few slivered almonds. Try your local farmer's market for extra fresh fruit. You can also drizzle with honey, but keep in mind that the dish is not vegan if you use honey.

Sawyer House B&B

INNKEEPER Ruth Norton
ADDRESS 101 S Lansing Avenue, Sturgeon Bay, WI 54235
TELEPHONE (920) 746-1640 | (888) 746-1614
CONTACT sawyerhouse@itol.com | www.bbonline.com/wi/sawyer
FEATURES 5 Rooms | No children | Pet-free environment

The Sawyer House B&B was initially built in 1902 by Dr. Albert Kreizer. The home is a Late Queen Anne Victorian that was renovated in 1999 and transformed into a B&B. This turn-of-the-century house is located in a quiet neighborhood in Sturgeon Bay, but is still close to all of the Door County attractions.

Experience warm hospitality with sweets in the evening and a homemade breakfast in the morning. All dishes have nutritional information available upon request and special dietary needs are not a problem to accommodate.

"We have enjoyed our stay. It was so relaxing and peaceful to be here. The hospitality is outstanding and the breakfast was wonderful. We love your home!"—Guest

Swedish Pancakes

Yield: about 8 pancakes

"This is a recipe used in my family for years and requested by family and guests alike."—Innkeeper

4	eggs, beaten
2	cups milk
2	Tbsp melted butter
2	Tbsp sugar
1	tsp cinnamon
1½	cups flour

In a bowl, add milk to beaten eggs, then add rest of ingredients, mix well with whisk. Make like a crêpe. Use a ladle (½ cup) of batter for each pancake, using a greased frying pan.

Tip: Serve with Door County Maple Syrup or fresh berries or jam.

Scofield House

INNKEEPERS Dan & Vicki Klein

ADDRESS 908 Michigan Street, Sturgeon Bay, WI 54235

TELEPHONE (920) 743-7727 | (888) 463-0204

CONTACT stay@scofieldhouse.com | www.scofieldhouse.com

FEATURES 6 Rooms | No children | Pet-free environment

Experience the welcoming warmth of a traditional and authentic B&B. At The Scofield House, a pleasing mix of old Victorian elegance and modern conveniences combine to provide the perfect place for relaxation. Our six guest rooms are distinctly decorated, inviting intimacy and romance. Each features a fireplace, double whirlpool, fine antiques, and comfortable bed.

We serve a full breakfast in the dining room each morning. Our menu may include White Chocolate Cherry Scones, Hashbrown Breakfast Casserole, a fresh fruit course, hot coffee or tea, and a selection of juices. After a day exploring Door County, guests may return to find our Triple-Flavored Big Batch Cookies and coffee, tea, or hot chocolate.

Triple-Flavor Big Batch Cookies

Yield: 7 dozen

"These cookies have been baked by The Scofield House innkeepers for over 15 years, the recipe having been passed on by Bill & Fran who first opened the B&B in 1987."—Innkeeper

- 3 cups all-purpose flour
- 2 cups rolled oats
- 3 Tbsp unsweetened cocoa powder
- 2 tsp baking soda
- ½ tsp salt
- 2 cups butter, softened
- 1 cup chunky peanut butter
- 1½ cups granulated sugar
- 1½ cups packed brown sugar
- 3 eggs
- 2 tsp vanilla
- 3 cups semisweet chocolate pieces

In a large bowl, stir together flour, oats, cocoa powder, baking soda and salt. In a very large mixing bowl, beat butter and peanut butter until smooth. Add sugars and beat until combined. Beat in eggs and vanilla. Gradually add flour mixture and mix well. Stir in chocolate pieces.

Drop by rounded teaspoonfuls 2 inches apart on ungreased cookie sheets. Bake in 350°F oven for 12–14 minutes, or until edges are lightly browned. Remove from oven and cool on cookie sheet for 1 minute. Transfer the cookies to wire racks and let cool.

Speckled Hen Inn

INNKEEPERS Pat & Bob Fischbeck
ADDRESS 5525 Portage Road, Madison, WI 53704
TELEPHONE (608) 244-9368 | (877) 670-4844
CONTACT innkeeper@speckledheninn.com | www.speckledhenninn.com
FEATURES 5 Rooms | Children age 12 and older welcome | Resident pets only | Will accommodate guests' special dietary needs

Located in Madison, Wisconsin, the Speckled Hen Inn is just 7.5 miles from the Capitol Square and University of Wisconsin campus. This B&B is the perfect place for a romantic retreat, reunion, celebration, travelers on business, or family visiting students at the university.

The 50-acre property features pastures with sheep and llamas, wetland and grassland areas, streams, pine and spruce plantations, orchards, walking trails and gardens.

Abundant, fresh, local, and seasonal describe the breakfast offerings at the Speckled Hen Inn. Start your day off right with a three-course breakfast; you choose your breakfast time. Eat early to get ahead of the crowds at the Dane County Farmers' Market, or sleep in and enjoy a leisurely breakfast at 10:00. Breakfast is served in the dining room under the big brass candelabra with real burning candles, or in the cozy library in view of the bird feeders on the back balcony.

Caramel Apple Scones

Yield: 12 servings

"Guests love this recipe because, due to the abundance of Wisconsin dairy products in it, the scones are never dry."—Innkeeper

- 2 cups unbleached all-purpose flour
- ¼ cup granulated sugar
- 2½ tsp baking powder
- 1 tsp cinnamon
- 6 Tbsp butter, chilled and cut in several small pieces
- 1 medium apple, peeled, cored and finely chopped
- ⅓ cup toffee bits
- 1 egg
- half & half
- ¼ cup milk

For the Caramel Glaze

- 1 tsp melted butter
- 1 Tbsp caramel flavored syrup (as used for flavoring coffee)
- 1½ cups powdered sugar

Preheat oven to 400°F. Place first 5 ingredients in the work bowl of a food processor. Pulse until the mixture resembles coarse crumbs. Place this mixture in a medium bowl and add the apple and toffee bits. Place the egg in a one-cup measure. Fill the cup with half & half to the ¾-cup line. Add the ¼ cup milk and mix well. Pour the egg mixture over the dry ingredients and mix just until moistened. Drop mounds of dough onto a nonstick baking sheet or a baking sheet lightly coated with cooking spray. Bake 12–15 minutes or until golden. Make the glaze by combining the melted butter, caramel syrup, and 1½ cups powdered sugar or the amount that will produce the desired glaze consistency. Blend until smooth and creamy. Drizzle the caramel glaze over the scones and serve warm.

Tips: Almost any combination of fruits, nuts, and baking chips will work well in these scones. Some of our favorites are dried cherries and white chocolate chips, dried apricots and almonds, fresh pears and candied ginger, and bananas and butterscotch chips. Just sprinkle the tops with coarse sugar before baking if you don't wish to glaze the scones.

St. Croix River Inn

INNKEEPERS Ben & Jennifer Bruno
ADDRESS 305 River Street, P.O. Box 356, Osceola, WI 54020
TELEPHONE (715) 294-4248
CONTACT innkeeper@stcroixriverinn.com | www.stcroixriverinn.com
FEATURES 7 Suites; Private baths | Children 16 and older welcome | No pets

"Guests at the St. Croix River Inn delight in a gourmet breakfast served privately to their room. The first course begins with a beautiful bread and beverage tray. Our St. Croix Streusel is a guest favorite. Enjoy!"—Innkeeper

The St. Croix River Inn is an elegant B&B nestled on the bluffs of the St. Croix River. With 7 luxury rooms, it offers a private, peaceful and relaxing environment. A sumptuous full gourmet breakfast, weekend wine and hors d'oevres, and nightly desserts to nurture a sweet tooth are all included with your stay. While the view from the dining room is spectacular, guests often prefer the privilege of breakfast in the private elegance of their room. Experience timeless luxury on the river.

St. Croix Streusel Cake

Yield: 12 servings

For the streusel topping:

- ¼ cup light brown sugar
- ¼ cup sugar
- ½ cup all-purpose flour
- 1 tsp ground cinnamon
- ¼ cup cold unsalted butter, cut into Tbsp-size pieces

For the coffee cake:

- 2 cups all-purpose flour
- 1 tsp baking powder
- 1 tsp baking soda
- 1 tsp salt
- ½ cup unsalted butter, room temperature
- 1 cup sugar
- 2 large eggs
- 1 cup sour cream
- ½ tsp vanilla extract
- ½ cup milk

Preheat oven to 350°F. Grease a 9-inch Bundt or springform pan with 2 tablespoons of butter.

For the streusel: Mix together the brown and white sugars, flour and cinnamon. Cut in the butter with a knife or pastry blender until the mixture is coarse and crumbly. Set aside.

For the cake: Sift together the flour, baking powder, baking soda, and salt and set aside. Using a hand-held mixer, or machine, beat the butter and the sugar in a separate bowl until light and fluffy, about 3 minutes. Add the eggs and beat lightly for another minute. Add the sour cream, vanilla extract, and milk and beat until smooth. Stir in the flour mixture and beat evenly.

Cake assembly: Pour a little less than half of the batter into the Bundt pan and smooth the top. Sprinkle in half of the streusel. Add the remaining batter, covering the streusel layer, and sprinkle the remaining streusel on top. Bake the cake on the middle shelf of the oven for about 45 minutes, until a cake tester comes out clean. Set on a rack and let cool in the pan for about 10 minutes. Invert onto a serving plate and serve warm or at room temperature.

Stewart Inn

INNKEEPERS Jane & Paul Welter
ADDRESS 521 Grant Street, Wausau, WI 54403
TELEPHONE (715) 849-5858
CONTACT innkeeper@stewartinn.com | www.stewartinn.com
FEATURES 5 Rooms | Children welcome/inquire | Pets welcome

The Stewart Inn offers upscale accommodations with a gourmet breakfast in an authentic National Register Arts and Crafts masterpiece. Incredible architectural detail, modern amenities, delicious food, and unobtrusive service make for a wonderful stay.

The inn is located in downtown Wausau. Nestled around the town square are shops and restaurants, the Grand Theater, which hosts a variety of live performances, and the Center for the Visual Arts gallery and gift shop. Nearby are an excellent YMCA, the Wisconsin River Walk, and the nation's only urban whitewater kayak course. At the top of East Hill is the Woodson Art Museum, known for its annual Birds in Art exhibit. Wausau is also home to Granite Peak Ski Area, the Sylvan Hills Tubing Facility, Rib Mountain State Park, and the Wisconsin Woodchucks baseball team.

Irish Oats with Fruit & Cranberry Syrup

Yield: 4 servings

- 1 cup water
- 1 cup milk or soy milk
- 1 Tbsp brown sugar or 1 package Splenda
- ¼ tsp cinnamon
- ⅛ tsp salt
- ¾ cup steel cut oats
- 1 can frozen cranberry juice concentrate

Fruit Topping

- ¾ cup water
- ⅛ tsp salt
- ¼ tsp cinnamon
- 2 each dried apricots, prunes, and dates, chopped
- ¼ cup Craisins
- ¼ Granny Smith apple, peeled and chopped pecans, and blueberries
- ½ banana, chopped
- 2 Tbsp cream or soy milk

Plan ahead, this dish needs to refrigerate overnight. In a saucepan over medium-high heat, combine the first five ingredients and bring to a boil. Stir in the oats, reduce heat, and continue cooking, stirring occasionally until thick, about 15 minutes. Pour into a bread pan sprayed with cooking spray. Cool to room temperature, then cover and refrigerate overnight. Thaw the cranberry juice overnight.

The following morning: Pour the juice into a saucepan and cook over medium heat for 20 minutes, or until juice has reduced by half and thickened. When it begins to foam, it is almost done. Set aside and it will thicken more as it cools. To prepare the fruit topping, bring the first three ingredients to a boil. Add the dried fruits, apples, and pecans to the mixture and heat 3–5 minutes, stirring gently. Add the remaining ingredients and stir just to mix. Cook one minute and set aside. Cut the chilled oats into 4 triangles. Melt 2 tablespoons butter on a nonstick skillet or griddle over medium heat. Add oat triangles and cook 3 minutes per side, or until golden brown and heated through. Put 1 triangle on a warm plate and top with ¼ cup warm fruit. Drizzle with 1–2 tablespoons of the cranberry syrup.

Sunnyfield Farm B&B

INNKEEPER Susanne Soltvedt
ADDRESS N6692 Batko Road, Camp Douglas, WI 54618
TELEPHONE (608) 427-3686 | (888) 839-0232
CONTACT soltvedt@mwt.net | www.sunnyfield.net
FEATURES 4 Rooms; Private & shared baths | Children welcome | Pets welcome

If you like country, you're sure to take pleasure from Sunnyfield Farm B&B. One hundred and sixty acres of rich farmland and scenic bluffs surround this impeccably decorated turn-of-the-century farmhouse. Enjoy panoramic views of the bluffs and wildlife from the old-fashioned porch swing.

This three-story home provides three roomy bedrooms, all located on the second floor, and each featuring hardwood floors, country décor, and handmade quilts. The Rose Room has an adjoining room with twin beds making it perfect for families or groups. The third floor offers a unique studio with accommodations for a romantic retreat, a writer's paradise, or a home away from home.

Redneck Caviar

Yield: about 6 Cups

"This recipe is adapted from one found in an Alabama church cookbook."—Innkeeper

1 (15 oz.) can black beans
1 (15 oz.) can black-eyed peas
1 (11 oz.) can shoepeg corn
2 (10 oz.) cans Ro-Tel
1 (14.5 oz.) can chopped tomatoes
1 tsp garlic salt
1 tsp garlic powder
1 tsp parsley flakes
1 tsp onion flakes
1 large bottle Italian dressing
Frito scoops

Plan ahead, this dish needs to be refrigerated overnight.

Open and drain the black beans, black-eyed peas, and corn and pour them together into a large bowl. Add, but do not drain, the Ro-Tel and chopped tomatoes. Stir in the garlic salt, garlic powder, parsley, and onion. Pour in the Italian dressing, cover the bowl, and refrigerate overnight. Serve with Fritos.

Sweet Autumn Inn

INNKEEPER Teri Nelson
ADDRESS 1019 S Main Street, Lake Mills, WI 53551
TELEPHONE (920) 648-8244 | (888) 648-8244
CONTACT innkeeper@sweetautumninn.com | www.sweetautumninn.com
FEATURES 3 Rooms | Children welcome/inquire | Pet-free environment

Sweet Autumn Inn offers three guest rooms, each with a fireplace, private bathroom, guest robes, slippers, guest refrigerator, and microwave.

No boring breakfasts here! In the morning you will enjoy a full and memorable meal. Teri easily accommodates special diets: No wheat, no eggs, no dairy, no problem! She also loves to use seasonal fruits and vegetables in her menu and grows many of them herself. From the asparagus and rhubarb in the spring to the pumpkin and apples in winter, the spicy aroma of cinnamon, cloves, nutmeg, and cardamom fill the air. Home baked breads and fresh eggs come together to make breakfast a feast. Are your taste buds tempted yet?

"The Sweet Autumn Inn offers the 'best beds' and 'best breakfasts!' "—Guest

"Teri's personalized service and attention to detail makes your stay extra special."—Guest

Sweet Autumn Inn's Easy Orange Cranberry Cinnamon Rolls

Yield: 10 Rolls

"I wanted to try a new Land O' Lakes recipe I'd found online, but didn't have enough orange marmalade and only one can of refrigerated biscuits. Since it was fall and cranberries are always on hand, I decided to add them to this recipe. I laid the biscuits flat over the jam and it turned out just like sticky rolls."—Innkeeper

- ¾ cup brown sugar
- ½ tsp cinnamon
- ½ cup cranberries, fresh or frozen
- ¼ cup sugar
- ½ cup orange marmalade
- ¼ cup chopped walnuts or pecans
- 1 can refrigerated flaky buttermilk biscuits
- ½ cup butter, melted

Preheat oven to 350°F and grease an 8- or 9-inch round baking pan. In a small bowl, stir together brown sugar and cinnamon and set aside. Place the cranberries and ¼ cup sugar together in a saucepan and cook until the berries pop and sauce thickens. Cool slightly and combine with the orange marmalade. Spoon the mixture evenly over the bottom of the baking dish and sprinkle with chopped nuts. Separate the biscuits and dip in the melted butter, then the brown sugar/cinnamon mixture. Lay the biscuits over the cranberry/marmalade. Sprinkle any remaining sugar/cinnamon mixture over the top and drizzle with any remaining butter. Bake 30–35 minutes, or until golden brown. Cool 5 minutes then invert onto a serving plate.

Token Creek Eco-Inn

INNKEEPERS Jean & Jason Schneider
ADDRESS 3919 Gray Road, Madison, WI 53532
TELEPHONE (608) 513-0016
CONTACT info@tokencreekecoinn.com | www.TokenCreekEcoInn.com
FEATURES 3 Suites | Children age 12 and over welcome | Resident pets only | Will accommodate guests' special dietary needs

Token Creek Eco-Inn is a tranquil, relaxing retreat situated on four acres just five minutes north of Madison and about 15 minutes from downtown Madison. Located near the headwater springs of Token Creek, we offer all the convenience of being near Madison without all the hustle, bustle and noise of the city. The craftsman style inn features three luxury guest rooms with private baths, some including a jetted tub or private deck.

We are a Travel Green Certified B&B that merges relaxation and luxury with sustainable living. Join us for our hearty locally grown organic breakfast, interesting workshops related to sustainability, or tour our permaculture grounds that include edible landscaping, water catchment systems, and free range chickens.

Zucchini Fritter Eggs Benedict

Yield: 12 servings

1	lb. zucchini, coarsely grated
1	large egg
½	cup onion, chopped
½–1	bunch chives (or scallions)
½	cup flour
	Salt and pepper
½	cup med/high temp oil (we use coconut or sunflower)
12	poached eggs
	Hollandaise sauce
	Fresh or dried chives for garnish

Fritters: Place zucchini in colander in sink and toss with 1 teaspoon salt. Let sit 10 minutes, then squeeze out excess water. Wisk egg in a bowl, mix in zucchini, optional onion, chives, flour and ¼ teaspoon pepper and some salt. Heat oil in large skillet over med/high heat. Drop about 2 tablespoon-size mounds in skillet and flatten. Brown, then turn over and brown other side. Sprinkle with sea salt immediately. Keep warm in a 250°F oven until ready to serve. Put two on a plate and top each with a poached egg. Pour hollandaise sauce over each and top with a sprinkle of chives and serve.

Hollandaise Sauce: Combine the following in a blender:

6	large egg yolks
4	tsp fresh lemon juice
	Pinch of pepper
1	tsp salt
2	sticks butter

Combine all ingredients except butter in a blender and blend on high for 3 seconds. In a pan, heat the butter just until bubbling. Turn blender on and slowly add butter. If sauce is too thick add a few drops of warm water. Serve immediately, or keep warm by putting blender container in a warm water bath.

Tufts' Mansion

INNKEEPERS	James & Dawn Voss
ADDRESS	26 Hewett Street, Neillsville, WI 54456
TELEPHONE	(715) 743-3346
CONTACT	info@tuftsmansion.com | www.tuftsmansion.com
FEATURES	4 Rooms | Children welcome | Pets welcome

Tufts' Mansion, located in Neillsville, Wisconsin, is a B&B like none you've ever experienced. Read a book in the parlour, sit on the front porch and relax, or stroll the beautiful grounds. You can even enjoy a soak in your own private claw-foot jetted tub.

A gourmet breakfast is served each morning in the formal dining area. On special Fridays and Saturdays you can enjoy some of the finest live music central Wisconsin has to offer before you retire to your suite for the evening. Owners James & Dawn Voss and James & Ellen Rickard are sure that an evening at Tufts' Mansion is a night you'll fondly remember.

Tufts' is also available for weddings, anniversaries, class reunions, and whatever special occasion you have in mind.

Crab & Onion Quiche

Yield: 1 Quiche

"This is one of our favorite recipes.
The original was found on the back of a bag of cheese."—Innkeeper

- 8 oz. shredded imitation crabmeat
- 3 sliced green onions
- 4 eggs
- 1¼ cups milk
- ¼ cup melted butter
- ½ cup Bisquick
- ½ cup shredded mozzarella
- 1/8 tsp pepper

Preheat oven to 350°F. Place the crabmeat and onions together in a large greased pie pan. In a medium bowl, beat together the eggs, milk, and butter. Add the Bisquick and mix to combine. Pour the mixture over the crab and onion mixture and sprinkle with cheese. Bake 30–40 minutes.

Tip: You can use real lump crabmeat in place of imitation in this recipe, but the cooking time may need to be adjusted as imitation crabmeat is already cooked—and the texture of the dish will be different.

Victoria on Main B&B

INNKEEPER Nancy Wendt
ADDRESS 622 W Main Street, Whitewater, WI 53190
TELEPHONE (262) 473-8400
CONTACT viconmain@sbcglobal.net | www.victoriaonmainbb.com
FEATURES 3 Rooms; Private & shared baths | No children | Resident pet cat only

It has been our pleasure to welcome guests to the Victoria on Main B&B for over twenty-two years. We are located in the historic district near downtown Whitewater, and across the street from the University of Wisconsin–Whitewater. Our Queen Anne revival home, built in 1895, features different woods in each room. The bedrooms are decorated with wallpapers, lace curtains, and antiques. The comfortable historic beds are covered with antique linens and lace trimmings, and down comforters and pillows. As a Shaklee distributor, we use all earth friendly products.

Everyone loves our small town and everything it has to offer. Hiking in the Kettle Moraine State Forest, swimming or boating at Whitewater Lake, attending plays at Young Auditorium or the Fireside, and eating at one of our many restaurants are just a few of the things to do. Check us out!

Easy Oven Omelet

Yield: 8 servings

¼ cup butter
18 eggs
1 cup sour cream
1 cup milk
¼ tsp basil leaves
2 tsp salt
2 cups shredded cheese
1 small can mushrooms, drained, or fresh
4 green onions, sliced
1 (2 oz.) jar pimentos, drained

Preheat oven to 325°F. Melt butter in a 9x13-inch baking dish in a preheated oven. In a large bowl, beat the eggs, sour cream, milk, basil and salt. Stir in cheese, mushrooms, onions, and pimentos. Pour into baking dish on top of the melted butter. Bake uncovered until omelet is set but still moist (40–45 minutes). Can make the night before and refrigerate (bake for 1 hour).

Variation: You can also add bacon or ham to this recipe.

Victorian Dreams B&B

INNKEEPERS John & Cindy Stevens
ADDRESS 115 Prairie Street, Lodi, WI 53555
TELEPHONE (608) 592-0362
CONTACT innkeeper@victoriandreamsbnb.com | www.victoriandreamsbnb.com
FEATURES 7 Suites | Children age 12 and older welcome | Pet-Free Environment | Will accommodate guests' special dietary needs

Victorian Dreams B&B consists of two 1897 Queen Anne Victorian homes. The main house features three lovely guest suites, each with its own private bath. Two of the suites have a two-person whirlpool tub; the third suite has a claw foot tub and a private veranda. The neighboring second house contains four large, luxurious suites, each with a private attached bath, two-person whirlpool tub and antique mantled gas fireplaces.

A full, hot breakfast is served in the dining room each morning, or for a small fee can be delivered to your suite. We accommodate all dietary restrictions and food allergies including lactose intolerant, gluten free, vegan and vegetarian. A complimentary wine and cheese reception is also offered each evening.

Gingerbread Pancakes

Yield: 18 medium-size pancakes

1¾ cups flour
½ cup whole wheat flour
¼ cup brown sugar
2 tsp baking powder
1 tsp ginger
1 tsp cinnamon
½ tsp baking soda
½ tsp salt
¼ tsp nutmeg
2 eggs
1½ cups buttermilk
1⅓ cups dark corn syrup
3 Tbsp canola oil

Combine flour, wheat flour, brown sugar, baking powder, ginger, cinnamon, baking soda, salt and nutmeg in a large bowl.

Whisk eggs, buttermilk, corn syrup and oil together in a separate bowl. Add this to dry mixture all at once. Stir until moistened—batter will be lumpy. You may need to add more buttermilk.

Heat a lightly greased griddle to medium heat. Cook for two minutes on each side. Serve immediately or keep warm in a loosely covered dish in a 200°F oven. Serve with apple or maple syrup.

Tip: This batter makes great Belgian waffles. This recipe makes 3 waffles.

VICTORIAN ROSE B&B

INNKEEPER Dee Davis
ADDRESS 323 S. Wisconsin Avenue, Muscoda, WI 53573
TELEPHONE (608) 739-4319
CONTACT vrosebb@mwt.net | www.thevictorianrosebedandbreakfast.net
FEATURES 3 Rooms | No children | Pet-free environment

Built in 1897 by local lumber baron, John Young, this beautiful Victorian mansion is the crown jewel of Muscoda, Wisconsin. The house features a grand, open staircase and oak, walnut, and maple hardwood floors. There are pocket doors, beveled crystal windows, and hand-carved entrance doors. In winter, guests enjoy breakfast by a cozy fire in the formal dining room. In summer, the morning meal is served outside on the half-moon deck.

Muscoda is a small but vibrant community located on the Wisconsin River in beautiful southwest Wisconsin. The area features year-round recreational opportunities such as canoeing, bicycling, snowmobiling, hunting, and fishing. There are numerous craft shows, antique galleries, and other festivals to delight you as well. The area is also a favorite with motorcycle riders who love to travel the beautiful Wisconsin River scenic byway and explore the many roads that wind through the magnificent hills.

Cranberry Coffee Cake

Yield: 1 Cake

"This is a real crowd pleaser and is often requested by our repeat guests."—Innkeeper

- ½ cup butter or margarine
- 1 cup sugar
- 2 eggs
- 1 cup sour cream
- 1 tsp baking soda
- 1 tsp baking powder
- 2 cups flour
- ½ tsp salt
- ¾ tsp almond extract
- 1 (16 oz.) can whole cranberry sauce
- ½ cup chopped nuts

Frosting

- ¾ cup powered sugar
- 1 Tbsp warm water
- ½ tsp almond extract

Preheat oven to 350°F and grease a 9x13-inch pan. In a medium bowl, using an electric mixer, cream together the butter and sugar. Add the eggs one at a time and mix at medium speed. Reduce speed and add the dry ingredients, alternating with the sour cream. Add the almond extract. Put half of the batter in the pan and spread to the edges. Swirl half of the cranberry sauce over the mixture and top with the remaining batter. Cover with the remaining cranberry sauce and sprinkle with nuts. Bake 50 minutes. Frost while warm.

For the frosting: Mix powdered sugar with warm water and almond extract. Drizzle over the cake.

WASHINGTON HOUSE INN

INNKEEPER Wendy Porterfield
ADDRESS W62N573 Washington Avenue, Cedarburg, WI 53012
TELEPHONE (262) 375-3550
CONTACT info@washingtonhouseinn.com | www.washingtonhouseinn.com
FEATURES 34 Rooms; 3 Suites | Children welcome | Pet-free environment

The Washington House Inn, located in the heart of historic Cedarburg, Wisconsin, offers guests an experience combining casual elegance with historic tradition. Our rooms offer tastefully appointed décor in a romantic country Victorian style mansion and feature antiques, cozy down quilts, luxury linens, whirlpool and steam baths. The inn is located within walking distance of unique shopping, art galleries, the Interurban Bike Trail, and fine coffee houses and restaurants.

The Washington House serves a complimentary deluxe continental breakfast for all guests. The breakfast includes homemade baked goods using local ingredients, healthy choices, seasonal fruits, plus a hot entrée daily. Some of our special dishes include Fresh Berry Trifle, Baked Oatmeal, Wisconsin Cheddar Egg Strata, and two award-winning scones—Cedarburg Breakfast Scones and Cherry Pecan Scones.

The Inn often get requests for recipes for the home-baked goods served at breakfast. The inn strives to accommodate all guests and has some gluten free items on hand for those who require this special diet. Breakfast is served buffet style in the Inn's warm and welcoming Gathering Room.

Egg Strata

Yield: 8 servings

- 12 eggs
- 2 cups milk
- 1 cup shredded Cheddar cheese
- 1 lb. cooked bacon
- 1 tsp salt
- ½ tsp pepper
- ½ tsp garlic powder
- 2 tsp Italian seasoning
- 8 small croissants, cubed

Plan ahead, dish needs overnight refrigeration.

In a large bowl, whisk eggs and milk until completely mixed, add remaining ingredients and combine. Pour into a greased 9x13-inch pan, cover and refrigerate overnight. In the morning, bake at 350°F for 40–50 minutes, or until set.

Westby House Inn & Restaurant

INNKEEPERS Mike & Marie Cimino
ADDRESS 200 West State Street, Westby, WI 54667
TELEPHONE (800) 434-7439
CONTACT info@westbyhouse.com | www.westbyhouse.com
FEATURES 9 Rooms; 2 Cabins/Cottages | Pet-free environment | Will accommodate guests' special dietary needs

This long-established Wisconsin B&B combines the right levels of history, comfort, and hospitality. Located in the quaint Norwegian community of Westby, and just minutes from the town of Viroqua, this La Crosse–area B&B is truly an inn steeped with replete period detail.

For restful and relaxing B&B accommodations choose from five guest rooms in the historic home that have their own style and atmosphere, with modern conveniences like wireless high speed Internet that make them ideal for today's traveler. Experience privacy in the Guest House suites with gas fireplaces, or a "refined touch of rustic in the city" in the Guest Lodge featuring loft bedrooms and mini-kitchenettes.

As you stroll into the formal dining room for your full gourmet breakfast, you will take in the scents wafting from the kitchen of perhaps cherry sundae French toast, lime-peppered bacon, fresh baked muffins or the aroma of just baked scones. Using the freshest ingredients available to savor your palette, you will experience creative culinary talents in the preparation of a gourmet breakfast that you will relish.

Chicken and Pear Waffle Sandwich

Yield: 4 servings

"This recipe gives the waffle grill a new use! A panini press can also be used. Be creative with the sandwich ingredients—like ham and Swiss cheese or apple and Cheddar cheese."—Innkeeper

4 Tbsp extra-virgin olive oil, divided
¾ lb. skinless, boneless chicken thighs or breasts
Salt and pepper
2 onions, thinly sliced
1 pear, cored and thinly sliced
1 cup shredded Monterey Jack cheese
4 dinner rolls, poppy seed or plain, split

Pre-heat waffle iron or panini press. In a large skillet, heat 2 tablespoons olive oil over medium-high heat. Season the chicken with salt and pepper. Add to the skillet and cook, turning occasionally, until golden, 6 to 8 minutes; transfer to a plate. Let cool slightly before thinly slicing.

In the same skillet, heat 2 tablespoons olive oil over medium-high heat. Add the onions, season with salt and pepper and cook until golden, about 7 minutes. Stir in the pear and cook until tender, 3–5 minutes. Remove from heat and toss with the chicken and cheese.

Divide the chicken mixture among the rolls. Using a waffle iron, cook the sandwiches in the same manner as cooking waffles. Press down on the iron to create waffle iron indents on the rolls. Cook until golden brown. Remove from iron and serve.

Tip: Can be served with a simple lettuce salad or as a side sandwich at breakfast.

Westphal Mansion Inn

INNKEEPERS	Garret & Pam Terpstra
ADDRESS	90 S Main Street, Hartford, WI 53027
TELEPHONE	(262) 673-7938
CONTACT	terpstra7938@sbcglobal.net | www.westphalmansioninn.com
FEATURES	8 Rooms | Children welcome/inquire | Resident pets only

The Westphal Mansion Inn is a fully restored and stately 1913 English Tudor mansion featuring romantic and luxurious accommodations with European ambiance. The charm of the inn offers the perfect setting away from the daily distractions of life and is a comfortable haven for a romantic getaway, travelers on business, or an elegant retreat. Each of the inn's eight unique suites is tastefully furnished in an old-world French-country style. Fine linens, antiques, fireplaces, air bubble massage tubs, and other upscale amenities can be found throughout.

In the morning, enjoy a delicious four-course breakfast with dessert. English afternoon teas and wine and cheese social hours are also offered. Stroll through the English gardens and make a wish at the 1917 fountain, or cozy up with a good book or a game of chess next to a crackling fire in the grand living room.

The inn is conveniently located within walking distance of Hartford's downtown shopping, theaters, and unique restaurants.

Thelma's Banana Nut Bread

Yield: 1 Loaf

"Thelma's Banana Bread recipe has been passed down for three generations. Over the past years, as a nanny for a family of seven, I have enjoyed many afternoons making this keepsake recipe with the third generation of children."—Innkeeper

- ½ cup vegetable oil
- 1 cup sugar
- 2 eggs, beaten
- 3 ripe bananas, mashed to a pulp
- 3 Tbsp milk
- ½ tsp vanilla extract
- 2 cups flour
- 1 tsp baking soda
- ½ tsp baking powder
- ½ tsp salt
- ½ cup mini chocolate chips (optional)
- ½ cup chopped nuts (optional)

Preheat oven to 350°F. In a medium bowl, beat together the oil and sugar. Add the eggs, bananas, milk, and vanilla and mix to combine. In a separate bowl, sift together the flour, baking soda, baking powder, and salt. Mix the dry ingredients into the wet mixture and fold in the chocolate chips and nuts. Grease a 9x5-inch loaf pan and place a waxed paper sheet on the bottom of the pan. Pour in the batter and bake 1 hour. Allow the bread to cool 5 minutes on a wire rack before removing from pan.

Variation: This recipe can be adapted for muffins. Simply bake 20 minutes at 350°F. Makes 2 dozen.

Westport B&B

INNKEEPERS Janice & Paul Zencka
ADDRESS 635 N 8th Street, Manitowoc, WI 54220
TELEPHONE (920) 686-0465 | (888) 686-0465
CONTACT info@thewestport.com | www.thewestport.com
FEATURES 4 Rooms | Children welcome/inquire | Pet-free environment

Relax in our 1879 Victorian home — a blend of elegance and comfort located in Manitowoc's Historic District, near Lake Michigan, museums, trails, shops, and dining.

Each of Westport's four guest rooms features a queen bed and private bath; spa suites have whirlpools and fireplaces. Rooms also include a stocked refrigerator, flowers, snack baskets, tea table, and fresh pastries. A four-course, candlelit breakfast is served in the dining room each morning of your stay.

Overnight Cinnamon Cranberry French Toast

Yield: 6–8 servings

"Guests seem to enjoy this recipe. We all remember the wonderful taste of cinnamon bread from when we were children. It brings back a favorite childhood taste, with extra added flavor."—Innkeeper

- 1 loaf of cinnamon swirl bread, cut into cubes (leave crust on)
- ¾ cup dried cranberries
- 6 eggs
- 3 cups half & half
- 2 Tbsp pure vanilla extract

Grease a 13x9 glass baking dish and add cubed bread. Sprinkle cranberries evenly over the bread cubes. In a medium bowl, whisk eggs together, add half & half and vanilla extract. Pour egg mixture over bread cubes and cranberries. Cover with foil and refrigerate overnight. Preheat oven to 350°F, remove foil, and bake for 45 minutes, until golden brown and set in the center. Remove from the oven and let stand for 5 minutes before serving. I serve this with a dollop of fresh whipped cream or Cool Whip and a sprinkle of cinnamon sugar. Sides include bacon and sausages.

WHITE LACE INN

INNKEEPERS **Dennis Statz, Mary & Marcia**
ADDRESS **16 N 5th Avenue, Sturgeon Bay, Door County, WI 54235**
TELEPHONE **(920) 743-1105 | (877) 948-5223**
CONTACT **Romance@WhiteLaceInn.com | www.WhiteLaceInn.com**
FEATURES **18 Rooms | Children welcome/inquire | Pet-free environment**

The White Lace Inn B&B is nestled in a quaint neighborhood in the heart of historic Sturgeon Bay, Wisconsin, on the well-known Door Peninsula. Innkeepers Dennis, Mary and Marcia and their staff invite guests to relax in one of their eighteen lovingly decorated Victorian rooms and suites. King and queen-size Victorian beds offer sweet dreams, and soothing colors with coordinated wallpapers create an inviting atmosphere. Each room has a private bath. Twelve of the rooms include oversize whirlpools and fifteen have a fireplace, while nine of the accommodations have both. A number of the rooms also feature porches or patios.

Each morning guests are treated to a delicious breakfast to start their day. Stroll through the beautifully landscaped, park-like setting and follow the redbrick path to a gazebo at the heart of the complex, the setting for more than 1,400 weddings since 1982.

We look forward to your visit.

Veggie Hashbrown Egg Bake

Yield: 10 servings

- 1 32-oz. pkg. frozen Southern-style hashbrowns (loose)
- 1 stick (½ cup) butter, melted
- 1 Tbsp onion salt
- 2 bunches green onions, chopped
- 2½–3 cups grated Cheddar cheese, divided
- ¾ loaf white bread cut into cubes, no crust
- ¼ cup chopped green pepper
- ¼ cup chopped red pepper
- ¼ cup chopped yellow pepper
- 1 8-oz. pkg. fresh mushrooms, thinly sliced
- 2 cups grated Monterey Jack cheese
- 1 large tomato, thinly sliced
- 7 eggs, beaten
- 1½ cups milk
- 1½ cups half & half
- 1 tsp dry mustard
- salt and pepper to taste
- garnish with a sprinkle of paprika or cayenne pepper and a dash of parsley flakes

Plan ahead, dish requires overnight refrigeration.

Thaw frozen hash browns in microwave for 2 minutes. Mix in ½ cup butter. Spread hashbrowns into greased 9x13-inch pan. Sprinkle with onion salt. Bake at 350°F for 20 minutes. Let cool.

Sprinkle chopped green onions and the 2 cups of the Cheddar cheese over hashbrowns. Place bread cubes over cheese. Microwave green, yellow and red peppers together for 2 minutes then sprinkle the pepper mixture and the sliced mushrooms over bread. Sprinkle Monterey Jack cheese over veggies. Place 10 slices of tomato over cheese then ½ cup (or up to 1 cup) additional grated Cheddar cheese over tomato.

Beat the eggs; add milk, cream, dry mustard, dash of salt and pepper and beat together. Pour over whole pan evenly. Sprinkle top with paprika or cayenne pepper and parsley flakes (optional). Cover and refrigerate overnight.

Bake at 350°F for 45 minutes covered with aluminum foil. Uncover for 15 minutes to let brown slightly. Let set for approximately 10 more minutes before slicing.

Willow Pond Bed, Breakfast & Events

INNKEEPERS Joe & Renee Wyngaard
ADDRESS E5490 North Shore Road, Weyauwega, WI 54983
TELEPHONE (920) 867-2493
CONTACT renee@willowpondevents.com | www.willowpondevents.com
FEATURES 5 Rooms | Children welcome | Pets welcome/inquire

Located halfway between Appleton and Stevens Point, just five miles north of Weyauwega, Wisconsin, a masterpiece of nature awaits your visit. Take a walk in the spectacular gardens, relax by the pond and waterfalls, and breathe in the fresh air of the country.

The farmhouse, built in 1901, has been a showcase for Renee's antique furniture collection. Recently, Joe & Renee took on the task of restoring the home to its original design with the goal of making the farmhouse available for the public to view and to provide a place for people in the area to stay. With more people wanting to hold their special events at Willow Pond, Joe and Renee decided to provide additional services such as event planning and receptions.

There are many locations on the twelve acres at Willow Pond to hold your reception or other celebration. From tea parties out in the garden to receptions by the pond and waterfalls, they can put up a tent and you can have your event, rain or shine. If you choose to have your party indoors, the reception room in the barn is also available for your group.

Pillowtalk Eggs

Yield: 12 servings

"I came up with this recipe for the Red Hat Ladies. They come to visit in their pajamas every year."—Innkeeper

1 roll puff pastry
½ cup onion, chopped
1 cup asparagus, chopped
½ cup red bell pepper, chopped
½ cup yellow bell pepper, chopped
½ cup chopped ham or sausage
1½ Tbsp butter
salt
pepper
12 eggs
hollandaise sauce
paprika

Preheat oven to 400°F. Line the bottom of 12 muffin cups with rounds of puff pastry, reserving 12 same-sized rounds for the "pillow tops." Sauté the onion, asparagus, bell peppers, and ham or sausage in a medium skillet with butter. Season with salt and pepper, and additional seasonings of choice, to taste. Divide the vegetable/ham mixture evenly between the 12 muffin cups and top with the reserved puff pastry rounds. Bake approximately 20 minutes, until nicely browned. Poach 12 eggs.

To serve: Carefully remove from the muffin cups and place on individual plates. Top each with a poached egg and cover with hollandaise. Sprinkle with paprika to garnish.

Wissahickon Farms Country Inn

INNKEEPER Sherilyn Litzkow
ADDRESS 2263 Maple Drive, St. Croix Falls, WI 54024
TELEPHONE (715) 483-3986
CONTACT stay@wissainn.com | www.wissainn.com
FEATURES 1 Cottage; Private baths | Children age 6 and over welcome | No pets

Built as a replica of an old country store from a bygone era, this cabin brings our guests into yesterday's world. This is your own private getaway, great for honeymoons, anniversaries or just escaping into your own private world. A gas fireplace casts a glow on the barn-plank floor and rough whitewashed walls. Braided rugs, rockers and the cast iron camel-back canopy bed topped with a handmade patchwork quilt make the place downright cozy and perfect for a St. Croix Falls romantic getaway. Wake up to a scrumptious continental breakfast.

Kick your feet up on the front porch and enjoy the peace on your scenic getaway or hit the great nearby routes on one of the available bikes. Both winter and summer have many outdoor activities available.

Cranberry Almond Muffins

Yield: 8 regular size muffins or 6 jumbo

1½ cups all-purpose flour
½ cup sugar
1 tsp baking powder
¼ tsp baking soda
¼ tsp salt
2 eggs
½ cup sour cream
¼ cup butter, melted
¼ tsp almond extract
¾ cup sliced almonds, divided
½ cup whole berry cranberry sauce

In a bowl, combine the flour, sugar, baking powder, baking soda and salt. In another bowl, whisk the eggs, sour cream, butter and extract; stir into dry ingredients just until moistened. Fold in ½ cup almonds.

Fill greased or paper-lined muffin cups half full; drop 1 tablespoon cranberry sauce into the center of each muffin.

Cover with enough batter to fill cups three-fourths full; sprinkle with remaining almonds.

Bake at 375°F for 20–25 minutes or until a toothpick inserted 1-inch from the edge comes out clean. Cool for 5 minutes before removing from pan to a wire rack. Serve warm.

Variation: Instead of cranberry sauce, other flavors of jellys or jams can be used.

Woodenheart Inn

INNKEEPERS John & Judy Hurlburt
ADDRESS 11086 State Highway 42, Sister Bay, WI 54234
TELEPHONE (920) 854-9097 | (877) 854-9097
CONTACT innkeeper@woodenheart.com | www.woodenheart.com
FEATURES 5 Rooms | Children welcome/inquire | Pet-free environment

Woodenheart Inn is located on the north side of Sister Bay, in beautiful Door County. As a guest in our log home you will find your surroundings to be elegant, private, and very comfortable. Each of the five guest quarters has its own unique charm. All of the rooms have a private bath and twin, king, or queen beds.

Guests enjoy early morning coffee in the guest loft or gazebo on the back deck, and there's plenty of space for late evening conversation in the great room with its large stone fireplace. A full country breakfast is served each morning in the dining room.

Raspberry Snowball

Yield: 8 servings

16 oz. cream cheese, softened
2/3 cup grated Swiss cheese
½ cup chopped nuts
10 oz. frozen raspberries
1 Tbsp cornstarch

In a medium bowl, combine the cream cheese, Swiss cheese, and nuts. Shape into a ball and refrigerate. Thaw the berries; drain and reserve the liquid. In a small saucepan over medium-high heat, combine the cornstarch and the reserved juice from the berries. Cook until thickened. Cool slightly and then add the raspberries. Chill.

To serve: Pour the berry sauce over the cheese ball and serve with crackers.

Variation: The classic cheese ball is so versatile, you can almost use any savory or sweet combination of ingredients. Try mixing 2 tablespoons port wine with the cream cheese. Substitute shredded Cheddar, dried cranberries, and chopped pecans in place of the Swiss, nuts, and raspberries, and drizzle with real Wisconsin maple syrup for a sweet variation. Another great combination is prepared pesto and chopped sun-dried tomatoes. Mix with the cheese and roll in a savory almond salad topper.

YE OLDE MANOR HOUSE B&B

INNKEEPERS Karen Fulbright-Anderson & John M. Anderson

ADDRESS N7622 US HWY 12, Elkhorn, WI 53121

TELEPHONE (262) 742-2450

CONTACT innkeeper@yeoldemanorhouse.com | www.yeoldemanorhouse.com

FEATURES 8 Rooms; Private baths | Children welcome/inquire | Pets welcome/inquire

Relax, renew, and rejuvenate at Ye Olde Manor House. Guests can luxuriate in one of our eight well-appointed guest rooms, surrounded by beautiful antiques and swim in our indoor heated swimming pool. The B&B sits on three acres of lush greenery and lovely gardens, just outside of Elkhorn, Wisconsin, and across the road from sparkling Lauderdale Lakes.

Ye Olde Manor House is the perfect spot for a weekend getaway or a week long retreat. Each morning, we prepare delicious breakfasts with the freshest ingredients and vegetarian, vegan, and special diet meals are happily prepared upon request. We have access to a sandy beach on nearby Pleasant Lake, a boat launch on Lauderdale Lakes, and biking and hiking in the nearby Kettle Moraine State Forest. Alpine Valley, only minutes away, offers downhill skiing in the snowy winter months and a renowned music venue in the summer. There are stables nearby for horseback riding and quaint towns with interesting antique shops, friendly cafes, and wonderful markets. There are also many fine restaurants within a short drive and the Friday night fish fry is a local tradition.

Oven Baked Apple Pancake

Yield: 6 servings

"This dish was prepared at our post-wedding brunch by a wonderful caterer who graciously gave us the recipe."—Innkeeper

- ½ cup unbleached flour
- ½ tsp baking powder
- ½ cup plus 1 Tbsp sugar, divided
- Pinch of salt
- 4 large eggs
- 1 cup milk
- 1 tsp vanilla extract
- ⅓ cup plus 2 Tbsp unsalted butter, divided
- ½ tsp cinnamon
- ½ tsp nutmeg
- 2 large green apples sliced into wedges

In a large bowl, mix together the flour, baking powder, 1 tablespoon sugar, and salt. In a separate bowl, blend the eggs, milk, vanilla, and 2 tablespoons melted butter. Mix the wet ingredients into the dry mixture and let stand 30 minutes at room temperature.

Preheat oven to 425°F. Melt the remaining ⅓ cup butter in an ovenproof skillet. In a small bowl, combine ½ cup sugar with the cinnamon and nutmeg. Sprinkle ¼ of the sugar mixture in the bottom of the skillet and set the skillet in the middle of the preheated oven. When the mixture bubbles, remove the skillet and spread the apple wedges evenly in the pan. Sprinkle the remaining sugar mixture over the apples and place the skillet over medium heat on the stove until the mixture bubbles again. Pour the batter over the apples and place in the oven for 15 minutes. Reduce oven temperature to 375°F and bake an additional 10 minutes, or until a toothpick inserted in the center comes away clean. Serve immediately.

Biscuits, Breads, Muffins & Scones

Port Washington Inn
Buttermilk Oat Biscuits

Yield: 12 servings

½ cup rolled oats
1¾ cups unbleached flour
½ tsp salt
1 tsp baking powder
½ tsp baking soda
4 Tbsp chilled butter
¾ cup buttermilk (or diluted plain yogurt)
¼ cup melted butter
raw sugar

Preheat oven to 425°F. Combine the dry ingredients in food processor and pulse to blend them. Cut the cold butter into pieces and pulse to blend it into the dry mixture only until the mixture is in coarse, irregular bits. Remove to a bowl, add the buttermilk and stir with a fork until the buttermilk is uniformly incorporated into the dry ingredients. A bit more buttermilk might be needed at this stage.

Using a tablespoon or a small ice cream dipper, drop mounds of the dough onto a baking sheet, spacing them at least an inch apart. Brush melted butter lightly on the tops of the biscuits and sprinkle them with raw sugar if desired.

Bake until lightly browned, approximately 12–15 minutes, depending upon the size of the biscuits.

Honeybee Inn B&B

Easy Quick Sticky Buns

Yield: 1 bun

"Make as many as you want. Just repeat the instructions for each one. Quick and very tasty. Guests rave about them!"—Innkeeper

1 tsp unsalted butter
1 thin slice of banana (optional)
sprinkle of chopped pecans
1 tsp brown sugar
1 tsp corn syrup
refrigerated or frozen biscuits

Preheat oven to 375°F. Drop butter in bottom of greased muffin tin and arrange banana slice on top. Sprinkle pecans, brown sugar and corn syrup over banana. Top each compartment with a biscuit. Bake 8–10 minutes. Remove from oven. Flip over immediately onto waxed paper. Serve immediately.

Riverside Manor B&B

Welsh Cakes

Yield: 24 servings

"An alternative to pancakes . . . "—Innkeeper

- 2 cups all-purpose flour
- ½ cup granulated sugar
- 2 tsp baking powder
- ½ tsp salt
- ¼ tsp nutmeg
- ¼ tsp cinnamon
- ½ cup butter or margarine
- ½ cup currants
- 1 egg
- ⅓ cup milk

Using a large bowl, combine flour, sugar, baking powder, salt, nutmeg and cinnamon. Cut in butter until crumbly. Stir in currants.

In another bowl, beat egg until frothy. Add milk. Stir into dough. Roll ¼-inch thick on floured surface. Cut into 3-inch rounds (a cookie cutter works well.) Lightly spray a frying pan or griddle with nonstick spray. Fry over medium heat, browning both sides.

Tip: You can add ¼ cup of peel and reduce the currants to ¼ cup.

Sawyer House B&B

Banana Blueberry Bread

Yield: 2 mini loaves

- 2/3 cup sugar
- 1½ cups flour
- 2 tsp baking powder
- ¼ tsp salt
- ¾ cup quick-cooking oats
- 1/3 cup canola oil
- 2 eggs
- 2 large bananas, mashed
- 1 cup blueberries

Preheat oven to 325°F. In a large bowl, sift together sugar, flour, baking powder, salt and oats. Mix in oil, eggs, and mashed bananas, stirring only until all ingredients are moist. Fold in blueberries. Pour batter into 2 greased mini loaf pans. Bake for 60–65 minutes or until a toothpick inserted in middle comes out clean. Cool in pan before removing.

Tip: This is a very moist bread and it freezes well.

Garden Gate B&B

Banana Tea Bread

Yield: 3 mini pans, 12 cupcakes or 8x5x5-inch pan

"This delicate treat is truly wonderful with a cup of tea."—Innkeeper

- 1 2/3 cups flour
- 1 tsp baking powder
- 1 tsp baking soda
- ½ tsp salt
- dash of cinnamon
- 4 oz. butter
- 1 cup sugar
- 2 eggs
- 1 cup banana (3 bananas)
- ½ cup sour cream or buttermilk
- ½ cup raisins (soaked in brandy or Kahlúa)
- ½ cup chopped pecans
- ½ cup coconut
- 1 tsp lemon juice or vanilla

Preheat oven to 350°F. Sift flour, baking powder, baking soda, salt and cinnamon in a large bowl. In a separate bowl, beat butter until fluffy. Add sugar and beat 1 minute. Add eggs one at a time. Add bananas and beat 30 seconds. Mix alternately with sour cream (buttermilk) and flour mixture, starting and ending with flour. Add raisins, nuts and coconut. Fold in lemon juice or vanilla and mix well. Bake as follows: 3 mini pans–45 minutes; cupcake pans–25 minutes; 8x5x5-inch pan–50–60 minutes.

Pedal'rs Inn
Cornbread

Yield: 12 single slices

"Once a year our community holds a chili cookoff with surrounding municipality employees. Nothing goes better with chili than cornbread, so I hit the ground running to my kitchen with flour flying and excitement in the air to make the best cornbread our residents have ever had."—Innkeeper

- ½ cup butter
- ⅔ cup honey
- 1 cup buttermilk
- 2 large eggs
- 1 tsp pure vanilla extract
- 1 cup yellow cornmeal
- 1 cup all-purpose flour
- ½ tsp baking soda
- 1 cup frozen corn

Preheat oven to 375°F. Coat an 8x8-inch bread pan with cooking spray and flour or line with parchment paper. Place butter in a large microwavable bowl. Melt butter in microwave at 30-second intervals. Do not boil. Stir in honey. Add buttermilk and eggs, alternating until everything is incorporated. Add vanilla and stir. In a separate bowl, combine dry ingredients with a whisk. Pour wet mixture into dry ingredients and stir until just wet. Add corn and continue to stir just until blended. Batter may be lumpy. Pour into prepared pan. Bake for 30–40 minutes until golden and cake tester inserted in center comes out clean.

Lake Ripley Lodge B&B

Jalapeño Cornbread

Yield: 8–12 servings

"This cornbread is a tasty addition to our Southwest-presented breakfast."—Innkeeper

- 3 eggs
- 2 cups milk
- 3 cups yellow cornbread mix
- ¼ cup oil
- 1 (no. 303) can cream-style corn
- 1 large onion, chopped
- 1 4-oz. can jalapeños, drained and chopped

Preheat oven to 425°F. Beat eggs lightly. Blend in remaining ingredients and pour into well-greased 9x13-inch pan. Bake for 30–40 minutes.

Inn at Pinewood

Crazy About Cranberry Bread

Yield: 16 servings

"This recipe was featured in a Midwest Living *article on the B&B in 2002. This bread is popular in the fall, and we usually serve it during the Eagle River Cranberry Fest the first weekend in October."*—Innkeeper

- 2 cups all-purpose flour
- 1 cup granulated sugar
- 1½ tsp baking powder
- ½ tsp salt
- ¼ tsp baking soda
- ⅓ cup butter or margarine
- 1 beaten egg
- 1 tsp finely shredded orange peel
- ⅔ cup orange juice
- 1½ cups fresh cranberries, halved
- 1 cup coarsely chopped walnuts

Preheat oven to 350°F. Lightly grease a 9x5x3-inch loaf pan, two 7½x3½x2-inch loaf pans or three 5¾x3x2-inch mini loaf pans. In a mixing bowl, stir together the flour, sugar, baking powder, salt and baking soda. Cut in butter or margarine until the mixture is crumbly. Add the egg, orange peel and juice to the mixing bowl, stirring until just combined. Fold in cranberries and nuts.

Turn the bread mixture into pan(s). Bake for 60–70 minutes for the large loaf or 40–50 minutes for the small loaves or until a toothpick inserted in the center comes out clean. Cool the bread completely on wire racks. Wrap in plastic wrap.

Tips: The bread is best if eaten the day after baking. It can be stored in the refrigerator for up to 3 days.

Amil's Inn B&B
Orange Cranberry Bread

Yield: 8–10 slices

"This recipe is so moist and delicious the bread never lasts too long at our B&B. It is also a great snack to take along biking, canoeing, hiking or traveling."—Innkeeper

- ½ cup vegetable oil
- ½ cup orange juice
- 1 Tbsp dried orange peel
- 2 eggs
- 1 cup sugar
- ½ tsp baking soda
- 1½ tsp baking powder
- ½ tsp salt
- 1⅔ cups all-purpose flour
- ¾ cup walnuts, chopped
- 1 cup cranberries, sliced

Preheat oven to 325°F. In a large mixing bowl, combine and cream together vegetable oil, orange juice, dried orange peel, eggs and sugar. Combine baking soda, baking powder, salt and flour and stir into creamed mixture. Gently stir in walnuts and cranberries. Spoon into a greased and floured 9x5x3-inch loaf pan. Bake for 60 minutes or until a toothpick inserted near the center comes out clean. Cool for 10–15 minutes; remove from loaf pan to wire rack.

Victorian Dreams B&B
Almond Poppy Seed Muffins

Yield: 1 dozen

½ cup sugar, plus 3 tsp
⅓ cup canola oil
1 egg
½ tsp almond extract
½ cup sour cream
¼ cup milk, plus 1 Tbsp
1⅓ cups flour
½ tsp baking powder
½ tsp salt
¼ tsp baking soda
2 Tbsp poppy seeds
2 Tbsp sliced almonds

Glaze

½ cup powdered sugar
2–3 tsp milk

Preheat oven to 365°F. Whisk together ½ cup sugar, oil, egg and almond extract in a large bowl. Whisk in sour cream and milk until blended. In a separate bowl, sift together flour, baking powder, salt, baking soda and poppy seeds until blended. Mix dry ingredients in with liquid ingredients. Spray a 12-count muffin pan with cooking spray. Divide mixture between 12 muffin cups. Sprinkle remaining 3 teaspoons of sugar and sliced almonds on top of each muffin. Bake 16 minutes or until toothpick inserted in center comes out clean. Remove muffins from the pan and cool several minutes before serving.

For the glaze: Mix together powdered sugar and milk. Drizzle over muffins before serving.

Lindsay House B&B

Banana Date Muffins

Yield: 6 large or 12 regular muffins

2½ cups flour (can use a combination of wheat and white)
1 tsp salt
2 tsp baking soda
2 cups sugar
2 cups mashed ripe banana (about 6 medium bananas)
4 eggs, slightly beaten
1 cup chopped nuts, any type
1 cup chopped dates

Preheat oven to 350°F. Grease the muffin tin. Stir together the flour, salt and baking soda. In a large bowl mix the sugar, mashed banana, eggs, nuts and dates. Add the dry ingredients and mix just until the batter is well blended. Don't over mix as that will give the muffins less of a tender and moist crumb. Fill muffin cups 2/3 full. Bake for 20–25 minutes. Remove from oven and let rest in pan for 5 minutes. Turn muffins on their side in the pan and let them cool. Serve warm.

Tip: These are excellent served warm with whipped cream cheese on the side.

Westport B&B

Blueberry Muffin Cake

Yield: 1 Bundt pan

"Guests enjoy this delicious cake and often ask for the recipe. A friend of mine gave me this recipe years ago. It is moist and light."—Innkeeper

- 1 box yellow cake mix
- 1 box vanilla pudding (small)
- 1 cup vanilla yogurt
- ½ cup vegetable oil
- ¼ cup water
- 1 tsp ground cinnamon
- 4 eggs
- 1 cup frozen blueberries (partially thawed and chopped)
- powdered sugar

Preheat oven to 350°F. Grease Bundt pan with shortening and flour. Blend all ingredients except 2 tablespoons cake mix and blueberries. Mix 1 minute on low speed to moisten. Then 2 minutes on medium speed. Combine reserved cake mix with chopped blueberries and fold into cake mixture. Pour into prepared pan. Bake 45–50 minutes. Cool in pan for 20 minutes. Remove from pan and cool completely. Dust with powdered sugar.

Inn at Pinewood Coffee Cake Muffins

Yield: 1 dozen

"This muffin was featured in an article about the Inn at Pinewood in Midwest Living *magazine in 2002 and again in 2007 when it was picked as one of* Midwest Living's *'20 Best Recipes of All Time.' It's our most requested muffin."*—Innkeeper

1½ cups flour
½ cup sugar
2 tsp baking powder
½ tsp salt
¼ cup shortening or margarine
1 egg, well beaten
½ cup milk
1 cup sour cream or plain yogurt

Topping

¼ cup brown sugar
2 Tbsp sugar
1 tsp cinnamon
¼ cup chopped pecans

Preheat oven to 350°F. Spray a muffin pan with nonstick cooking spray. In a large bowl, mix together the flour, sugar, baking powder and salt. Cut in the shortening until it resembles coarse crumbs. Add the egg, milk, and sour cream and stir until just moistened.

For the topping: In a medium bowl, combine brown sugar, sugar, cinnamon and pecans. Spoon half of the muffin batter into the muffin tins and sprinkle half of the topping evenly over the tops. Spoon the remaining batter on top and sprinkle with the remaining topping. Bake 20–25 minutes or until a toothpick inserted in the center comes away clean.

Lindsay House B&B

Cream Cheese Carrot Muffins

Yield: 12 regular or 6 large muffins

- 1 14½-oz. can sliced carrots, drained
- 1¾ cups flour (can use a combination of wheat and white)
- 1 cup sugar
- 1¼ tsp baking soda
- ½ tsp salt
- ½ tsp ground cinnamon
- 1/8 tsp ground allspice
- 1/8 tsp cloves
- 1/8 tsp nutmeg
- ½–1 tsp crystallized ginger, depending on taste
- 1 egg
- 1/3 cup vegetable oil (can substitute applesauce for the oil)

Filling

- 1 8-oz. pkg. cream cheese, softened
- 1 egg
- ¼ cup sugar

Preheat oven to 350°F. Place carrots in a food processor, cover and process until smooth. In a large bowl, combine the flour, sugar, baking soda, salt and spices. In a small bowl, whisk the puréed carrots, egg and oil. Stir into the dry ingredients just until moistened. Fill 12 greased muffin cups 1/3 full.

For the filling: In a small mixing bowl, beat the filling ingredients until smooth. Drop by tablespoon into the center of each muffin. Top with remaining batter. Bake for 20–25 minutes or until a toothpick comes out clean. Cool for 5 minutes before removing from pan to a wire rack. Serve warm.

Variation: Substitute 1½ cups puréed pumpkin for the carrots for another delicious muffin.

CANYON ROAD INN

Margarita Muffins

Yield: 30–36 mini muffins

"Moving back to Wisconsin from Arizona to enjoy the four seasons again, we brought some of our Southwest flavors with us. Guests get a kick out of our Margarita Muffins, which are a great accompaniment to our Eggchiladas."—Innkeeper

- 2 cups flour
- 2 tsp baking powder
- ¼ tsp baking soda
- ¼ tsp salt
- ½ cup butter, softened
- ¾ cup sugar
- 2 eggs
- ¾ cup sour cream
- ½ Tbsp orange zest
- ¼ cup lime juice
- 1 Tbsp tequila
- powdered sugar

Preheat oven to 375°F. Sift together flour, baking powder, baking soda and salt in a bowl. Set aside. Cream together butter and sugar until light and fluffy. Add eggs, beating well. Fold in sour cream and orange zest. Combine lime juice and tequila. Alternately add to creamed mixture with combined dry ingredients, blending just until combined. Do not over mix. Spoon into mini muffin pans. Bake 15–18 minutes until center springs back when lightly touched. Cool 5 minutes. Remove from pans. Dust with powdered sugar.

Variation: For a light lemon muffin, skip the tequila, use lemon zest in place of orange zest and lemon juice in place of lime juice.

Garden Gate B&B

Piña Colada Muffins

Yield: 6 large or 12 small muffins

"A jewel of a muffin. Awake to the aroma of these muffins as guests begin their day."—Innkeeper

½ cup sugar
1 egg
¼ cup oil
1 cup sour cream
1 tsp rum extract
1½ cups flour
1 tsp baking powder
½ tsp baking soda
1 cup crushed canned pineapple, undrained
½ cup coconut

Preheat oven to 375°F. Mix all ingredients together. Spoon mixture into greased muffin tin and bake for 20–30 minutes. Bake, enjoy and share!

Wissahickon Farms Country Inn

Raspberry Cream Cheese Muffins

Yield: 12 regular 6 jumbo muffins

- 2/3 cup cream cheese, softened
- 1/3 cup butter, softened
- 1½ cups sugar
- 2 egg whites
- 1 egg
- 1½ tsp vanilla extract
- 2 cups all-purpose flour
- 1 tsp baking powder
- ¼ tsp baking soda
- ½ cup buttermilk
- 2 cups fresh or frozen raspberries (no need to thaw)
- ¼ cup of walnuts, chopped

Preheat oven to 350°F. In a large mixing bowl, beat the cream cheese, butter and sugar until light and fluffy. Add the egg whites, egg and vanilla and beat well. Combine the flour, baking powder and baking soda. Add to creamed mixture alternately with buttermilk. Roll fresh or frozen raspberries in a little flour or sugar before folding in; this will prevent the color from bleeding into the batter. Fold in the raspberries and walnuts. Fill paper-lined muffin cups ¾ full. Bake for 20–24 minutes or until a toothpick comes out clean. Cool for 5 minutes before removing from pans to wire racks. Serve warm.

Forest Moon B&B
Raspberry Muffins

Yield: 6 huge muffins

"I have added wheat bran to the recipe to make it healthier and to give the muffins a chewier texture."—Innkeeper

- 1½ cups white flour
- ½ cup wheat bran
- 1 Tbsp baking powder
- 1/8 tsp salt
- ½ cup sugar, plus some for the top
- 2 large eggs
- 1 cup milk
- 6 Tbsp oil or melted butter
- 1 tsp vanilla extract
- 1 cup frozen raspberries

Preheat oven to 400°F. Grease a 6-cup muffin pan for extra-large muffins. Mix together the flour, wheat bran, baking powder, salt and sugar in a large bowl. Lightly beat the eggs in a smaller bowl, then beat in the milk, oil and vanilla extract. Make a well in the center of the dry ingredients and pour in the liquid ingredients. Add the raspberries and stir gently. Do not over mix. Spoon the batter into the prepared muffin pan. Sprinkle the top with sugar. Bake for 20 minutes.

Amil's Inn B&B

Almond Cranberry Scones

Yield: 12 scones

"This recipe came from Janice Knutson at Grapevine Log Cabins, Sparta, Wisconsin."—Innkeeper

- 2½ cups flour
- 2½ tsp baking powder
- ½ tsp baking soda
- ¾ cup cold butter, sliced
- 1 cup fresh or frozen cranberries, sliced
- ⅔ cup sugar
- ¾ cup buttermilk

Almond Frosting

- 1 Tbsp butter, softened
- 12 tsp almond flavoring
- 1½ cups powdered sugar
- 3 Tbsp milk

Preheat oven to 400°F. In a large bowl, mix the flour, baking power and baking soda. Cut in butter until the mixture is pea sized. Add the cranberries and sugar and stir well. Add the buttermilk a little at a time, mixing until blended. Divide the dough in half and roll each piece out into an 8-inch circle, about ½-inch thick. Cut each circle into 6 wedge-shaped pieces. Put wedges on two cookie sheets and bake for 12–15 minutes.

For the frosting: In a medium bowl, cream the butter and almond flavor with an electric mixer. Gradually add the powdered sugar, scraping the sides and bottom of the bowl often. Slowly add the milk, mixing until light and fluffy. After the scones have cooled, drizzle with almond-flavored frosting.

Cameo Rose Victorian Country Inn

Cherry Berry Breakfast Scones with Berry Honey Butter

Yield: 12 scones

- 3 cups flour
- ½ cup sugar
- 2 level Tbsp baking powder
- 1 tsp salt
- ⅔ cup dried cherries and berries
- 1 stick cold butter, cut into small pieces
- 1¼ cups cold heavy whipping cream
- 2 large eggs
- mint leaves, garnish

Berry Honey Butter

- 1 stick butter, softened
- 2 Tbsp seedless raspberry jam
- 1 Tbsp honey

Preheat oven to 400°F. In a large mixing bowl, combine the flour, sugar, baking powder and salt. Add the dried cherries and berries. Cut in the stick of cold butter with a pastry cutter or knife until coarsely blended. In a separate, smaller bowl, stir together the whipping cream and eggs.

Pour the cream and egg mixture on top of the flour mixture. Use a large fork to gently fold and stir in the liquid until it is formed into dough. Do not over stir. Divide the dough into two equal parts and place on a floured counter space. Gently shape each part into a large ball and flatten into a circle, about 1-inch thick. Take a sharp knife and cut the dough into 6 equal pie-shaped wedges. Place each scone on a floured baking sheet. Bake for 10 minutes, then reduce the heat and bake for another 5 minutes at 350°F. Serve immediately with the berry honey butter.

For the berry honey butter: Blend butter, jam and honey together with a fork, then whip with a small wire whisk until smooth. If butter is too hard to work with, soften it on the defrost setting in the microwave for a few seconds so it will be easier to work with. If it gets too soft, just chill it a bit.

Parkview B&B

Cranberry Scones with Cranberry Cream Cheese Butter

Yield: 12 scones

- ½ cup fresh or frozen cranberries, drained and coarsely chopped
- 2 Tbsp sugar, plus 1/3 cup
- 2½ cups flour
- 2 tsp baking powder
- ½ tsp salt
- 1 tsp orange zest
- ½ cup unsalted butter, chilled
- 2 large eggs
- 5 Tbsp heavy cream
- 1 tsp vanilla

Cranberry Cream Cheese Butter

- ½ cup butter
- ½ tsp orange zest
- 3 oz. cream cheese
- ¼ cup powdered sugar

Preheat oven to 375°F. In a small bowl, stir together chopped cranberries and 2 tablespoons sugar. Let stand about 5 minutes. In a large bowl, stir together flour, 1/3 cup sugar, baking powder, salt and orange zest. Cut the butter into ½-inch cubes and distribute over the flour mixture. Cut in the butter until the mixture resembles coarse crumbs. In a small bowl, stir together eggs, cream and vanilla. Add the egg mixture to the flour mixture and stir to combine.

Turn out the mixture onto a lightly floured surface, knead in the cranberries. Pat the dough into a 9-inch circle. Place the dough on a lightly greased baking sheet. Score into 12 wedges with a serrated knife. Sprinkle with sugar if desired. Bake for 18–22 minutes or until lightly brown. Serve with cream cheese butter.

For the cranberry cream cheese butter: Combine butter, orange zest, cream cheese and powdered sugar in a bowl. Beat until smooth. Refrigerate until 30 minutes before serving.

Variation: Use blueberries and lemon zest instead of cranberries and orange zest.

Riverside Manor B&B
Traditional English Scones

Yield: 24 depending on size

"Visiting in England a few years ago I fell in love with the traditional scone. I bought a cookbook there that had the recipe and was so excited that I didn't really take a look at the recipe I was most interested in. I arrived home and couldn't wait to get to bake my new-found scone recipe. And found out I couldn't figure out the ingredient list much less some of the measurements. They included items such as a walnut of butter, demerara sugar … You get the picture. So, I started looking online and wonders of wonders, I found a recipe in a very old cookbook that I had for years. I adapted it to suit my needs and the end result is here."—Innkeeper

- 4 cups all-purpose flour
- ½ cup sugar
- 10 tsp baking powder
- 1 tsp salt
- 1 cup golden raisins, currants or combination
- 2 eggs, beaten
- 1 cup heavy cream
- 1 cup milk
- additional milk and sugar for brushing the tops

Preheat oven to 425°F. Combine flour, sugar, baking powder and salt. Stir in raisins. In another bowl, beat eggs until frothy. Add to flour mixture. Add cream and milk. Stir until a soft ball of dough is formed. Turn out on a lightly floured surface. Knead 8–10 times. Pat or roll out to 1-inch thick. Cut with a round cookie cutter. Arrange on lightly sprayed cookie sheet close together for soft sides, or 1 inch apart for crisp sides. Brush tops with milk and sprinkle with sugar. Bake for 15 minutes until risen and browned.

Variations: Omit the raisons and/or currants if desired. This recipe also works well with blueberries. Try with Devonshire cream.

Scofield House White Chocolate Cherry Scones

Yield: 8-12 scones

"Door County is famous for its cherries. This is just one way to use the sweetened dried cherries sold all over the county. Our guests love these!"—Innkeeper

- 2 cups flour
- 1 Tbsp baking powder
- ½ tsp salt
- ¼ cup sugar
- 1⅓ cups cream
- ⅔ cup dried cherries
- ½ cup white chocolate chips

Preheat oven to 425°F. In a medium bowl, combine the flour, baking powder, salt and sugar. Using a fork, stir in the cream until the dough holds together; this dough will be sticky. Fold in the cherries and white chocolate chips, mixing just until incorporated. Lightly flour a board and place the dough on it. Knead 8–9 times and then divide the dough in half. Pat and roll the dough out into two 7–8 inch diameter circles. Cut each circle into 4–6 wedges and place on ungreased cookie sheets. Sprinkle with additional sugar and bake 11–12 minutes, until golden brown on the edges.

Coffee Cakes, Pastries & Cereals

Amil's Inn B&B Apple Kuchen

Yield: 6–8 servings

"This recipe came from a friend, Beverly Pralle."—Innkeeper

- ½ cup butter
- ½ cup sugar
- 2 eggs
- 1 cup flour
- ½ tsp baking powder
- ½ tsp vanilla
- 3 apples, firm (Granny Smith)

Topping

- ¼ cup butter
- ¼ cup flour
- ½ tsp cinnamon
- ⅓ cup sugar

Preheat oven to 350°F. Cream butter and sugar. Beat in eggs one at a time until creamy. Add flour, baking powder and vanilla. Spread in a 7½x11-inch greased baking pan. Slice apples and put on top of dough.

For the topping: Mix together the butter, flour, cinnamon and sugar and sprinkle over the top. Bake for 25–30 minutes.

Variation: This recipe is also excellent with peaches.

Hamilton House B&B
Baked Oatmeal

Yield: 8 servings

"Baked Oatmeal does not sound very glamorous, but it is very yummy. Great when you need to feed a crowd early in the morning. I searched around for something satisfying I could make for a group that was staying with me but wanted a very early breakfast before going off to a full day of seminars. I took several different ideas and added a little personal touch to come up with this recipe that could be prepared the night before and tweaked, depending on preferences of that day's guests."—Innkeeper

- 2 cups oatmeal, quick or regular
- 1½ tsp baking powder
- ½ tsp salt
- 1 cup milk
- 2 eggs
- ½ cup applesauce
- ¼ cup brown sugar
- ½ cup dried cranberries
- 1 tsp vanilla
- ½ cup almonds
- fresh fruit and steamed milk to garnish

Preheat oven to 325°F. Combine the oatmeal, baking powder and salt. In a separate bowl, mix the milk, eggs, applesauce, brown sugar and vanilla until blended. Combine the dry and wet ingredients. Add cranberries and almonds. Refrigerate overnight. Pour into a greased 9-inch pie pan. Bake for 45–60 minutes or until done. Serve hot, topped with steamed milk and fresh fruit.

Variations: Substitute a milk option or fruit and nut combination. Try topping with honey-flavored Greek yogurt for additional protein. Use soy, almond or coconut milk, depending on dietary restrictions.

WASHINGTON HOUSE INN

Baked Oatmeal

Yield: 4 servings

"A great start to a holiday morning with the family!"—Innkeeper

- 2 cups milk
- 1 Tbsp butter
- 3 Tbsp brown sugar, packed
- ¼ tsp salt
- ¼ tsp cinnamon
- 1¼ cups old-fashioned rolled oats
- ½ cup raisins, dried cranberries or other dried fruit
- 1 cup peeled, diced apple

Preheat oven to 350°F. Combine the milk, butter, sugar, salt and cinnamon in a saucepan and bring to a boil. Stir in oats and fruit and heat until bubbles appear along edge of pan. Turn into a buttered casserole dish and bake for 20 minutes, covered. Serve warm with milk, cream or maple syrup and your favorite oatmeal toppings.

Scofield House Cherry Coffee Cake

Yield: 9x13-inch cake pan

1 box yellow or white cake mix
4 eggs
½ cup oil
¾ cup sour cream
1 pint jar cherry pie filling

Topping

¾ cup firmly packed brown sugar
½ cup all-purpose flour
½ cup uncooked oatmeal
⅓ cup butter, softened

Preheat oven to 350°F. Place cake mix in a large mixing bowl and add eggs, oil and sour cream. Blend well. Spread ⅔ of the batter into a greased 9x13-inch pan. Spoon dollops of pie filling over the batter. Top with dollops of remaining batter.

For the topping: Combine brown sugar, flour and oatmeal in a small mixing bowl. Cut in butter to make a crumbly mixture. Sprinkle over top of batter mixture. Bake for about 35 minutes.

Parkview B&B Cinnamon Crunch Coffee Cake

Yield: 10–12 servings

"This was the coffeecake that my mother frequently made and it is our family's favorite coffeecake recipe!"—Innkeeper

- 2 cups flour
- 1 Tbsp baking powder
- ¼ tsp salt
- ¾ cup sugar
- 5 Tbsp butter/margarine
- ¾ cup milk
- 1 egg
- 1 tsp vanilla

Topping

- ⅓ cup sugar
- 1½ Tbsp Butter
- 1½ Tbsp flour
- 2 tsp cinnamon

Preheat oven to 375°F. Combine the flour, baking powder, salt, sugar and margarine. In a separate bowl, beat the milk, egg and vanilla. Combine liquid ingredients with dry ingredients. Pour into a greased 8x8-inch pan.

For the topping: Combine the sugar, butter, flour and cinnamon until well blended. Spread topping over the batter. Bake for 25–35 minutes or until brown.

Variations: Put some topping in the middle of the cake by pouring half the batter in the pan, some topping, then the remainder of the batter and the rest of the topping. Try adding thinly sliced fruit in the middle, like apples or peaches.

Inn at Pinewood
Danish Pastries

Yield: 2 pastries

"My Mom would bake this pastry at Christmas time and now every time I bake it and smell the almond wafting through the air, I'm reminded of her. This pastry freezes well but if your family is at all like mine, the second one never makes it to the freezer!"—Innkeeper

2 cups flour, divided
1 cup butter, divided
2 Tbsp water, plus 1 cup water
1 tsp almond extract
3 eggs

Frosting

½ stick butter
2 cups (approx) unsifted powdered sugar
small amount of water to make icing
toasted almond slices (optional)

Preheat oven to 350°F. Mix 1 cup flour, ½ cup butter and 2 tablespoons water and crumble like pie crust. Divide this dough into 2 equal parts and pat on cookie sheets in 2 long strips, about 3 inches wide. Bring to a boil in a saucepan the ½ cup butter and 1 cup water. Once boiling, add 1 teaspoon almond extract. Remove from heat and stir in 1 cup flour into a ball. Add 3 eggs, one at a time, and beat well after each addition. Spread the dough onto each of the 2 strips of crust already on the cookie sheet. Bake for 1 hour or until golden brown. Cool and frost.

For the frosting: Combine the butter, powder sugar and water to make a spreadable frosting. Spread on cooled baked pastries and garnish with toasted almond slices, if desired.

Victorian Dreams B&B
Hot Quinoa Breakfast Cereal

Yield: 2 small servings

"This is a great vegan or vegetarian recipe."—Innkeeper

½ cup quinoa
1 cup water
¼ cup apples, cut into small chunks
small handful of dried cranberries
¼ tsp cinnamon
milk or half & half
brown sugar or honey

Rinse quinoa and put in saucepan with the water. Bring to a boil. Reduce heat and simmer for 5 minutes. Add apples, cranberries and cinnamon. Simmer until water is absorbed, about 10 minutes. Serve with milk or half & half. Sweeten to taste with honey or brown sugar.

Variation: Raisins can be used in place of the dried cranberries.

Token Creek Eco-Inn
Jean's Cinnamon Rolls

Yield: 8 rolls

- 2¼-2½ cups Gold N White or all-purpose flour
- 2 Tbsp sugar
- 1¼ tsp baking powder
- ½ tsp baking soda
- ¼ tsp sea salt
- 1¼ cups organic buttermilk
- 2 Tbsp melted butter
- extra butter for greasing the pan and brushing rolls

Filling

- ½ cup sugar
- 4 Tbsp Penzeys cinnamon
- 3-4 Tbsp melted butter

Frosting

- 3 oz. cream cheese, softened
- 6 Tbsp butter, softened
- 1 tsp organic buttermilk
- 1 tsp Penzeys vanilla
- 1½ cups powdered sugar

Preheat oven to 425°F with the rack in the upper middle position. Butter a springform pan. Wisk flour, sugar, baking powder, baking soda and salt together in a large bowl. Add buttermilk and butter and mix with a wooden spoon until liquid is mixed in and dough is shaggy. On a lightly floured surface, knead dough just until smooth. Pat dough with your hands until it is about 12x9 inches. Combine the ingredients for sugar/cinnamon filling, using only enough butter to combine. Spread filling, avoiding the outer 1 inch of the dough. Starting at the 9-inch side, roll the dough up tightly. Spray a large, sharp knife with oil and slice the roll into 8 equal pieces.

Arrange rolls in springform pan with one roll in the middle. Lightly press rolls down with your hand. Brush rolls with butter. Bake rolls covered for 15 minutes, then remove foil and bake an additional 5–10 minutes or until lightly browned.

For the frosting: While the rolls are baking, use an electric mixer to whisk cream cheese and butter, then add buttermilk and vanilla. Slowly add powdered sugar and whisk until smooth. Use about half the frosting to frost the rolls and place the extra in a bowl on the table.

Angel Inn B&B
Lavender Coffee Cake

Yield: 8–12 servings

"I grow and dry my own lavender, which makes this recipe even more special to me."—Innkeeper

- 2¼ cups flour
- 2 cups sugar
- ½ tsp salt
- ½ tsp baking soda
- 3 eggs
- 1 cup butter, softened
- 1 small container of lemon yogurt
- 2 tsp natural dried lavender

Preheat oven to 325°F. In a large bowl, mix all the ingredients at low speed until evenly blended. Increase speed to medium and beat for 3 more minutes. Pour batter into a greased Bundt pan. Bake for 60–70 minutes. Let cake cool on a wire rack before inverting it onto a serving plate.

Variations: Top coffee cake with lemon juice and powdered sugar frosting. Add sprinkles of dried lavender on top of the frosting.

Franklin Street Inn, LLC

Quinoa Granola

Yield: Varies by amount used per serving

"There is a high demand for gluten-free breakfast items. I received this recipe for my special diet guests. It is very interesting that Quinoa Granola is now a favorite of all of our guests and not just those requesting special diets."—Innkeeper

- ¼ cup vegetable oil, canola or sunflower
- ¼ cup honey
- ½ tsp salt
- 1 tsp vanilla
- 4 cups or 1 box of quinoa flakes
- 1½ cups sliced almonds
- 1 cup coconut
- ½ cup brown sugar, packed
- 1 tsp ground cinnamon
- 1½ cups raisins or dried cranberries

Preheat oven to 250°F. Set oven rack on 3rd level from bottom. Line a jelly roll pan with parchment paper.

In a small bowl, whisk oil, honey, salt and vanilla. Set aside. In a large bowl, toss together flakes, almonds, coconut, brown sugar and cinnamon. Fold oil mixture into dried mixture until combined. Spread mixture evenly over baking sheet and bake, stirring every 15 minutes until golden brown for about 50 minutes. Remove pan from the oven and allow to cool on a wire rack. Stir in raisins or dried cranberries, when cooled. Store in an airtight container in the freezer.

Tip: The granola makes an attractive and tasty garnish for parfaits!

Cream Pitcher B&B

Raspberry Cream Cheese Coffee Cake

Yield: 10–12 servings

- 2 1/3 cups flour
- 2 Tbsp sugar
- 1 Tbsp baking powder
- ½ tsp salt
- 6 Tbsp butter
- 3 oz. cream cheese
- ¼ cup shortening
- ½ cup, plus 2 Tbsp milk
- 2/3 cup raspberry preserves
- ¼ cup walnuts, chopped
- 1 cup powdered sugar
- ¼ tsp vanilla

Preheat oven to 400°F. Stir together flour, sugar, baking powder and salt. Cut in butter, cream cheese and shortening until mixture resembles peas. Stir in ½ cup milk. On a lightly floured board, knead dough gently 20 times. Roll to 12x8-inch rectangle on waxed paper. Spread preserves down the middle 1/3 of the rectangle. Sprinkle nuts over preserves. Make 2½-inch cuts at 1-inch intervals on the long sides. Fold the strips over the center portion. Bake on a greased baking sheet for 12–15 minutes.

Make a glaze of the powdered sugar, 2 tablespoons milk and vanilla. Drizzle over coffee cake while warm.

Tips: Any jam or preserves can be used with this recipe. It is yummy with apple butter. Instead of rolling the dough out on waxed paper, it can be rolled out on the cookie sheet then it won't need to be transferred.

Fountain Chateau B&B
Rhubarb Berry Coffee Cake

Yield: 12–15 servings

"I'm always looking for quick and easy recipes. This is so easy and the aroma brings people to the kitchen to check it out."—Innkeeper

- 1 18¼-oz. pkg. yellow cake mix, divided
- ⅔ cup packed brown sugar
- 2 Tbsp cold butter
- ¾ cup chopped walnuts
- 2 eggs
- 1 cup sour cream
- 1½ cups finely chopped fresh rhubarb
- 1½ cups sliced fresh strawberries
- ½ cup cream cheese frosting (optional)

Preheat oven to 350°F. In a bowl, combine ⅔ cup cake mix and brown sugar. Cut in butter until crumbly. Add walnuts; set aside.

Place remaining cake mix in another bowl. Add the eggs and sour cream. Fold in rhubarb and strawberries. Spread into a greased 12x9-inch baking dish. Sprinkle with reserved crumb mixture. Bake for 40–50 minutes. Cool on a wire rack. If desired, place frosting in a microwavable bowl and heat for 15 seconds. Drizzle over cake.

French Toast, Pancakes, Waffles & Crêpes

Inn on Hillwind

Baked Apple French Toast

Yield: 6–8 servings

"This is one of the recipes from our website. It's a tasty combination of Wisconsin dairy products, maple syrup produced just over the hill from the Inn, and our home-grown apples."—Innkeeper

1 loaf French bread, cut in cubes
1 8-oz. pkg. cream cheese, cut in cubes
2 cups apples, peeled and diced
1 tsp cinnamon
4 Tbsp butter, melted
6 eggs
½ pint heavy cream
2 cups milk
¼ cup maple syrup, plus extra to serve

Preheat oven to 325°F. Coat a 9x13-inch pan with cooking spray. Arrange half of the bread in bottom of the pan. Sprinkle the cream cheese over the bread. Top with apples. Sprinkle cinnamon on top. Pour melted butter over bread and apples. Top with remaining bread. In a large bowl, beat together eggs, cream, milk and syrup. Pour over bread mixture. Press bread down so all pieces are soaked. Cover with plastic wrap and refrigerate for at least 2 hours. Bake uncovered for 45 minutes. Let stand for 10 minutes before serving. Serve with warm maple syrup.

Variations: Drizzle with caramel sauce and top with whipped cream.

Inn at Lonesome Hollow
Baked Orange French Toast

Yield: 6–8 servings

"This recipe was originally given to us by a friend and we have tweaked it. We make pats of butter and melt them in the pan on low heat on the stove to ensure the pan is completely covered with the butter. Pete usually makes this recipe and he never measures. He tends to go heavy on the butter and cinnamon. I have to say, it tastes better his way!!"—Innkeeper

- 1/8-¼ cup butter
- ½ cup sugar
- 1 tsp cinnamon
- 1 Tbsp orange zest
- 2/3 cup orange juice
- 4–5 eggs, beaten
- 8–10 slices French bread
- powdered sugar for garnish

Preheat oven to 325°F. Melt butter in a 9x13-inch glass pan. Combine the sugar, cinnamon and orange zest, and sprinkle mixture over the melted butter in the pan. Mix the eggs and juice. Dip bread in the egg mixture and arrange in the pan. Bake until brown, about 25 minutes. Turn bread pieces over onto serving plate, so that caramelized sugar is on the top. Garnish with powdered sugar.

Garden Gate B&B
Cherry Baked French Toast

Yield: 9x13-inch pan or 7 ramekins

"This recipe is easy to make overnight and can also be made with different pie fillings. It's a real treat, almost like dessert for breakfast."—Innkeeper

- 1 loaf white bread
- 1 cup sugar
- 1 16-oz. pkg. cream cheese, softened
- 1 can cherry pie filling
- 7 eggs
- 1½ cups milk
- 1½ cups half & half
- 2 tsp vanilla extract
- ½ tsp nutmeg
- ½ tsp cinnamon
- ½ loaf French bread
- powdered sugar

Grease either a 9x13-inch pan or 7 ramekins. Cut white bread into cubes. Place in bottom of pans. Mix sugar and cream cheese. Spread on top of bread. Spread pie filling over top. Mix eggs, milk, half & half, vanilla, nutmeg and cinnamon. Set aside.

Slice French bread into ½-inch slices. Dip in egg mixture and place over pie filling. Pour the remaining mixture over bread. Cover and set overnight in fridge.

In the morning, preheat oven to 350°F. Bake uncovered for 50–60 minutes for a 9x13-inch pan or 30 minutes for ramekins. Dust with powdered sugar.

Brayton B&B

Crème Brûlée French Toast with Streusel Topping

Yield: 4 servings

"This recipe is a combination of two recipes that I found in a magazine years ago and put together as one dish."—Innkeeper

- 1 stick butter
- 1 cup brown sugar
- 2 tsp corn syrup
- 1 loaf cinnamon bread
- 5 large eggs
- 1½ cups half & half
- 1 tsp vanilla extract
- strawberry jam

Crumb Topping

- ¼ cup brown sugar
- ½ stick butter
- ½ tsp cinnamon
- ¼ cup chopped pecans

Plan ahead, this dish needs to refrigerate overnight.

In a saucepan over medium-high heat, bring the butter, brown sugar and corn syrup to a boil. Stir frequently. Pour the mixture into an 8x8-inch baking dish. Layer the bread over the glaze, 2–4 slices high, making them fit the pan. In a medium bowl, whisk together the eggs, half & half and vanilla until combined. Pour over the bread and cover. Chill overnight.

Preheat oven to 500°F. Bake uncovered for 15 minutes. In a small bowl, mix together the crumb topping. Sprinkle over the baked French toast. Bake an additional 10 minutes. Serve with strawberry jam.

Token Creek Eco-Inn Pumpkin French Toast

Yield: 6 servings

"This recipe is absolutely delicious made with either challah or gluten-free bread. Check your spices and pumpkin can to make sure they are gluten free if you are making a gluten-free version."—Innkeeper

1 loaf brioche or fresh softer-crusted ciabatta or sourdough (see above)
8 eggs
2 cups whole milk
½ cup real maple syrup
2 cups cooked puréed pumpkin (fresh) or 1 full can pumpkin
2 Tbsp pumpkin pie spice
chopped nuts (walnuts, hickory or hazelnuts) (optional)
maple syrup

Preheat oven to 350°F. Butter a 9x9-inch pan. Cut thick slices of the bread then slice in half or quarters (serving-size slices). In a large bowl, lightly beat eggs then add milk, syrup, pumpkin and spices. Arrange half of the bread slices in one layer at the bottom of the pan. Pour half of the egg mixture over the bread. Then arrange the second half of the bread on top of the first. Pour the remaining mixture over the last layer of bread. The egg mixture should cover all the bread. The pan will look almost too full. Sprinkle optional nuts over top. Let the pan sit for about an hour or however long you have. Bake for 30–45 minutes until browned. Serve with warm maple syrup.

Variation: Add diced apples on top before cooking.

O'Neill Manor, LLC
Stuffed French Toast with Fruit

Yield: 6 servings

"I make this the night before and have used a variety of fruit, including peaches, strawberries and raspberries. I think most anything will do."—Innkeeper

- 2/3 loaf dense bread (French, potato, sourdough, etc.)
- 5 large eggs
- 1 cup milk
- ½ cup heavy cream or half & half
- ¼ cup sugar
- ½ cup dark brown sugar, divided
- 1 tsp vanilla
- 1 tsp cinnamon
- 3 cups fruit
- real maple syrup

Butter a 9-inch round glass baking dish. Arrange bread into a tight, flat layer about 1-inch deep (remove crust from bread for a smoother dish). In a large bowl, mix eggs, milks, sugar, ¼ cup brown sugar and vanilla. Blend well and pour over top of bread. It is important that it looks like there is still a good amount of liquid to be absorbed by the bread overnight. If there's not enough liquid, add more. The consistency should end up like custard; it should not be served dry. For added moisture, mix in some preserves or crushed fruit. Top with a consistent layer of fruit. Arrange in a nice pattern if you are using something like peaches. Top this with the remaining brown sugar and cinnamon. Cover tightly and refrigerate overnight.

Remove dish from fridge and let stand for 30 minutes. Preheat oven to 350°F. Bake uncovered for 45–55 minutes until lightly browned and center is firming up. Let stand for 5 minutes before serving with real maple syrup.

Tip: The amount of fruit used—3 cups—will vary with the type of fruit used. You want good coverage on the top of the bread.

Lindsay House B&B Ebelskivers (Danish Pancakes)

Yield: approximately 40

- 2 cups all-purpose flour, or a combination of wheat and white
- 1 tsp baking powder
- ½ tsp salt
- 1 Tbsp sugar
- 4 eggs, separated
- 2 cups milk, or 1 cup buttermilk and 1 cup regular milk for a bit of a tang
- 4 Tbsp butter, melted

In a bowl, whisk together the flour, baking powder, salt and sugar. In a small bowl, lightly whisk the yolks, then whisk in the milk and the melted butter. Whisk the yolk mixture into the flour mixture until combined. Batter will be lumpy. In another bowl, using an electric mixer, whisk the egg whites on high speed until stiff, but not dry, peaks form, about 2 to 3 minutes. Using a rubber spatula, gently fold the whites into the batter in two additions.

Put ¼ teaspoon butter in each well of the ebelskiver pan. Set over medium heat and heat until the butter begins to bubble. Pour 1 tablespoon batter into each well. Put 1 teaspoon of the filling of your choice in the center of each pancake and top with 1 tablespoon batter. Cook until the bottoms are golden brown and crispy, about 3 to 5 minutes. Using 2 wooden or bamboo skewers, flip the pancakes over and cook until golden and crispy, about 3 minutes more. Transfer to a plate. Repeat with the remaining batter and fillings. Serve immediately with topping, if desired.

Filling suggestions: Nutella, jam, bananas, berries, curd or cheese, ham and Swiss, horseradish and jam (sounds weird but it's really tasty).

Topping suggestions: Syrup, fruit sauce, maple syrup or powdered sugar for sweet; a dusting of kosher salt and cracked pepper for savory.

McConnell Inn Gingerbread Pancakes

Yield: 24–30 pancakes

"Pancakes are regularly on the menu at McConnell Inn. I enjoy trying new ingredients and new combinations of flavors, from buckwheat to sour cream to lemon zest to cottage cheese. This recipe is always a hit, especially on a cold autumn or winter morning."—Innkeeper

- 4 eggs
- 2 cups buttermilk
- 4 Tbsp brown sugar
- ¼ cup melted butter
- 4 cups flour
- 4 Tbsp baking powder
- 1 Tbsp cinnamon
- 1 tsp salt
- 1 tsp ginger
- 1 tsp nutmeg

Mix eggs, buttermilk, brown sugar and melted butter. In a separate bowl, mix flour, baking powder and spices. Create a well in center of the dry ingredients. Pour in egg mixture and mix until blended. Spray griddle and preheat. Scoop ¼ cup of batter onto hot griddle and cook until brown. Flip and cook until set.

Tip: This recipe can be mixed the night before. Refrigerating overnight seems to make for a lighter pancake.

Bowman's Oak Hill B&B

Nancy's Gourmet Pancakes with Lemon Sauce

Yield: 12 pancakes, 1½ cups sauce

"I got this recipe from a neighbor on the 4th of July, 45 years ago, when I was a very young mother. From that day forward, my girls did not think pancakes were truly pancakes without this sauce."—Innkeeper

- 1¼ cups flour
- 1/3 cup sugar or sugar substitute
- 1 tsp baking soda
- ½ tsp baking powder
- dash of salt
- 1 cup light cottage cheese
- ½ cup plain yogurt
- ½ cup light sour cream
- 1 tsp vanilla extract
- 2 eggs

Nancy's Secret Lemon Sauce

- 1 egg, beaten
- 1 cup sugar
- ¼ cup water
- ½ cup butter
- zest of 1 lemon
- juice of 1 lemon, or ¼ cup bottled lemon juice
- dash of salt

In a large bowl, combine the flour, sugar, baking soda, baking powder and salt. In a second bowl, combine the cottage cheese, yogurt, sour cream, vanilla and eggs. Heat a griddle to medium. Once heated, combine the wet and dry mixtures. Butter or spray the griddle with nonstick cooking spray. Place ¼ cup of batter on the griddle; the batter will be thick. Turn when the top bubbles and the edges begin to dry. It will take about 3 minutes per side to cook. Continue until all the batter has been used.

For the sauce: In a medium saucepan over medium-high heat, combine all the ingredients, stirring occasionally. Bring just to a boil before pouring into a small pitcher. Serve with warm pancakes.

Variations: Serve with fresh berries or maple syrup.

Hamilton House B&B
Oven-Baked Buttermilk Pancakes

Yield: 8 servings

"I discovered this recipe while leafing through one of my many breakfast cookbooks (which by the way I read instead of romance novels like some women. Much more satisfying!). I was delighted that I could finally serve my houseful of guests pancakes or sit down to enjoy hot fluffy pancakes with my family instead of standing at the stove while the family enjoyed their pancakes. This basic recipe can be changed up seasonally. You can mix it all up and put it in the fridge the night before or mix it up quickly in the morning while the coffee brews."—Innkeeper

- 2 cups flour
- 3 Tbsp sugar
- 1 tsp baking soda
- 1 tsp baking powder
- ¼ tsp salt
- 1 large egg
- 1½ cups buttermilk
- 3 Tbsp vegetable oil
- fresh fruit, nuts or sugar of choice, as topping

Preheat oven to 350°F. Spray a 9x13-inch pan with nonstick spray. Sift together the flour, sugar, baking soda, baking powder and salt. In another bowl, mix the egg, buttermilk and oil. Combine the wet and dry ingredients. Spread batter into pan. Sprinkle with choice of topping: cinnamon/sugar, vanilla sugar, nuts and/or fresh fruit. Bake for approximately 25 minutes. Serve with powdered sugar, syrup and/or fresh fruit.

Variations: Top with lemon zest and powdered sugar in the summer, apples and cinnamon in the fall and blueberries and vanilla sugar in the spring. Other ideas are cherries, raspberries, pecans and apricot jam. Or, top with warmed seasonal fruit compote. Heat fruit in a small pan until thick and bubbly. Remove from heat. Add butter, lemon zest and a splash of brandy or whisky.

Altemus Corners B&B International Waffles

Yield: 6 servings

"This is easy to make since half is prepared the day before and it's also healthy for the guests with the soaked whole grains."—Innkeeper

Day 1

- 1¾ cups buttermilk
- 3 Tbsp melted ghee (melt butter and carefully skim off white casein from top)
- 1 tsp vanilla
- 2/3 cup brown rice flour (grind about ½ cup brown rice)
- 2/3 cup oat flour (grind about 2/3 cup rolled oats)
- 1/3 cup millet flour (grind about ¼ cup millet)
- 1/3 cup buckwheat flour (grind about ¼ cup toasted buckwheat)

Day 2

- 2 tsp baking powder
- ½ tsp baking soda
- ½–1 tsp salt
- 4 eggs, separated
- ½–1 tsp cinnamon (optional for cinnamon whole grain waffles)
- maple syrup
- butter

Day 1: Blend together buttermilk, ghee, vanilla and flours in mixing bowl. Cover and let stand 12–24 hours.

Day 2: Sift baking powder, baking soda and salt through a small strainer into a small bowl and set aside. Separate 4 eggs; blend yolks into soaked batter. Beat egg whites until stiff but not dry. Briefly blend leavenings and salt mixture into batter just until evenly mixed. Fold in beaten egg whites. Bake waffles and serve. May be kept warm in oven. Serve with maple syrup and butter.

Crystal River Inn B&B

Waffles at the Crystal River Inn

Yield: 4 servings (recipe doubles or halves)

- 2 large eggs
- 2 cups cultured buttermilk (use less if using milk plus vinegar substitute)
- ¼ cup canola oil
- 1⅓ cups all-purpose flour
- good pinch of salt
- 1 Tbsp sugar
- ¼ tsp baking soda
- 2 tsp baking powder
- ½ tsp ground cinnamon

Mix eggs, buttermilk and canola oil together in a bowl until well blended. Sift flour, salt, sugar, baking soda, baking powder and cinnamon together. Start preheating waffle iron.

Very shortly before baking, mix the wet and dry ingredients together. Don't over mix, just enough to make a wet batter.

Ladle enough batter into hot waffle iron and close. Depending on iron, baking may take 4 minutes, give or take a bit. Learn how long the iron takes to get done and use a kitchen timer to get uniform results.

Holding the waffles: Put the cooked waffles on the rack of a 200°F oven with the door propped open. This will let the waffles crisp up if needed. Most importantly, it holds the cooked waffles well until you make more, but not much longer than 10–15 minutes.

Tips: Dust with powdered sugar. Cover with real Wisconsin maple syrup. Serve with sides of breakfast meat and fresh fruit.

Apple Tree Lane B&B

Strawberry Cheese Crêpe with Lavender Cream

Yield: 6 servings

1½ cups flour
1 Tbsp sugar
½ tsp baking powder
½ tsp salt
2 cups milk
2 eggs
½ tsp vanilla
2 Tbsp melted butter
fresh strawberries, garnish

Filling
2 cups ricotta cheese
½ cup strawberry jam

Strawberry Sauce
½ cup strawberry jam

Lavender Cream
2 cups heavy whipping cream
½ cup confectioners' sugar
1 tsp culinary-grade lavender

Measure flour, sugar, baking powder and salt into bowl. Stir in milk, eggs, vanilla and melted butter. For each crêpe, lightly butter an 8-inch skillet and heat until bubbly. Pour ¼ cup batter into skillet, rotating to cover pan bottom. Cook until light brown, turn and brown on other side. Crêpes may be used immediately or frozen for future use.

For filling: Mix ricotta cheese with strawberry jam.

For strawberry sauce: Melt strawberry jam in microwave until pourable.

For lavender cream: Beat heavy whipping cream with confectioners' sugar and lavender, until thick.

Fill middle of crêpe with ⅓ cup filling. Bring 2 sides up forming log shape. Microwave for about 15 seconds. Drizzle heated strawberry sauce over crêpe. Place a large dollop of lavender cream on crêpe and garnish with fresh strawberries.

Variation: This recipe is equally good using apricot jam, and fresh or canned apricots for garnish.

Breakfast Entrées

Heaven Scent B&B

Bacon Omelet Roll with Salsa

Yield: 8 servings

"If you are looking for an egg dish that makes a great presentation and tastes even better, try this dish, it is quickly becoming a favorite of my guests."—Innkeeper

- 8 eggs
- 1 cup milk
- 1/3 cup flour
- 1 red pepper, finely chopped
- 8 slices bacon, cooked, crumbled
- 3 green onions, finely chopped
- 1 tsp dried oregano leaves, crushed
- 1 cup shredded sharp Cheddar cheese
- 1 cup thick salsa, warmed

Preheat oven to 350°F. Line a 15x10x1-inch pan with parchment paper, with ends extending over the shortest sides of the pan. Spray with cooking spray. Beat eggs, milk and flour in a large bowl with a whisk until well blended. Stir in red pepper, bacon, green onions and oregano. Pour into prepared pan. Bake 14–16 minutes or until edges are almost set. Top with cheese. Bake 2 minutes or until melted. Roll up omelet immediately, starting at one short end and peeling off paper as omelet is rolled. Place on platter and cut into slices. Serve with salsa.

Sawyer House B&B

Baked Egg/Potato Dish

Yield: 6 servings

- ¾ lb. shredded potatoes
- 8 oz. sausage links or 8 slices cooked bacon, cut or sliced
- 2 cups cheese (cheddar, Swiss or other)
- 4 eggs
- 1 cup milk (1%)
- salt and pepper to taste
- 1 Tbsp ground mustard

Preheat oven to 350°F. Spray an 8-inch square baking dish with non-stick cooking spray. Line the bottom with potatoes. Spread the sausage or bacon over the potatoes. Spread the shredded cheese on top. Combine the eggs and milk. Add salt, pepper and ground mustard and beat well. Pour evenly over mixture. Cover with foil and bake 45 minutes. Uncover and bake an additional 10–15 minutes or until knife inserted in center comes out clean. Let stand 5 minutes before serving.

Variation: Add sliced tomatoes on top during last 10–15 minutes of cooking.

Hamilton House B&B

Baked Omelet

Yield: 8 servings

"This recipe was developed to fulfill the need for a healthy, versatile egg dish to serve to my guests before they headed out for a day of hiking and biking along the state park trails. The basic recipe can be tweaked depending on what is in season. I like to serve it with a small fresh micro green salad, grape tomatoes and white balsamic vinegar along with hearty multigrain toast or roll. It can be assembled the night before or whipped up quickly in the morning."—Innkeeper

1 cup shredded cheese
1 small red pepper, chopped
1 small yellow pepper, chopped
1 cup baby spinach
9 eggs, whisked
¾ cup cream
Tbsp brown mustard
Mrs. Dash Tomato Basil Garlic or seasoning to taste

Preheat oven to 350°F. Spray a 9x13-inch pan. Sprinkle shredded cheese in pan. Chop vegetables and add to pan. Mix eggs, cream and mustard. Pour egg mix in pan and season to taste. Bake for 30 minutes.

Tip: Serve with fresh tomatoes, baby spinach and whole-grain bread.

Variations: Use a combination of cheese and vegetables. Try adding shaved ham. Using sour cream or plain yogurt in place of the cream will give a creamier texture. Try hot sauce in place of mustard if you like a little zing in your morning.

Lake Orchard Farm B&B

Basil Potatoes

Yield: 8–10 servings

"Served with our Italian sausage casserole (pg. 105), these potatoes are simply delicious!"—Innkeeper

- 5 Tbsp butter, unsalted
- 1½ cups yellow onions, chopped
- 2 lbs. potatoes, cubed
- 2 tsp kosher salt
- 1 tsp pepper
- 2 Tbsp basil, fresh or dried

Cut butter into pieces and melt in large skillet on medium heat and sauté onions. Add potatoes and seasonings. Cook on medium low heat until potatoes are browned.

O'Neill Manor Breakfast Casserole

Yield: 6–8 servings

- 8 strips bacon, crumbled, plus drippings
- ¼ cup crushed corn flakes
- ¼ cup onion
- ¼ cup green pepper
- 6 large eggs
- ½ cup milk
- ½ cup small-curd cottage cheese
- 1 8-oz. pkg. shredded cheddar cheese
- salt
- pepper
- seasonings to taste (oregano, basil, thyme, etc.)
- 2 cups frozen cubed hash brown potatoes

Plan ahead as dish requires overnight refrigeration.

In a large skillet, cook bacon until crisp. Set aside and crumble. Mix 2 teaspoons of bacon drippings with corn flakes. Set aside. Cook onion and green peppers until softened. Mix eggs, milk, cottage cheese, cheddar cheese, onion and peppers together. Season with salt, and pepper and other seasonings to taste. Grease a 9-inch round baking dish and layer bottom with hash browns. Pour egg mixture over top evenly. Top with bacon crumbles and sprinkle corn flake mixture over. Cover tightly and place in refrigerator overnight.

Remove casserole from fridge and let stand for 30 minutes. Preheat oven to 350°F. Bake uncovered for 45–55 minutes until lightly browned and center is firming up. Knife inserted into center should come out clean. Remove from oven and let stand for 5 minutes before serving.

Inn on Hillwind

Breakfast Pizza

Yield: 6–8 servings

"This recipe remains a guest favorite, even though it's been around a while. While we serve our entrées meatless (sausage on the side), any type of brown-and-serve sausages could be cut up and added to the recipe. We garnish each serving with a tomato wedge sprinkled with oregano and serve it with warm baking powder biscuits and fresh fruit."—Innkeeper

1 pkg. refrigerator crescent rolls
8 extra-large eggs
¾ tsp dried oregano
¾ tsp dried basil
½ tsp fennel seed
¾ cup chopped red onion
¾ cup chopped red pepper
¾ cup chopped green pepper
6 oz. fresh or canned mushrooms, sliced
4 cups shredded pizza cheese

Preheat oven to 350°F. Unroll crescent dough and press into bottom of an ungreased 13x9-inch baking pan; set aside. In a large bowl, beat eggs. Add oregano, basil and fennel. Stir in red onion, red pepper, green pepper, mushrooms and cheese. (Mixture will be thick.) Pour over crescent roll crust and spread evenly to edges. Bake for 35–45 minutes until cheese is slightly browned and eggs are set.

Westport B&B

Breakfast Strata with Spinach & Gruyère

Yield: 6 servings

- 8 slices French or Italian bread
- 4 Tbsp unsalted butter
- 4 shallots minced
- 1 pkg. frozen chopped spinach, thawed and squeezed dry
- 1 tsp salt
- additional salt and pepper to taste
- ½ cup dry white wine (Chardonnay or Sauvignon Blanc)
- 6 eggs
- 1¾ cups half & half
- 8 oz. Gruyère cheese, grated

Preheat oven to 225°F. Put bread in single layer on baking sheet. Bake 40 minutes, turning once to dry. Remove and let cool. Spread one side of slices with 2 tablespoons of butter. Tear into pieces. Meanwhile, heat remaining 2 tablespoons of butter in medium skillet over medium heat. Cook shallots until soft, about 3 minutes. Add spinach and salt and pepper to taste. Cook, stirring occasionally until combined, about 2 minutes. Transfer to bowl and set aside. Add wine to skillet. Increase heat to medium high and simmer until reduced to about ¼ cup, about 3 minutes. Set aside. Whisk eggs in medium bowl. Whisk in wine, half & half and 1 teaspoon of salt and pepper to taste. Set aside.

Arrange half of the bread pieces in a greased 8-inch square baking dish. Top with half the spinach mixture and ¼ cup of grated cheese. Arrange remaining bread pieces in a single layer over cheese. Sprinkle with remaining spinach and ¼ cup of cheese. Pour egg mixture evenly over bread layers. Cover surface with plastic wrap and refrigerate at least 1 hour, or preferably overnight.

Let strata stand at room temperature at least 20 minutes. Preheat oven to 325°F. Uncover and sprinkle with remaining ½ cup of cheese. Bake until puffed and edges have pulled away slightly from sides of dish, about 55 minutes. Cool on wire rack 5 minutes before serving.

Inn on Hillwind

Cheesy Egg Puffs

Yield: 2½ dozen

"This recipe was found in 'Quick Cooking's Clip and Keep Recipe Cards.' They are 'melt-in-your-mouth' delicious when served piping hot, easy to reheat as leftovers and even make good finger-food snacks."—Innkeeper

- ½ lb. fresh mushrooms, sliced
- 4 green onions, chopped
- 1 Tbsp, plus ½ cup butter or margarine
- ½ cup all-purpose flour
- 1 tsp baking powder
- ½ tsp salt
- 10 eggs, lightly beaten
- 4 cups (16 oz.) shredded Monterey Jack cheese
- 2 cups (16 oz.) small-curd cottage cheese

Preheat oven to at 350°F. In a skillet, sauté the mushrooms and onions in 1 tablespoon butter until tender. In a large bowl, combine the flour, baking powder and salt. In another bowl, combine eggs and cheeses. Melt remaining butter; add to egg mixture. Stir into dry ingredients along with mushroom mixture. Fill greased muffin cups three-fourths full. Bake for 35–40 minutes or until a knife inserted near the center comes out clean. Carefully run the knife around edge of muffin cups before removing.

Riverview B&B
Cranberry and Sausage Quiche

Yield: 6 servings

"Because Wisconsin is a top cranberry grower, I like to serve this to all my guests, especially those who come here from out of state as a sense of local pride."—Innkeeper

- 1 sheet puff pastry, thawed
- 1 lb. seasoned pork sausage (we use Reetz Meats, of course!)
- ¼ cup chopped onion (optional)
- 1½ cups Monterey Jack cheese, shredded
- ¾ cup dried cranberries
- 5 eggs, beaten lightly
- 2 cups half & half or milk

Preheat oven to 400°F. Spray a 9-inch square baking pan with nonstick oil. Carefully unfold the pastry and line the baking pan, pressing firmly into place. Set aside. In medium skillet, crumble and cook sausage and onion over medium heat until sausage is browned. Remove from heat. In square baking pan, sprinkle cheese on the pastry. Top with sausage and cranberries. This can be refrigerated overnight before adding the eggs and milk. When ready to bake, combine the eggs and milk or half & half and pour over the prepared pastry mix. Bake 35–40 minutes or until a knife inserted into the center comes out clean.

Franklin Street Inn

Creamy Ham & Egg Toasted Butter Cups

Yield: 8 servings

- 5 eggs, boiled, divided
- 1 cup finely diced ham cubes (optional)
- 1/3 cup finely diced mushrooms, canned
- 1/8 cup finely chopped onions (optional)
- 1 can cream of celery soup, undiluted
- salt and pepper to taste
- 8 slices white bread or preference
- fresh soft butter or Smart Balance
- paprika or fresh parsley, garnish

Preheat oven to 350°F. Boil eggs, cool and peel. Keep separate 1 egg, diced, and hold back for the garnish on the egg cup top. Dice the last 4 eggs, ham, mushrooms and onions. Mix all of the first 7 ingredients that you have chosen to include. Set aside in refrigerator until ready to use. Trim the bread crusts away. Butter each slice of bread on both sides. Push the center of each bread slice down into the bottom of a ramekin or muffin cup so the corners point up just over the rim. (The recipe may be prepared to this point in the evening.)

Set the ramekins on a cookie sheet and bake for 10 minutes to lightly toast the crusts. Do not overcook the bread crust because they will be returning to the oven. Fill each toasted butter cup with the egg mixture. Spoon small amounts of the extra unmixed egg over the top. Sprinkle with paprika or fresh parsley for garnish. Bake for 10 more minutes or until heated through. Serve in the white ramekins or remove the egg cups from the muffin pan and place on plates.

Variations: Substitute 1 cup of white sauce or a can of cream of mushroom soup for the cream of celery soup. This recipe can be varied by using fried chopped bacon instead of the ham. Sprinkle grated cheddar cheese on the top of each egg cup before the paprika is added. For a vegetarian version, omit the meat and add another vegetable, if desired.

Westport B&B

Early Morning Wake-Up Casserole

Yield: 8 servings

"This is a great recipe to make in the morning. It is easy to put together, and guests always seem to enjoy the blend of flavors that come together in this casserole."—Innkeeper

- 8 frozen hash brown patties
- 4 cups shredded cheddar cheese (16 oz.)
- 1 lb. cubed ham
- 7 eggs
- 1 cup milk
- ½ tsp salt
- ¼ tsp Mrs. Dash

Preheat oven to 350°F. Grease a 13x9-inch baking dish. Place hash brown patties in a single layer. Sprinkle with cheese and cubed ham. In a bowl, beat eggs, milk, salt and Mrs. Dash. Pour over ham, cheese and hash browns. Cover with foil and bake for 1 hour. Uncover and bake 15 minutes longer or until edges are golden brown and a knife inserted comes out clean.

Variations: Try adding sautéed chopped green and red pepper and sautéed mushrooms. Serve casserole with thick sliced bacon, and English muffins.

Riverside Manor B&B

Egg Strata

Yield: 8 servings

- 1 medium onion, chopped
- 1 cup mixed bell peppers, chopped
- 4 Tbsp butter or margarine
- 18 eggs
- 1 cup plain yogurt
- 1 tsp Lawry's Seasoned Salt
- 1 lb. diced ham
- 1 lb. shredded cheese
- 2 cups thawed frozen hash browns

Preheat oven to 350°F. Sauté onions and peppers in 4 tablespoons butter or margarine. In a large mixing bowl, beat eggs until frothy. Add yogurt, seasoning salt, ham and cheese. Add hash browns to pepper and onion mix to slightly brown. Add to egg mixture. Place combined mixture into a 9x13-inch baking pan. Bake for 30 minutes or until done.

Tips: This can be made the night before and placed in the refrigerator overnight. Increase baking time to 1 hour.

O'Neill Manor

Ham & Broccoli Quiche

Yield: 1 pie

"This can be made with or without a crust. If I make without a crust, I use individual quiche pans. I also like to make sure the florets and ham are cut into relatively small pieces for a nicer texture."—Innkeeper

- 1 pie crust (optional)
- 1 cup half & half or milk
- 4 eggs, beaten
- ½ tsp dry mustard
- 1 cup cubed, cooked ham
- 8 oz. shredded Cheddar cheese
- 1 cup fresh broccoli florets, blanched and drained

Preheat oven to 350°F. Prepare pie crust per package instructions. Combine milk, eggs and dry mustard in a bowl and mix well. Layer ham, cheese and broccoli in cooked crust. If desired, brown ham in a little bacon grease before using. Pour in egg mixture. Bake for 40–50 minutes or until knife comes out clean. Cool 5 minutes and serve.

Brayton B&B

Ham & Cheese Vegetable Omelet Bake

Yield: 8 servings

"This is a great recipe for a big crowd in the morning. It does not take long to throw together and you can add whatever vegetables are your favorite."—Innkeeper

- ½ box (5 oz.) frozen broccoli and cheese flavored sauce
- 1 can Pillsbury Grands! refrigerated biscuits
- 10 eggs
- 1½ cups milk
- 1 tsp ground mustard
- salt and pepper to taste
- 2 cups diced ham (optional)
- ⅓ cup chopped onion
- ½ cup chopped zucchini
- 1 cup shredded Cheddar
- 1 cup shredded Swiss
- 1 4.5-oz. can or fresh mushrooms

Preheat oven to 350°F. Thaw broccoli pouch completely. Spray bottom of a 9x13-inch glass baking dish. Separate dough into 8 biscuits and lay in greased baking dish. In a large bowl, beat eggs, milk, mustard and salt and pepper until blended. Stir in ham, onion, zucchini, cheeses, mushrooms and broccoli and cheese sauce. Pour mixture over biscuits and press down with back of a spoon to make sure all biscuits are covered. Bake 40–50 minutes until edges are golden brown and puffed. Let stand 10 minutes before serving to make sure everything is held together.

Parkview B&B
Hash Brown Egg Bake

Yield: 10–12 servings

"I have been using this recipe for more than 20 years now. It is versatile and ingredients are usually available."—Innkeeper

- 1 lb. hash browns, thawed (about 4 cups)
- 10–12 large eggs
- 2 cups milk
- ½ cup sour cream
- 1 tsp seasoning salt
- 2 cups shredded Cheddar cheese
- ¼ cup chopped onion
- pepper, as desired
- paprika

Preheat oven to 350°F. Mix hash browns, eggs, milk, sour cream, seasoning salt, cheese, onions and pepper together in a large bowl. Pour into a greased 9x13-inch pan or individual ramekins. Sprinkle with paprika. Bake for 35–40 minutes (less if baking in individual ramekins). Cut into squares.

Variations: Add broccoli, mushrooms, green pepper, ham, sautéed sausage, etc. Use different kinds or combinations of cheese for variety.

Riverview B&B
Hash Brown Egg Bake

Yield: 8 servings

"Because many of my guests stay for an extended time and several are gentlemen, I like to serve this to those who are truly meat-and-potato guys, even though they have delighted in and willingly indulged in the fruit and quiche recipes served previously."—Innkeeper

- 1 32-oz. pkg. frozen cubed hash browns potatoes, thawed
- 1 lb. sliced bacon, cooked and crumbled
- 1 cup shredded Cheddar cheese (or other), divided
- ¼ tsp salt
- 8 eggs
- 2 cups milk
- dash paprika

Preheat oven to 350°F. In a large bowl, combine hash browns, bacon, ½ cup cheese and salt. Spoon into a greased 13x9-inch baking dish. In another bowl, beat eggs and milk until smooth and pour over hash brown mixture. Sprinkle with paprika. Bake uncovered for 45–50 minutes until golden. Top with remaining cheese.

Tips: This dish may be prepared in advance, covered and refrigerated overnight. Remove from refrigerator 30 minutes before baking.

Inn at Lonesome Hollow Italian Sausage Breakfast Casserole

Yield: 12 servings

2 lbs. bulk Italian sausage
1 medium green pepper, chopped
1 cup sliced fresh crimini mushrooms
½ cup chopped onion
2½ cups onion and garlic croutons
8 eggs
1½ cups milk
1 cup shredded mozzarella cheese
1 cup shredded Cheddar cheese
3–4 Roma tomatoes, thinly sliced
½ cup shredded Parmesan cheese

Cook sausage, green pepper, mushrooms and onion in a large skillet until meat is browned and vegetables are tender; drain. Place croutons in a greased 9x13-inch baking dish and top with sausage mixture. Beat eggs and milk; pour over sausage. Cover and chill 8 hours or overnight.

Remove from refrigerator 30 minutes before baking. Preheat oven to 300°F. Bake uncovered for 1 hour. Remove from the oven and sprinkle with the mozzarella and cheddar cheeses. Place tomato slices over top. Sprinkle with Parmesan cheese. Bake 20 minutes longer or until a knife in the center comes out clean. Let stand 5 minutes before cutting.

Tip: Roma tomatoes work best for this dish because they are firm and compact, but any fresh tomatoes will do.

Inn at Lonesome Hollow

Mexican Frittata

Yield: 12–18 servings

- ¼ cup butter
- ½ cup onion, chopped
- 1 17-oz. can corn
- 2 8-oz. cans chopped green chilies, drained
- 1¼ tsp chili powder
- 18 eggs
- 1 cup sour cream
- ½ tsp salt
- dash red pepper
- 3 cups shredded sharp Cheddar cheese
- 2½ cups shredded Monterey Jack cheese
- medium salsa
- sour cream

Preheat oven to 350°F. Grease three 9-inch pie plates. In a skillet over medium heat, melt the butter and sauté the onion, corn and chilies until the flavors blend. Mix in chili powder. In a bowl, whisk the eggs with the sour cream. Add the sautéed mixture and the salt, red pepper and cheeses. Pour into prepared pans. Bake for about 40 minutes. Cut the frittatas into wedges and serve with salsa and sour cream on each wedge.

Variations: For a non-vegetarian version of this dish, put chopped fried bacon or Canadian bacon on the bottom of the pie plates.

Lake Ripley Lodge B&B

Muffin Frittatas

Yield: 10–12 servings

"An easy to-go breakfast snack for the up-early travelers, kayakers or fishermen."—Innkeeper

- 1 English muffin
- 8 eggs
- 2 Tbsp milk
- 1 cup grated Cheddar cheese
- 1¼ cups cooked ground sausage
- 1 4-oz. can diced green chilies
- fresh cilantro, as desired

Preheat oven to 350°F. Using a blender or food processor, blend muffin into very fine crumbs. Beat eggs with a fork. Add milk, bread crumbs, cheese, cooked sausage and green chilies. Mix thoroughly. Spoon mixture into greased muffin pans ¾ full and bake until plump and firm, 20–25 minutes. Enjoy!

Cream Pitcher B&B
Mushroom Crust Quiche

Yield: 4–6 servings

5 Tbsp butter, divided
½ lb. mushrooms, sliced
½ cup finely crushed saltine crackers
¾ cup finely chopped green onions
2 cups shredded baby Swiss cheese
1 cup cottage cheese
3 eggs
¼ tsp ground cayenne
¼ tsp paprika

Preheat oven to 350°F. In a skillet, melt 3 tablespoons butter over medium heat; add mushrooms and cook until limp. Stir in crushed crackers. Turn mixture into well-greased 9-inch pie pan, pressing mixture evenly over pan bottom and up sides. In same skillet, melt remaining 2 tablespoons butter over medium heat, add onion and cook until transparent. Spread onions over mushroom crust, then sprinkle evenly with shredded cheese. In a food processor or blender, whirl cottage cheese, eggs and cayenne pepper until smooth. Pour mixture into crust and sprinkle with paprika. Bake for 20–25 minutes or until knife inserted in the middle comes out clean. Let stand for 10 minutes before serving.

Sweet Autumn Inn
Northwoods Omelet

Yield: 1 serving

- 2 eggs
- parsley
- ¼ cup shredded Monterey Jack cheese
- ¼ cup shredded Swiss cheese
- paprika
- sour cream
- Sweet Red and Ancho Chili Pepper Spread (Harry & David's), for garnish
- chives and parsley

Northwoods Filling

- 1½–2 cups cooked wild rice
- 1 rib celery, diced
- 3–4 chopped green onions or ¼ cup chopped yellow onion
- 1 cup sautéed sliced portobello mushrooms (optional)
- 12 oz. bulk breakfast sausage
- 1/3 cup dried cranberries (optional)

Beat the eggs with a fork and add in a pinch of parsley. Pour the eggs into a piping hot omelet pan sprayed with nonstick cooking spray. Cook the omelet and top with the cheeses. Spread ½ cup Northwoods filling on half of the omelet. Fold the omelet over the filling and slip from the pan onto a warm plate. Sprinkle with paprika, garnish with sour cream, relish, pepper spread and sprinkle with chives and parsley. Serve warm with toast and jam.

For the Northwoods filling: Cook the rice according to package directions. Sauté the celery and onion until soft. Remove from pan and keep warm. Sauté the mushrooms in a bit of butter and olive oil. Remove from pan and mix with the celery and onion. In a large sauté pan, brown the sausage until no longer pink. Drain well. Stir in the wild rice and the celery mixture. Set aside but keep warm. If using the dried cranberries, soften 5 minutes in enough hot water to cover. Drain, chop and add to the wild rice mixture. Filling is enough for several omelets.

Victorian Rose B&B
Breakfast Kielbasa

Yield: 6–8 servings

- 2 rings (1 lb. each) kielbasa sausage
- ¼ cup apricot preserves
- 2 Tbsp orange juice

Preheat oven to 350°F. Cut kielbasas at angles into about 48 pieces. Place in ovenproof dish. Mix preserves and juice and pour over kielbasas, turning to coat. Bake for 45 minutes. Check periodically and if dry, continue to brush on glaze.

Hillcrest Inn & Carriage House

Poached Egg on Hash Browns with Sausage

Yield: 8 servings

- 1 32-oz. pkg. frozen hash browns
- 1 can Cream of Mushroom soup
- ½ cup milk
- 1½ cups shredded Cheddar cheese, divided
- ½ Tbsp seasoning salt
- 1 lb. pork sausage
- 8 eggs

Preheat oven to 350°F. Mix together hash browns, soup, milk, 1 cup cheese and salt. Spread half of mixture in a greased 9x13-inch pan. Place chunks of pork sausage on potatoes. Spread remaining potatoes over meat. Bake for 1 hour. Poach eggs and place on top of potato-meat casserole. Sprinkle with remaining cheese.

Tip: Serve with fresh vegetables and herbs.

Honeybee Inn B&B
Puff Pastry Ham & Cheese with Hollandaise

Yield: 4–6 servings

"Makes a fantastic presentation and guests love it!"—Innkeeper

- 1 sheet of Pepperidge Farm Puff Pastry
- 10 eggs
- 4 oz. cream cheese
- seasoning, as desired
- 8 slices ham
- 4 slices Swiss cheese
- 1 egg mixed with 1 Tbsp water for egg wash
- hollandaise sauce
- paprika

Preheat oven to 400°F. Thaw puff pastry for 25 minutes or overnight in fridge. Roll out to a 17x12-inch rectangle. Soft scramble eggs with cream cheese and seasonings, as desired. Let cool. Put puff pastry on a pre-sprayed cookie sheet; it will hang off edges. Place 4 slices of ham down middle of pastry sheet. Place eggs on top. Place Swiss cheese and final layer of ham slices. Wash all surfaces of pastry with egg wash. Flip one side of pastry over ham. Wash the top with egg wash. Flip other side over and seal ends. Wash the whole top and sides with egg wash. Bake until golden brown and puffy, about 20–25 minutes. To serve, cut slices crosswise and place on plates. Spoon hollandaise sauce over top and sprinkle with paprika.

McConnell Inn
Quiche with Potato Crust

Yield: 10–12 servings

- 4 potatoes, grated
- ½ cup shredded Cheddar cheese
- 1 Tbsp butter
- 6 oz. Jimmy Dean pork sausage with sage
- ½ cup chopped green and red peppers
- ½ cup chopped mushrooms
- 1 cup any type shredded cheese
- 9 eggs
- 1¾ cups milk
- 1 Tbsp flour
- 1 tsp basil or oregano
- salt and pepper to taste

Grate potatoes with skins and soak in salt water for 15 minutes; drain. In a microwavable bowl, mix shredded Cheddar cheese, grated potatoes and butter. Heat for 1 minute. Press into bottom and up sides of a 9x13-inch ungreased pan. Fry Jimmy Dean sausage, drain, and layer on crust. Chop peppers and mushrooms and layer on sausage. Sprinkle 1 cup shredded cheese on top. Cover and refrigerate overnight.

Next morning, preheat oven to 375°F. Beat eggs, milk, flour and spices. Pour into pan. Bake for 45–55 minutes until brown and puffed up. Cut in squares.

Variations: Substitute chopped ham for sausage and 10 oz. frozen chopped spinach, thawed and drained, for peppers. To make a 9-inch pie pan, use 5 eggs and 1 cup milk, decrease all other ingredients by ⅓ and cut into slices instead of squares. Yield: 6–8 servings.

Miller's Daughter B&B Red Pepper & Spinach Frittata

Yield: 6–8 servings

2 Tbsp (¼ stick) unsalted butter
2 leeks, whites only, thinly sliced
1 red bell pepper, sliced
8 large eggs, beaten
2 cups cooked fresh or frozen spinach, thawed, squeezed of water
½ cup fresh basil, chiffonaded
4 oz. Jarlsberg cheese
½ cup grated Parmesan cheese
½ tsp kosher salt
¼ tsp freshly ground black pepper
¼ cup dry bread crumbs

Preheat oven to 350°F. In a medium skillet over medium heat, melt the butter. Add the leeks and sauté about 10 minutes. Add in sliced red bell pepper in the last 5 minutes of sautéing. Remove from heat and cool completely. In a large mixing bowl, combine the eggs with the leeks, red pepper, spinach, basil, Jarlsberg cheese, Parmesan, salt and pepper. Mix well. Spray a 9-inch nonstick cake pan or springform pan with nonstick cooking spray. Add the bread crumbs and shake until the pan is evenly coated. Pour the egg mixture into pan. Bake for 30–35 minutes, until solid and a toothpick comes out clean. Cool in the pan over a wire rack for 5 minutes. Invert the frittata onto a plate, then flip right side up onto a serving plate or remove sides of springform pan and transfer to a serving plate. Serve warm or at room temperature.

Scofield House

Sausage Breakfast Casserole

Yield: 8–12 servings

- 1 box (6 oz.) seasoned croutons
- 1 cup shredded Cheddar cheese
- 1 cup shredded mozzarella cheese
- 1 lb. breakfast sausage, browned, crumbled and drained
- 10 eggs
- 2 cups half & half
- 1 can cream of mushroom soup

Plan ahead—dish needs overnight refrigeration.

Preheat oven to 350°F. Spray a 9x13-inch pan with cooking spray. Fill bottom with croutons. Layer cheeses and sausage on top of croutons. Mix eggs, milk and soup thoroughly. Pour over ingredients in pan. Cover and refrigerate overnight. Uncover and bake 45 minutes to 1 hour.

Amil's Inn B&B

Sausage Gravy Over Homemade Biscuits

Yield: 6–8 servings

1 lb. pork sausage
2 Tbsp chopped onion
6 Tbsp flour
4 cups milk
½ tsp poultry seasoning
½ tsp ground nutmeg
¼ tsp salt
dash Worcestershire sauce
dash hot pepper sauce
homemade biscuits, warmed
grapes, garnish
orange slices, garnish

In a skillet, brown sausage and onion over medium heat. Cook the sausage until no longer pink. Drain off grease. Stir in flour, milk, poultry seasoning, ground nutmeg, salt, Worcestershire sauce and hot peeper sauce. Bring to a boil and stir for 2 minutes. Serve over biscuits and garnish with grapes and a slice of orange.

Tip: To prevent lumps, stir milk into the flour gradually. Once a smooth paste has been made, more milk may be added for desired consistency.

Red Forest B&B
Smoked Salmon Benedict with Potato-Chive Cake

Yield: 8 servings

8 oz. cold smoked cured salmon fillet, sliced thin

Potato-Chive Cakes

1½ lbs. Idaho russet potatoes
1 egg, beaten
salt, to taste
pepper, fresh ground, to taste
1 clove garlic, minced
2 Tbsp chives, fresh, sliced fine
2 Tbsp all-purpose flour
blend of equal parts extra virgin olive oil and clarified butter for pan frying

Hollandaise Sauce (Yield: ¾ cup)

2 Tbsp white wine vinegar
4 black peppercorns
2 Tbsp water
2 egg yolks
4 fluid oz. clarified butter, warm (about 120°F)
sea salt, to taste
lemon juice, fresh squeezed, to taste

Poached Eggs

8 eggs
2 Tbsp chives, finely sliced

For potato-chive cake: Boil the unpeeled potatoes until a knife is easily inserted. Remove from water and cool for several hours. Peel and grate the potatoes and place in a mixing bowl. Add the eggs, salt, pepper, garlic, chives and flour. Blend well. Heat a wide sauté pan or cast iron skillet with the olive oil and clarified butter. Spoon and press out little cakes in your hands. Fry on both sides until crisp. Drain on paper towel and serve hot.

(Continued next page)

For hollandaise sauce: Combine vinegar and peppercorns in a 1- or 2-quart heavy sauce pot, stainless steel lined and thick on bottom and sides. Cook over medium heat, reducing the vinegar to almost dry. Remove from heat and cool the bottom of pan under cold water to stop cooking. Spoon the peppercorns out. Add 2 tablespoons water to the pan, then add the yolks. Whisk to combine and put over low heat, whisking constantly. Continue cooking the yolks, whisking always, and managing the heat of the pot by pulling it off and on the burner. Cook until ribbons form when the whisk is pulled through the yolks. Take off burner and cool bottom of pan again to stop cooking. Drizzle warm clarified butter into the yolks slowly, a few drops at a time at first, until all the butter is in. Season with sea salt and lemon juice to taste.

For poached eggs: Bring water to a boil in a stainless steel lined pan (water should be about 4 inches deep). Add vinegar to the water (ratio is 1 Tbsp vinegar to 1 quart water). Crack eggs in individual cups. Lower heat to a simmer and pour eggs into water, keeping them separated. When the eggs are in, lift them slightly to be sure they do not attach to the bottom of the pan. Cook about 3–4 minutes. Remove with slotted spoon. Place on prepared potato and smoked salmon stacks. Spoon warm hollandaise sauce over egg and garnish with chives.

Tips: The finished hollandaise should taste of rich butter with a light lemon brightness, but not overpowering the butter. The consistency should be creamy, foamy, light and velvety smooth in the mouth.

Grapevine Log Cabins B&B

Spring Breakfast Strata

Yield: 12 servings

"This will work well if you have a bunch of people. It is a delicious dish."—Innkeeper

8 eggs
3 cups milk
1 Tbsp Dijon mustard
2 tsp dried basil
1 tsp salt
2 Tbsp butter or margarine, melted
2 Tbsp flour
2 cups shredded Cheddar cheese
2 cups cubed ham
2 cups cut fresh cooked asparagus
2 cups sliced fresh mushrooms (sautéed)
10 cups cubed bread
breadcrumbs

Plan ahead—dish needs overnight refrigeration.

In a large bowl, beat eggs. Add milk, mustard, basil and salt. Stir in butter, flour, cheese, ham, asparagus, mushrooms and bread. Put bread crumbs in the bottom of a 9x13-inch (or larger) pan. Pour the ingredients over the top. Cover and refrigerate overnight.

Remove strata 30 minutes before baking. Preheat oven to 350°F. Bake uncovered for 1 hour or until knife comes out clean. Let stand 5 minutes before cutting.

White Lace Inn
Stuffed Croissants

Yield: 6 servings

3 large eggs
1½ cups milk
6 large croissants
12 slices Canadian bacon
6 slices Monterrey Jack cheese
1½ Granny Smith apples, sliced thin (optional)
powdered sugar (optional)

Preheat oven to 350°F. Whisk together eggs and milk. Spray baking dish with cooking spray. Slice croissants in half lengthwise. Lightly dip bottom half in egg and milk mixture and place on prepared pan. Layer bacon, cheese and apple on top of croissant. Lightly dip top half of croissant in egg and milk mixture and place on top. Secure with toothpicks. Repeat the procedure with remaining croissants, then bake for 30 minutes. Remove toothpicks and sprinkle lightly with powdered sugar, if desired.

Appetizers, Soups, Salads & Sides

Brewery Creek Inn & Brewpub

Brandied Creole Cream

Yield: 12 ounces or 1½ cups

- ¼ cup butter
- 1–4 Tbsp blackening or Creole spice (amount depends on the heat of spice)
- ⅓ cup brandy
- 4 cups heavy whipping cream
- green onion or cilantro, garnish

Melt the butter over medium-high heat and add the seasoning. Cook for 2–3 minutes. Remove from heat and add the brandy. Return to the heat and cook until the brandy is almost gone, about 1 minute. Add the whipping cream and bring to a boil. Stir and reduce by half or until the mixture is thick enough to coat the back of a spoon, about 5 minutes. Garnish with green onion or cilantro.

Brewery Creek Inn & Brewpub

Beer Cheese Spread

Yield: 12 servings

"We are a brewpub and we live in a town with one of the best cheese factories in the state. This extremely simple recipe combines our beer and Hook's cheese into a remarkably good and very popular appetizer spread."—Innkeeper

1 lb. Hook's One Year Sharp Cheddar
1½ cups (approx.) Brewery Creek light draught beer
Tabasco sauce to taste

Cut up cheese into chunks that your food processor can handle. Put cheese into the bowl of your food processor. Pour in the beer. Mix thoroughly until smooth. If desired, add more beer or more cheese. Sprinkle a little Tabasco sauce to taste. Serve with crispy crackers or toast.

Old Rittenhouse Inn

Bruschetta

Yield: 4 servings

½ cup fresh tomato, chopped
1 tsp chopped garlic
1 Tbsp minced red onion
2 Tbsp olive oil
3 Tbsp fresh chopped basil (6–10 leaves)
2 Tbsp kalamata olives, diced
splash of lemon juice or vinegar
pinch of salt, cracked black pepper
4 slices French bread
Parmesan or mozzarella cheese (optional)

Combine tomato, garlic, onion, olive oil, basil, olives, lemon juice and seasoning. Rub 4 slices French bread (or sourdough baguette) with a slice of garlic clove. Grill dry (no butter or oil) until toasted. Cover toasted bread with mixture. Top with Parmesan and mozzarella cheese (optional). Finish in warm oven to melt cheese.

Heaven Scent B&B

Cowboy Caviar

Yield: 12–18 servings

"I serve this appetizer as a snack for my guests when they arrive at the Inn. Put a generous serving of scoop chips with a bowl of caviar and you will have happy guests. I keep several copies of this recipe handy, as I am asked for it often."—Innkeeper

- 1 can pinto beans
- 1 can black-eyed peas
- 1 can diced jalapeños
- 1 can shoepeg corn
- ½ cup celery, diced
- ½ cup green pepper, diced
- ½ cup onion, diced
- ¾ cup vinegar
- ¼ cup vegetable oil
- 1 cup sugar
- 1 Tbsp water

Mix together canned ingredients and drain. In a large serving bowl, add mixture to celery, green pepper and onion. In a small saucepan, combine vinegar, oil, sugar and water. Bring mixture to a boil, stirring frequently. Boil for 3 minutes. Let mixture cool completely. Once cooled, pour mixture over veggies. Cover and chill for at least 2 hours (preferably overnight). Drain before serving. Serve caviar with chips. Enjoy!

Phipps Inn B&B

Martha's Vineyard Shrimp Dip

Yield: 6–8 servings

"We had this delicious dip at a restaurant on Martha's Vineyard. They wouldn't give us the recipe; however, we figured out the basic ingredients and perfected it ourselves. Make sure you have plenty of crackers to scrape up every last bit!"—Innkeeper

- 7 oz. frozen baby shrimp
- 8 oz. cream cheese, softened
- 2–3 oz. Gorgonzola cheese, softened
- 1 clove minced garlic
- 1 shallot, minced
- ½ teaspoon thyme
- ½ cup chopped fried pancetta

Preheat oven to 450°F. Thaw and rinse shrimp and place in the bottom of a shallow baking dish. Mix cream cheese, Gorgonzola, garlic, shallots, thyme and pancetta and pour over shrimp. Spread evenly. Bake for 15–20 minutes until lightly browned and bubbly. Serve with crackers or crostini.

Port Washington Inn Puréed Potato Cauliflower Soup

Yield: 6–8 servings

"As far as I know, this recipe is unpublished. Our daughter made it for us and she had first had it on the menu of Tapioles 53 restaurant in Barcelona where she served as pastry chef for two years. I've added chives and powdered white Cheddar cheese to our version."—Innkeeper

1 head cauliflower
baking potatoes (amount equal to cauliflower)
1 large sweet onion (not red)
white Cheddar cheese powder (not the popcorn topping variety)
salt and pepper to taste
finely minced chives

Clean one head of cauliflower and break into florets. Measure. Peel baking potatoes and cut into sizes similar to the cauliflower florets. Peel the onion and divide each half into 6 equal chunks.

Place the cauliflower, potato and onion mixture in a pan and add water to the level of the vegetables. Simmer until vegetables are tender. Using an immersion blender, purée the hot soup, adding white cheddar cheese powder, salt and pepper to taste. Stir in minced fresh or frozen chives.

Tips: This delicious soup is wonderful served in a soup mug. It freezes well but expands as it freezes so place it in a generous and/or non-breakable container. We get our powdered white cheddar cheese from Frontier Natural Products Co-op in Norway, Iowa.

Phipps Inn B&B

Adrienne's Salad

Yield: 8 servings

"My sister-in-law Adrienne introduced this salad to family gatherings and it became a hit. One nephew now refers to it as "The Salad" because there are no others that he likes as well."—Innkeeper

- 1 head romaine or red leaf lettuce, broken into bite-size pieces
- ½ cup chopped celery
- 6 green onions, thinly sliced
- 1 11-oz. can Mandarin oranges, drained

Dressing

- 2 Tbsp sugar
- 1 Tbsp chopped fresh parsley
- ½ tsp salt
- dash of pepper
- ¼ cup vegetable oil
- 2 Tbsp white wine vinegar

Topping

- ¼ cup sliced almonds
- 4 tsp sugar

Combine lettuce, celery, onion and Mandarin oranges in a bowl.

For the dressing: Combine all ingredients in a jar and shake well.

For the topping: Combine almonds and sugar in a nonstick pan. Stir over medium-low heat until sugar is melted and almonds are coated. Cool, then crush or break apart. Toss salad with dressing and sprinkle almonds on top.

Variation: Use 1 cup sliced fresh strawberries in place of the oranges.

Pedal'rs Inn Garden Blueberry Salad

Yield: 6 servings

"My family loves my cooking and sometimes too much! This recipe came as a last-minute save when family members ate my fruit course intended for the guests. Desperation begets inspiration!"—Innkeeper

- 6 cups washed and chopped mixed greens
- 1 cucumber, washed and diced (½-inch pieces)
- 1 avocado, diced (½-inch pieces)
- 2 stalks celery, julienne
- 1 pint blueberries, washed
- ¼ cup pine nuts

Blueberry Poppy Seed Dressing

- ½ cup plain yogurt
- ¼ cup milk
- ¼ cup honey
- 1/8 cup white vinegar
- ¼ cup blueberry syrup
- 1 Tbsp poppy seeds

Gently toss greens, cucumber, avocado, celery and berries in large mixing bowl. Over tossing will smash avocado and berries. Chill until ready to serve. Dish evenly onto 6 salad plates. Sprinkle pine nuts over each salad. Drizzle with blueberry poppy seed dressing and serve.

For the dressing: Whisk together all ingredients in small bowl. Chill dressing in refrigerator until served.

Bowman's Oak Hill B&B
Raw Corn Salad

Yield: 6 servings

"This recipe came from one of my daughters years ago. Even though this is not a dish that I serve for breakfast, it is one that I have often shared with our guests when we are talking about simple summer dish ideas. Many have called or emailed to let me know what a hit it was with their family and friends."—Innkeeper

- 4 large ears of very fresh sweet corn
- 4 Roma tomatoes, cubed
- 4–6 green onions, sliced
- 1 Tbsp mayonnaise
- salt and pepper to taste

Using a sharp knife, cut the kernels of corn off of the cobs. Add tomatoes, green onions, mayonnaise and salt and pepper to taste. Stir well and chill in refrigerator for a while or serve right away.

Tips: Cut the corn off right into a large bowl so as not to lose any of the juice. It mixes in with the mayonnaise to make the dressing. This dish is just as good the next day.

Fountain Chateau B&B
Wild Rice and Cranberry Salad

Yield: 6–8 servings

"Customers say 'yummm!'"—Innkeeper

- 1 16-oz. pkg. long-grain and wild rice mix
- 1 cup dried cranberries
- 1 cup chopped fresh broccoli florets
- 4 green onions, chopped
- 3 celery ribs, thinly sliced
- ½ cup sweet and sour dressing
- 1 cup chopped dry roasted peanuts

Prepare rice mix according to package directions and cool. Combine rice, cranberries, broccoli, onions and celery. Add dressing. Stir gently. Cover and chill at least 2 hours. Stir in peanuts just before serving.

Speckled Hen Inn

Corn Fritters with Jalapeño Pepper Jelly

Yield: 10 servings

- 2 cups buttermilk baking mix or Bisquick
- 1 tsp ground cumin
- 1 egg
- ½ cup milk
- 1 Tbsp salsa
- 1 cup frozen corn kernels, thawed (or fresh corn in season)
- oil for frying

Jalapeño Pepper Jelly

- 12 fresh jalapeño chili peppers
- 1 large red bell pepper
- 1½ cups cider vinegar
- 1/3 cup freshly squeezed lemon juice
- 6 cups granulated sugar
- 4 oz. Certo liquid fruit pectin

Combine the baking mix and cumin in a medium bowl. Beat the egg, milk and salsa together and add to the baking mix. Add the corn kernels and stir just until all ingredients are combined. Drop by rounded teaspoons full into 365°F oil in a deep fryer. Cook about 3 minutes until dark golden brown, turning once. Drain thoroughly and serve hot with a small saucer of jalapeño pepper jelly.

For the jalapeño pepper jelly: Wearing protective gloves, stem and seed the jalapeños. Chop in a fine dice. (Hand chopping will make a clearer, prettier jelly than a food processor). Stem, seed and chop the bell pepper. In a large stainless steel pot, combine the peppers and vinegar. Bring to a hard boil and boil for 10 minutes, stirring occasionally. Remove from the heat and stir in the lemon juice and sugar. Place the pot back on the heat and bring back to a hard boil. Add the liquid pectin and boil for 1 minute. Remove from heat and skim off any foam. Cool and store in the refrigerator until needed.

Tip: Make the jalapeño jelly at least one day before you plan to serve it.

Variation: Replace the corn with a corn, black bean and pepper blend for a little spice.

McConnell Inn

Oven-Roasted Potatoes

Yield: 8–12 servings

6–10 potatoes, large Wisconsin russet
olive oil
2 tsp basil or oregano
salt and pepper

Preheat oven to 350°F. Wash and cut up potatoes into 1-inch chunks. Spread in a 9x13-inch glass pan. Sprinkle with olive oil and herbs, salt and pepper. Stir to coat. Bake for 45–50 minutes, stirring once or twice while baking.

Variation: Substitute Yukon gold or baby red potatoes. Baking time will decrease by approximately 10 minutes.

Lunch & Dinner Entrées

Angel Inn B&B

Amazing Meatball Appetizers

Yield: 10–12 servings

"This is my daughter Amanda's recipe and she was so kind to share it with me."—Innkeeper

- 2 16-oz. cans "whole berry" cranberry sauce
- ¾ cup ketchup
- ½ cup beef broth
- 3 Tbsp brown sugar
- 1 onion chopped
- 2 tsp apple cider vinegar
- 1 bag frozen meatballs

In a bowl, mix together the cranberry sauce, ketchup, beef broth, sugar, onion and vinegar to create the sauce. Fill a crock pot to the top with frozen meatballs. Pour all the sauce over the meatballs and stir until completely coated. Cook 4 hours on low, stirring every ½ hour.

Phipps Inn B&B Corn & Cheese Casserole

Yield: 1-quart casserole

"This is the most popular 'vegetable' dish at Thanksgiving and Christmas, especially among the younger crowd. As our family has grown, so has the amount of 'cheesy corn' that must be made for dinner. Luckily it's a recipe that is easily doubled or tripled."—Innkeeper

- 1 cup crushed saltine cracker crumbs
- 2 Tbsp melted butter
- 2 eggs, beaten
- 1 15–16-oz. can creamed corn
- ½ cup milk or cream
- ½ tsp salt
- ¼ tsp paprika
- ¼ cup chopped onion (or 1 Tbsp dry onion)
- 1 cup shredded Cheddar cheese

Preheat oven to 350°F. Toss cracker crumbs with butter. Reserve ¼ cup. Beat eggs until thick and creamy. Add creamed corn, milk, salt, paprika, onion, cheese and cracker mixture. Pour into a 1-quart greased casserole. Sprinkle with reserved cracker crumbs. Bake for 55 minutes.

Fountain Chateau B&B Grilled Veggie Sandwich

Yield: 4 servings

"We serve this recipe in the Harmony Bistro restaurant inside the Fountain Chateau. Both vegetarians and non-vegetarians enjoy it."—Innkeeper

- ¼ cup mayonnaise
- 3 cloves garlic, minced
- 1 Tbsp lemon juice
- 1/8 cup olive oil
- 1 cup sliced red bell peppers
- 1 small zucchini, sliced
- 1 red onion, sliced
- 1 small yellow squash, sliced
- 2 pieces focaccia bread (4x6-inch), split horizontally
- ½ cup crumbled feta cheese

In a bowl, mix the mayonnaise, minced garlic and lemon juice. Set aside in the refrigerator. Preheat skillet sprayed with cooking spray. Brush vegetables with olive oil on each side. Arrange veggies singly in skillet and cook 3 minutes. Turn and cook another 3 minutes. Spread some of the mayo mixture on cut sides of the bread. Sprinkle with cheese. Place in skillet cheese side up and cover with lid 2–3 minutes. This will melt the cheese and warm the bread. Remove from skillet and layer with veggies.

Cream Pitcher B&B Heirloom Tomato Pie

Yield: 1 pie

- 1 cup flour
- ¾ cup yellow cornmeal
- ¾ tsp salt
- 1 stick cold, unsalted butter (cut into ½-inch pieces)
- ¾ cup, plus 3 Tbsp shredded Manchego cheese
- 4 Tbsp ice water
- dried beans (as weights)

Filling

- 2 Tbsp olive oil, divided
- 1 large onion, thinly sliced
- 2¼ lbs. mixed heirloom tomatoes
- ¾ cup shredded mozzarella cheese
- ¼ cup mayonnaise
- 3 Tbsp breadcrumbs
- 3 Tbsp chopped fresh chives
- 3 Tbsp chopped fresh parsley
- 1 tsp chopped fresh thyme
- kosher salt
- freshly ground pepper

Pulse the flour, cornmeal and salt in a food processor to combine. Add the butter and 3 tablespoons Manchego. Pulse until the mixture resembles coarse meal with pea-size bits of butter. Drizzle in 4 tablespoons of ice water and pulse until the dough comes together. Add 1 more tablespoon ice water if necessary. Turn out onto a sheet of plastic wrap and pat into a disk. Wrap and refrigerate until firm, about 45 minutes.

Put the dough between 2 sheets of parchment paper and roll into a 13-inch round. Transfer the dough to a 9½-inch deep-dish pie plate. Fold the overhang under itself and crimp the edges. Pierce the bottom of the crust all over with a fork. Refrigerate until firm, about 20 minutes. Meanwhile, preheat oven to 350°F. Line the crust with foil, then fill with dried beans. Bake until the edges are golden, about 20 minutes. Remove the foil and beans and continue baking until golden all over, 10–15 more minutes. Transfer to a rack to cool.

(Continued next page)

Heirloom Tomato Pie (*Continued*)

For the filling: Heat 1 tablespoon olive oil in a large skillet over medium heat. Add the onion and cook, stirring until golden, about 15 minutes. Let cool. Meanwhile, thinly slice the tomatoes. Toss with 1 teaspoon kosher salt in a colander. Let drain about 30 minutes, gently tossing occasionally.

Increase oven temperature to 375°F. Combine the remaining ¾ cup Manchego, mozzarella, mayonnaise, breadcrumbs, 2 tablespoons each chives and parsley, thyme, ¼ teaspoon each kosher salt and pepper and the sautéed onion in a bowl. Spread in the crust. Arrange the tomatoes on top. Drizzle with remaining 1 tablespoon olive oil and season with pepper. Bake until the tomatoes are browned, about 50 minutes. Top with remaining 1 tablespoon each chives and parsley.

Bay Point Inn
Peanut Stew

Yield: 8 servings

"Our innkeeper, Myles Dannhausen, developed a menu of African specialties while he was a Peace Corps volunteer in Sierra Leone. Once home, Myles introduced his family and friends to African cuisine. Peanut stew is a main course and is a fricassee of chicken and/or meat, flavored and thickened with tomato purée and peanut butter. It may be served with white rice or with skewered chicken/beef."—Innkeeper

- 1 stewing chicken, cut into pieces
- 1 lb. round steak, cubed
- 2 small onions, chopped
- 2 small hot peppers, freshly ground
- 4 cups water
- 1 tsp salt
- ½ cup tomato purée
- ½ cup peanut butter
- pepper
- cayenne pepper
- oregano

Place the cut up chicken, beef cubes, onion, and peppers in a large stew pot with a lid. Add water and 1 teaspoon salt. Cover and simmer until meat and chicken are tender. Stir in the tomato purée and peanut butter. Simmer for 20 minutes. Add seasonings to taste. Serve over plain or Jollof rice.

Tip: Jollof rice is a one-pot rice dish from Africa that includes ingredients like onions, tomatoes, spices and sometimes vegetables and meat.

Sabamba Alpaca Ranch and B&B

Pork Loin with Coriander & Garlic Crust

Yield: 4-6 servings

"This dish is inspired by Elizabeth David, who makes a coriander crust for lamb, and by a dish made at the Heathman Hotel in Portland."—Innkeeper

¼ cup coriander seeds
1 cup fresh bread crumbs
2 large cloves garlic, peeled
½ teaspoon salt
freshly ground pepper
¼ cup extra virgin olive oil, more if needed
1 boneless pork loin (2¼ lbs.)
½ cup water

Preheat oven to 400°F. Crush the coriander seeds in a food processor for about 30 seconds. Add the bread crumbs and garlic and process to combine. With the processor running, add the salt, pepper and ¼ cup olive oil and process just until mixture is combined. Mixture should be moist enough to hold lightly together when pressed. If not, add another tablespoon of oil and continue adding oil until the desired moisture is attained. Place the pork on a rack inside a roasting pan. Press the crumbs on the top, ends and down the sides. Cook until pork is nearly pink in the center (145–150°F) about 1 hour 10 minutes. Let the pork rest for 10 minutes before adding the water to the pan. Reduce to a dark sauce and serve with the pork.

Cream Pitcher B&B

Roast Pork with Sherry Plum Sauce

Yield: 12 servings

- 4 lbs. pork, boneless loin roast
- 2 Tbsp olive oil
- 1 cup dry sherry
- 1 Tbsp ground (dry) mustard
- 2 Tbsp soy sauce
- 1½ tsp dried thyme leaves
- 1¼ tsp ground ginger
- 1 tsp salt
- ¼ tsp pepper
- 3 cloves garlic, finely chopped
- ½ cup plum jam

Trim excess fat from pork. Heat oil in a 10-inch skillet over medium-high heat. Cook pork in oil about 10 minutes, turning occasionally until brown on all sides. Place pork in slow cooker. Mix sherry, mustard, soy sauce, thyme, ginger, salt, pepper and garlic. Pour over pork. Cover and cook on low heat setting 7–9 hours or until pork is tender. Remove pork from cooker. Cover and keep warm. Skim fat from pork juices in cooker, if desired. Stir jam into juices. Cover and cook on high setting about 15 minutes or until jam is melted. Serve with rice.

Bowman's Oak Hill B&B

Stir-Fry Frittata

Yield: 1 pie

"This is a very simple but flavorful dish that my guests who are newlyweds or just very busy women love to have to add to their recipe collections. It is also a huge hit with our vegetarian guests."—Innkeeper

- 1 1-lb. bag frozen stir-fry blend vegetables, thawed
- 2 tsp Mrs. Dash Tomato Basil Garlic or other herb blend seasoning
- 2 cups grated sharp Cheddar cheese
- 7 large eggs
- ½ tsp sea salt
- ½ cup half & half
- 1 Tbsp chopped dry or fresh basil

Preheat oven to 350°F. Spray a 10-inch pie pan with cooking or baking spray. Place stir-fry vegetables in pan and sprinkle with seasoning. Layer cheese over top. Whip eggs, salt and half & half together in a bowl just until blended well. Pour over cheese and vegetables. Sprinkle with basil. Bake for 45 minutes or until set. Check in about 30 minutes and put a slice in the center of the pie with a sharp knife to let the steam from the vegetables out because the cheese will make a delightful crust that will trap it in.

Inn on Hillwind

Veggie Pie

Yield: 4 servings

"This dish showcases our local cheese makers, an industry for which Plymouth is famous."—Innkeeper

2 cups Sargento shredded 4-Cheese Mexican
¼ cup fresh broccoli florets, chopped
¼ cup fresh mushrooms, sliced
¼ cup chopped green onion
¼ cup halved cherry or grape tomatoes
½ cup Bisquick
2 eggs
1 cup milk
tomato, garnish

Preheat oven to 400°F. Grease a 9-inch glass pie plate. Spread 2 cups shredded cheese on bottom. Place broccoli, mushrooms, onion and tomatoes on top of cheese. Set aside. Blend together Bisquick, eggs and milk for 2–3 minutes with electric mixer, making sure Bisquick is dissolved. Pour mixture over vegetables and cheese. Bake for 20–25 minutes. Top of pie should be golden when done. Cut into 4 equal wedges and garnish with slice of tomato.

Tips: Serve with ham, bacon or sausage and fresh baking powder biscuits.

Variations: This recipe works equally well with gluten-free Bisquick. Substitute veggies as desired.

Franklin Street Inn

Wisconsin Cheese Curd & Brat Strata

Yield: 12 servings

"Come to Wisconsin to enjoy our local cuisine—brats and cheese curds!"—Innkeeper

- 6 brats
- 1 loaf French bread (cut into 1½-inch cubes)
- 2 cups mozzarella cheese, shredded
- 2 cups cheese curds
- 1 cup green pepper, diced
- 8 eggs
- 2½ cups milk
- ¼ tsp pepper
- ½ tsp garlic salt
- ¼ tsp dry mustard

Preheat oven to 350°F. Brown brats in a skillet. Cut the skin and remove. Cut into ½-inch pieces. Spray a 9x13-inch pan with cooking spray. Place half of the cubed bread in baking dish. Cover with cheese, brats and peppers. Top with remaining cubed bread. Beat eggs with milk, pepper, garlic salt and mustard. Pour over bread, making sure to coat all the cubes. Cover and refrigerate overnight or at least 4 hours. Bake for 1 hour or until knife inserted in center comes out clean.

Fruit Specialties

Bowman's Oak Hill B&B

Banana Supreme

Yield: 4 servings

"I was serving a baked banana dish in the fall and winter but I wanted one to serve in the warmer months that would be just as interesting, so I came up with this idea."—Innkeeper

4 just-ripe bananas
1 cup orange juice
4–6 oz. vanilla yogurt
3–4 Tbsp granola
¼ cup dried cranberries
mint leaves

Slice 1 banana each into 4 stemmed dessert dishes. Drizzle ¼ cup orange juice over each dish. Make sure each banana is touched with some juice. Place a large spoon of vanilla yogurt over that and sprinkle with granola and cranberries. Top with mint leaves.

Variation: Try using toasted almonds and coconut for a topping instead of the cranberries.

HONEYBEE INN B&B

Blueberries Brûlée

Yield: 1 serving that's easy to multiply

"Delicious and a guest favorite!"—Innkeeper

granola
fresh blueberries
vanilla yogurt
brown sugar
powdered sugar
whipping cream

In a small ramekin or fancy small dish, layer, in order, ½-inch granola, 1-inch blueberries, ¼-inch yogurt and a sprinkly of brown sugar. Use a brûlée torch or put under broiler and lightly broil or torch the brown sugar to crisp as with brûlée. Be careful that brown sugar doesn't catch fire! When done, sprinkle powdered sugar on top with a dollop of whipping cream. Make sure guest goes down through all layers to eat.

Honeybee Inn B&B

Fresh Pineapple with Maple Cream Sauce

Yield: 8–10 servings

"My guests swoon over this simple fruit dish, and it has become our signature fruit dish at the inn. It is not unheard of for grown men to pick up their dish and lick the sauce up!"—Innkeeper

1 fresh pineapple, cut into small chunks
½ cup pure maple syrup
½ cup whipping cream
toasted coconut
whipped cream

Cut up pineapple and set aside. Bring ½ cup pure maple syrup (only works with real) to a low boil. Watch carefully so it doesn't boil over. Let low boil for about 4–5 minutes until slightly thickened. Take off heat and add ½ cup whipping cream and mix well. Refrigerate overnight. In the morning, spoon thickened sauce over pineapple chunks in pretty serving dish. Sprinkle toasted coconut over top lightly. Add a dollop of whipped cream.

Tip: Sauce can be refrigerated for up to 2 weeks.

Inn On Maple

Just Peachy Soup

Yield: 8 servings

1 bag (1 lb. or 1 can) peaches, peeled and sliced
2 cups orange juice
2 Tbsp honey
16 oz. low-fat vanilla yogurt
1–2 cups blueberries, frozen or fresh

Blend peaches in blender. At a lower speed, slowly add juice, honey and yogurt. Drop in blueberries to finished soup.

Pedal'rs Inn B&B

Sautéed Plums with Cardamom

Yield: 4 servings

4 medium or 6 small seasonal plums
2 Tbsp butter
¼ cup sugar
6 cardamom pods
pinch of nutmeg
2 Tbsp Grand Marnier

Rinse fruit. Slice into wedges ½-inch thick. In a skillet, melt butter over medium-high heat. Add plums, sugar, cardamom pods and nutmeg to melted butter. Turn heat to high. Sauté fruit, moving plums around frequently so meat of fruit takes on color while caramelizing. Pluck out pods and discard. Add in liqueur.

Tip: Serve warm over yogurt or top with ice cream, yellow cake or yogurt.

Franklin Victorian Inn

Strawberry Soup

Yield: 6–8 servings

"Great way to use your fresh strawberries and frozen berries. This is a wonderful start to any meal you may have all year."—Innkeeper

- 5 cups fresh strawberries, washed, cleaned and hulled (or 1 bag frozen)
- 1/3 cup white sugar
- ½ tsp almond extract
- 1 Tbsp strawberry Schnapps
- 1 cup heavy whipping cream
- ½ cup 2% milk
- ½ tsp cinnamon
- fresh mint, garnish

Put clean berries in blender. Add sugar, almond extract, Schnapps, whipping cream, milk and cinnamon. Whirl until mixture looks like buttermilk, then pulse a few times more to be sure all ingredients are well blended. Store in refrigerator overnight before serving. Garnish with fresh mint.

Riverview B&B

Erdbeersuppe (Strawberry Soup)

Yield: about 4 servings

"What a chilled treat on a hot summer morning!"—Innkeeper

- 1½ quarts fresh strawberries (or 1½ pkg. frozen)
- 5 Tbsp honey, divided
- 2½ Tbsp cornstarch
- ½ cup orange juice
- ½ cup vanilla yogurt

Wash and slice strawberries, enough to make 3¾ cups. Add 3 tablespoons honey and stir to coat berries evenly. Set aside for about 1 hour. Drain berries, saving about 1½ cups juice. Put juice into a blender and add half the berries for a liquid purée. Heat purée to boiling. Dissolve cornstarch in the orange juice, then stir into the boiling purée. Cook 1–2 minutes until mixture is clear and thick. Cool slightly. Add remaining honey and berries. Chill entirely and serve with yogurt as topping for each bowl.

Phipps Inn B&B

Sweet & Sour Grapefruit

Yield: 4 servings

2 grapefruit, red preferred
¼ cup sour cream
1 Tbsp dark brown sugar
ground nutmeg
4 maraschino cherries with stems

Cut grapefruit in half. Section and place in individual bowls. Warm all 4 grapefruit halves at one time in microwave for 1 minute. Blend sour cream and brown sugar well. Place a tablespoon of the sour cream sauce in the middle of each grapefruit. Warm all four halves again for 30–40 seconds. Sprinkle sparingly with nutmeg. Garnish each half with a cherry.

Westby House Inn & Restaurant

Strawberries with Banana Dressing

Yield: 4 servings

2 ripe bananas, peeled, sliced
1 cup sour cream
¼ cup firmly packed brown sugar
1½ tsp lemon juice
1 cup strawberries
1 cup green grapes

Combine bananas, sour cream, brown sugar and lemon juice in blender. Blend 15–20 seconds until smooth. Refrigerate 2 hours. Cut strawberries and grapes in half lengthwise and combine in a large bowl. Add dressing and toss together gently.

Desserts

Amil's Inn B&B

Almond Bars

Yield: 24 bars

- 1 cup butter
- 2 cups flour
- ½ cup powered sugar

Filling

- 8 oz. cream cheese
- ½ cup sugar
- 2 eggs
- 1 tsp almond extract

Frosting

- 1½ cups powdered sugar
- ¼ cup butter
- 1½ tsp almond extract
- 1 Tbsp milk
- slivered almonds

Preheat oven to 350°F. Mix butter, flour and powdered sugar well. Form crust in a 9x13-inch pan. Bake for 15 minutes.

For the filling: Mix cream cheese, sugar, eggs and almond extract. Spread over crust. Bake another 15 minutes.

For the frosting: Blend powdered sugar, butter, almond extract and milk until smooth. Spread on bars and sprinkle with slivered almonds.

Inn at Lonesome Hollow

Any Berry Cobbler

Yield: 6–8 servings

- ¼ cup butter
- 1¼ cups white sugar, divided
- 1 cup flour
- 2 tsp baking powder
- 1 cup milk
- 3 cups berries

Preheat oven to 350°F. Melt butter in a 9x13-inch baking dish. Mix 1 cup sugar, flour, baking powder and milk. Pour over melted butter. Cover top of batter with fruit (blackberries, raspberries, peaches or rhubarb). Sprinkle ¼ cup (or less) sugar over fruit. Bake about 30 minutes or until batter is golden brown.

Tip: Serve warm with whipped cream or ice cream.

Speckled Hen Inn
Apple Fritters

Yield: 3½ dozen

1 egg, beaten
1 cup finely chopped, unpeeled, cored apples
1 cup milk
¼ cup granulated sugar
¼ tsp salt
1 Tbsp fresh, grated orange peel
3 Tbsp orange juice
½ tsp vanilla
2 cups flour
1 Tbsp baking powder
oil for frying
sifted powdered sugar or a sugar-cinnamon mixture

Combine the egg, apple, milk, sugar, salt, orange peel, orange juice and vanilla in a mixing bowl. Sift together the flour and baking powder. Fold it into the apple mixture, stirring just until all the flour is moistened. Drop batter by rounded teaspoons into deep hot oil. Fry until deep golden brown, about 3 minutes, turning once. Drain the fritters thoroughly. Roll in powdered sugar or a cinnamon-sugar mixture. Serve warm.

Variation: Rather than rolling the cooked fritters in a sugar, try drizzling them with pure Wisconsin maple syrup.

Washington House Inn

Banana Sour Cream Bundt Cake

Yield: 1 Bundt pan

- ½ cup butter
- 1 cup sugar
- 2 eggs
- 1 cup mashed bananas (about 3)
- ½ tsp vanilla
- ½ cup sour cream
- 2 cups flour
- 1 tsp baking powder
- 1 tsp baking soda
- ¼ tsp salt
- ½ cup chopped nuts or chocolate chips (optional)

Preheat oven to 350°F. Cream butter and sugar. Beat in eggs. Mix in bananas, vanilla and sour cream. Sift together flour, baking powder, baking soda and salt. Add to banana mix. Fold in nuts and/or chocolate chips. Pour into a greased and floured 10-cup Bundt pan. Bake for 40 minutes or until toothpick comes out clean.

Tip: For a bigger cake, triple the recipe and cook in two 12-cup tube pans. Bake for 1 hour.

Washington House Inn

Berry Trifle with Yogurt

Yield: 18–20 servings

- 6 cups leftover blueberry or other plain muffins or cake
- 4 cups honey-flavored yogurt
- 2 cans blueberry pie filling
- 2 cups fresh sliced strawberries
- 1 cup fresh raspberries
- 1 cup fresh blackberries
- 1 cup fresh blueberries

Crumble muffins into large crumbs. In a trifle dish, layer half of the crumbs, half of the yogurt, 1 can pie filling and half of the berries. Repeat. Keep chilled until ready to serve. Best when served within 6 hours.

Hillcrest Inn & Carriage House

Black Cherry Merlot Sorbet

Yield: 12 small bowls

- 1 16-oz. can black cherries
- 1 cup Merlot
- ¼ cup sugar
- ½ cup orange juice
- 12 mint leaves, garnish

Combine cherries, Merlot, sugar and orange juice in a blender until puréed. Pour into plastic container, cover and freeze. To serve, scrape with a spoon and place sorbet into small, footed compote bowls. Garnish with mint leaf.

Hamilton House B&B

Boiled Cookies

Yield: 3 dozen

- 2 cups sugar
- 1/3 cup cocoa
- 1 stick butter
- ½ cup milk
- 1 tsp vanilla
- ½ cup peanut butter
- 3 cups quick oats

Combine sugar, cocoa, butter and milk in saucepan over low heat. Bring to a boil and continue boiling for exactly 1½ minutes. This part is important or they won't set up. Remove from heat. Add vanilla, peanut butter and oats. Mix well. Spoon onto wax paper and cool. Try to wait until set before serving!

Fountain Chateau

Butter Cream Eggs

Yield: 15 pieces

- 1 stick butter
- 16 oz. powdered sugar
- 1 tsp vanilla
- 1–2 Tbsp whipping cream
- dipping chocolate

Mix together butter, sugar and vanilla. Mixture will be stiff. Add cream and mix well. Turn out on surface with powder sugar. Knead until smooth. (The more you knead, the smoother the cream.) Shape into balls or eggs. Dip in dipping chocolate. Decorate as desired.

Apple Tree Lane B&B

Caramel Apple Bars

Yield: 36 bars

"We received The Joy of Apples *cookbook from a guest and have found many great recipes in it. The modified caramel apple bars recipe is a favorite!"*—Innkeeper

- 1 cup dark brown sugar, packed
- ½ cup butter, softened
- ¼ cup solid shortening
- 1¾ cups all-purpose flour, plus 3 Tbsp
- 1½ cups quick-cooking oatmeal
- ½ tsp baking soda
- 1 tsp salt
- 4 cups apples, peeled, cored and coarsely chopped (Granny Smith or a combination)
- ½ tsp pure vanilla extract
- 1 14-oz. bag caramels, melted

Preheat oven to 400°F. Mix sugar, butter and shortening in a large bowl until well blended. Stir in 1¾ cups flour, oatmeal, soda and salt. Reserve 2 cups of the mixture and set aside. Press remaining mixture into an ungreased 13x9-inch baking pan.

Mix apples, 3 tablespoons flour and vanilla. Spoon over crumbly mixture. Pour melted caramels over apples. Sprinkle with reserved mixture and press down lightly. Bake 25–35 minutes or until apples are tender and topping is lightly browned. Cool slightly, then cut into bars. Refrigerate leftovers.

St. Croix River Inn Centennial Cupcakes

Yield: 2 dozen

- 1½ cups self-rising flour
- 1¼ cups all-purpose flour
- 1 cup (2 sticks) unsalted butter, softened
- 2 cups sugar
- 4 large eggs, room temperature
- 1 cup milk
- 1 tsp vanilla extract

Frosting

- ¼ stick unsalted butter, room temperature
- 4 oz. plain cream cheese
- 4 oz. tiramisu mascarpone cheese
- 2 cups sifted powdered sugar
- 1 tsp vanilla
- cinnamon-sugar mixture (1 part cinnamon to 3 parts sugar)

Preheat oven to 350°F. Line muffin tins with cupcake papers. In a small bowl, combine the flours. Set aside. In a large bowl, on the medium speed of an electric mixer, cream the butter until smooth. Add the sugar gradually and beat until fluffy, about 3 minutes. Add the eggs 1 at a time, beating well after each addition. Add the flour mixture in 3 parts, alternating with the milk and vanilla. With each addition, beat until the ingredients are incorporated, but do not over beat. Using a rubber spatula, scrape down the batter in the bowl to make sure the ingredients are well blended. Carefully spoon the batter into the cupcake liners, filling them about ¾ full. Bake for 20–25 minutes or until a cake tester inserted into the center of the cupcake comes out clean. Cool the cupcakes in tins for 15 minutes. Remove from the tins and cool completely on a wire rack before icing.

For the frosting: Beat butter vigorously with an electric mixer. Scrape the bowl and add the cream cheese. Beat until combined. Add the sifted powdered sugar and vanilla. Beat until smooth. Add mascarpone cheese. Gently mix until blended. Spread frosting on cupcake and sprinkle with cinnamon-sugar mixture.

Garden Gate B&B
Chocolate Carrot Cake

Yield: 12–16 servings

"A very scrumptious treat for a late-night dessert craving."—Innkeeper

- 2 cups all-purpose flour
- 2 cups sugar
- ½ cup baking cocoa
- 1 tsp baking soda
- ½ tsp salt
- 4 eggs
- 1¼ cups vegetable oil
- 3 cups finely shredded carrots

Frosting

- 1 8-oz. pkg. cream cheese, softened
- ½ cup butter, softened
- 3¾ cups confectioners' sugar
- ¼ cup baking cocoa
- 3 tsp vanilla extract
- ¼ cup chopped walnuts
- ¼ cup semi-sweet chocolate chips

Preheat oven to 350°F. Line two 9-inch round baking pans with waxed paper. Grease the paper and set aside. In a large mixing bowl, combine the flour, sugar, cocoa, baking soda and salt. Add the eggs, oil and carrots; beat until combined. Pour into prepared pans. Bake for 25–30 minutes or until a toothpick inserted near the center comes out clean. Cool for 10 minutes before removing from pans to wire racks to cool completely.

For the frosting: In a large mixing bowl, beat cream cheese and butter until fluffy. Beat in the confectioners' sugar, cocoa and vanilla until smooth. Place one cake layer on a serving plate. Spread with half of the frosting. Repeat layers. Sprinkle with nuts and chocolate chips.

Pedal'rs Inn B&B

Chocolate Sorbet

Yield: 4–6 servings (2–3 ounces)

- 1/3 cup Dutch-process cocoa
- ½ cup baker's sugar
- 1 cup water
- 4 oz. dark chocolate (I use ADM out of Milwaukee)
- salt
- 1 egg white, whisked until foamy

Combine cocoa and sugar. In a small saucepan, whisk water and cocoa/sugar mixture over low heat. Combine well. Raise heat to medium then bring to a boil. Meanwhile, place dark chocolate in glass container. Melt in microwave on high 30 seconds at a time. Be careful not to create hot spots. Stir between intervals until melted. Add melted chocolate and salt to cocoa/sugar mixture in saucepan. Stir thoroughly. Cool in refrigerator. Place in sorbet maker. Process/freeze according to manufacturer's instruction. When sorbet begins forming, add egg white.

Variations: Add small amount (¼ tsp) vanilla or 1 oz. chilled liqueur during processing.

Port Washington Inn Cornmeal Thyme Cookies

Yield: 36–48 cookies

1¾ cups all-purpose flour
1 tsp baking soda
1 cup stone-ground yellow cornmeal
½ tsp salt
8 oz. softened butter
1¼ cups sugar (turbinado or other)
2 eggs
¾ cup dried currants
1 Tbsp finely chopped fresh thyme

Preheat oven to 350°F. Whisk together flour, baking soda, cornmeal and salt. Use an electric mixer on medium speed to cream together butter, sugar and eggs (1 at a time) until fluffy. With the mixer on low speed, add flour mixture, currants and thyme.

Drop rounded balls of dough (approx. 1 tablespoon) 2 inches apart on baking sheets. Bake 10–12 minutes, rotating and switching pan positions halfway through.

Lake Orchard Farm B&B

Cream Cheese Bars

Yield: 16 servings

"A delicious dessert to complement any breakfast."—Innkeeper

2 tubes crescent roll dough (seamless)
2 8-oz. pkg. cream cheese
1 egg yolk (save the white for later)
1 tsp almond extract
1 cup sugar, plus ½ cup for topping

Preheat oven to 350°F. Grease jelly roll pan and press 1 tube of crescent roll dough in bottom of pan. Beat cream cheese, egg yolk, almond extract and sugar. Spread over dough. Spread second tube of dough over top of the cream cheese mixture. Beat egg white until foamy and spread over top with a brush. Sprinkle ½ cup sugar over top. Bake for 35 minutes. Serve warm or chilled.

Port Washington Inn
Fruit Crisp Topping

Yield: 3 (10-inch) deep dish pie plates

"We make all kinds of fruit crisps using this topping. Our idea of a delicious fruit crisp is that the fruit is the star and retains its signature fruit flavor. The crisp topping perfectly complements the baked fruit, adding the texture of the oats and the flavor of the butter without making it overly sweet."—Innkeeper

2 cups turbinado sugar
3 cups unbleached flour
1 lb. butter straight from the freezer
3 cups thick rolled oats

Place sugar and flour in a large food processor and blend together. Cut sticks of butter lengthwise into fourths, then slice. Add butter to dry ingredients and pulse until butter is incorporated into flour and sugar. Small lumps of butter will remain. Add 3 cups oats and pulse just until mixed. Freeze in a container from which it will be easy to scoop out the amount required.

Lake Orchard Farm B&B Grandma's French Apple Cake

Yield: 9 servings

"A family favorite passed down from Grandma Doris. Our apple orchard provides fresh apples for this cake. Delicious served warm or chilled."—Innkeeper

- 6 cups sliced apples, peeled and cored
- 1 tsp cinnamon
- ½ tsp nutmeg

Custard

- 1 cup sugar
- ¾ cup milk
- 2 eggs
- ½ cup Bisquick
- 2 Tbsp softened butter

Topping

- 1 cup Bisquick
- 1/3 cup brown sugar
- 3 Tbsp softened butter

Preheat oven to 325°F. Grease a 9x9-inch baking dish. Place 6 cups sliced apples in bottom of dish. Sprinkle with cinnamon and nutmeg. Beat custard ingredients in mixer until blended. Pour custard mixture over apples. Mix topping ingredients and sprinkle over top of the apples and custard. Bake for 1 hour.

Phipps Inn B&B

Gretchen's Bars

Yield: 48 bars

"When our children were in high school, I was on a school committee with a woman named Gretchen who made these wonderful bars. They are a little like Seven Layer bars only not so rich, so you can eat more of them! We serve dessert with breakfast at the Phipps Inn and one of these bars on a small plate with a smear of caramel syrup is just the right ending."—Innkeeper

8 oz. (approximately 32) caramels (unwrapped of course!)
3 Tbsp butter, plus ¾ cup, melted
3 Tbsp cream or whole milk
1 cup flour
1 cup oatmeal (quick oatmeal, not instant or old-fashioned)
¾ cup brown sugar, packed
tsp baking soda
1 cup chocolate chips (mix semi-sweet and white)
½ cup chopped walnuts

Preheat oven to 350°F. In a double boiler, melt caramels, 3 tsp butter and cream. While this is melting, mix together ¾ cup melted butter, flour, oatmeal, brown sugar and baking soda. Pat ¾ of mixture into a 9x3-inch pan. Bake for 10 minutes.

Remove from oven. Pour caramel mixture carefully over crust. Sprinkle with 1 cup chocolate chips and ½ cup chopped walnuts. Crumble remaining oatmeal mixture over the top. Bake 15 minutes more. Cool completely before cutting.

Lindsay House B&B

Island Bananas

Yield: 4 servings

4 bananas (1 per person)
butter for sautéeing
1 can coconut milk (left in fridge overnight)
2–4 Tbsp powdered sugar (or more if desired for sweetness)
1 tsp vanilla
¼ cup shredded coconut, toasted
¼ cup sliced almonds, toasted
whipped cream

Slice bananas into discs or split down the middle. Sauté in a nonstick pan with some butter for a few minutes, until the sugars begin to caramelize and the bananas begin to brown. Open coconut milk and drain the liquid. Whip the remainder with powdered sugar and vanilla. Toast coconut and almonds in a dry frying pan. Assemble the banana slices/split halves in a shallow bowl or banana split dish. Top with coconut milk, whipped cream and toasted coconut and almonds.

Variation: Enjoy this as a dairy-free treat by using vegetable oil instead of butter.

Sunnyfield Farm B&B

Jewels Under Cake Dessert

Yield: 15 servings

"Guests have asked me to serve only this at breakfast so that they can eat more of it. I have made boxes to go for hiking and biking and I often halve the recipe for smaller groups. The original recipe was a 1991 winner at the Warrens Cranfest cookoff. I found it in a church cookbook."—Innkeeper

20 oz. crushed pineapple
6 cups cranberries, fresh or frozen
3½ cups sugar
3½ Tbsp cornstarch
1 Tbsp vanilla extract
¾ tsp salt
1 box yellow cake mix
1 cup melted butter
1 cup chopped nuts
1 cup coconut

Preheat oven to 325°F. Slightly drain the crushed pineapple and set aside. Mix the cranberries, sugar and cornstarch together in a saucepan over low heat. Cook until the berries are tender, being careful not to burn them. When the mixture is thick, add the vanilla and salt. Pour the mixture into a 9x13-inch baking dish and allow to cool. Pour the drained pineapple over the cooled cranberries. Sprinkle the cake mix over the top and drizzle with butter. Top with nuts and coconut. Bake for 1 hour. Serve warm or cold.

Apple Tree Lane B&B
Lavender Shortbread Cookies

Yield: 2 dozen

"Guests love this recipe and often comment that they have never cooked with lavender!"—Innkeeper

1½ cups butter, softened
2/3 cup white sugar
¼ cup sifted confectioners' sugar
2 Tbsp finely chopped fresh lavender
1½-2 Tbsp chopped fresh mint leaves
2 tsp grated lemon zest
2½ cups all-purpose flour
½ cup cornstarch
¼ tsp salt
powdered sugar

In a medium bowl, cream together the butter, white sugar and confectioners' sugar until light and fluffy. Mix in the lavender, mint and lemon zest. Combine the flour, cornstarch and salt. Mix into the batter until well blended. Divide dough into two balls. Wrap in plastic wrap and flatten to about 1-inch thick. Refrigerate until firm, about 1 hour.

Preheat oven to 325°F. On a lightly floured surface, roll the dough out to ¼-inch thickness. Cut into shapes with cookie cutters and place on cookie sheets. Bake for 18–20 minutes just until cookies begin to brown at the edges. Cool for a few minutes on the baking sheets, then transfer to wire racks to cool completely. Dust lightly with powdered sugar, if desired.

Tips: Experiment to your taste with the amount of lavender, mint and lemon. Also, make sure cookies are at least ¼-inch thick or they will get too brown and crunchy. Watch baking time closely so they do not over bake.

Grapevine Log Cabins B&B

Lemon Poppy Seed Dessert

Yield: 12 servings

"This recipe was just given to me by a good friend in the Bangor Garden Club, of which we're both members."—Innkeeper

- 1 stick of butter
- 1 cup flour
- ¼ cup sugar
- ½ cup chopped pecans (toast if desired)

Filling

- ¾ cup brown sugar, packed
- 1 tsp vanilla
- 2 eggs, well beaten
- 1 cup sour cream
- ¼ cup Durkee poppy seeds

Topping

- 2 cans lemon pie filling
- 1 10-oz. tub Cool Whip, thawed

Preheat oven to 350°F. Mix butter, flour, sugar and nuts. Grease only the bottom of a 9x13-inch glass pan with Crisco. Press the crust into the pan.

For the filling: Beat brown sugar and vanilla into eggs until creamy. Add sour cream and beat slightly. Add poppy seeds. Pour over crust and bake for 25–30 minutes. Let cool and freeze. Remove from freezer and top with lemon pie filling and Cool Whip. Freeze again. Partially thaw and cut into pieces, running a thin-blade knife under hot water between each row. Sprinkle top with poppy seeds and serve.

Tips: Freeze in plastic wrap. Store poppy seeds in freezer.

Brayton B&B

Mini Pineapple Upside Down Cake

Yield: 4 servings

"I stopped using butter as a condiment a couple of years ago and switched to coconut oil which is much better for my health and my waist line. I have learned to add it in many of my desserts for a little extra sweetness. This recipe it works particularly well with."—Innkeeper

- coconut oil or butter
- brown sugar
- 1 small can ring pineapple (save juice)
- 1 egg
- ½ pineapple juice from the canned pineapple
- 3 Tbsp melted butter
- vanilla
- ½ cup flour
- 6 Tbsp sugar
- ½ tsp baking powder
- ⅛ tsp baking soda
- salt
- powdered sugar
- maraschino cherries

Preheat oven to 350°F. Brush 4 small ramekins or custard cups with coconut oil or butter. Sprinkle brown sugar in bottom of each cup. Line each cup with 1 pineapple ring. Whisk egg, pineapple juice, butter and vanilla together. Stir in flour, sugar, baking powder, baking soda and salt. Divide batter among the 4 cups. Bake for 20 minutes. Let cool slightly and flip over on a plate dusted with powdered sugar. Top with a cherry and serve.

Brewery Creek Inn & Brewpub

Old-Fashioned Sour Cream Blackberry Blueberry Pie

Yield: 1 pie

1 unbaked 9-inch pie crust
2 Tbsp lemon juice
2 Tbsp cinnamon
½ tsp allspice
2 cups fresh or frozen blackberries
2 cups fresh or frozen blueberries
1 cup flour
1½ cups sugar
1 cup sour cream

Preheat oven to 350°F. Prepare the shell or simply use a purchased shell. Sprinkle lemon juice, cinnamon and allspice over the fruit. Spread the fruit out evenly into the pie shell. Combine flour and sugar with a whisk. Add sour cream and blend. The mixture will be thick. Spoon over the berries, distributing evenly. Bake for about 1 hour or until the top is golden brown.

Franklin Street Inn Peach Custard

Yield: 12 or more servings

"The extracts used in this recipe make this custard very delicious. This fruit medley keeps very well in the refrigerator for one week."—Innkeeper

- 1/3 cup flour
- 1 cup sugar
- 1/8 tsp salt
- 2 cups milk
- 2 egg yolks
- 2 egg whites
- 1 tsp vanilla extract
- ½ tsp lemon extract
- ½ tsp almond extract
- 3 cups peeled and sliced fresh peaches or sliced canned peaches

Stir flour, sugar and salt together in pan. Add milk and 2 beaten egg yolks. Cook until thickened, stirring constantly. Add vanilla, lemon and almond extracts. Beat 2 egg whites until stiff. Fold into thickened, hot mixture. Place sliced peaches in 2-quart dish. Use a spoon to evenly distribute the peaches. Pour custard mixture over top. Chill and serve.

Heaven Scent B&B Peaches & Cream Dessert

Yield: 15 servings

"I serve this recipe to my guests instead of a fruit cup or baked goods when peaches are in season—fresh peaches are best. The pecan shortbread crust makes it irresistible. I have had many requests for this recipe, which I am happy to share.—Innkeeper

- 1 16-oz. pkg. pecan shortbread cookies, crushed
- ½ cup butter, melted
- 1 cup sugar
- 1 3-oz. pkg. peach gelatin
- 2 Tbsp cornstarch
- 1 12-oz. can lemon-lime soda
- 1 8-oz. pkg. cream cheese, softened
- 1 cup confectioners' sugar
- 1 8-oz. tub frozen whipped topping, thawed
- 3 large peaches, fresh if in season
- 1/3 cup unsweetened pineapple juice

In a small bowl, combine cookie crumbs and butter. Press onto bottom of an ungreased 9x13-inch dish. In a small saucepan, combine sugar, gelatin and cornstarch. Stir in soda until smooth. Bring to a boil. Cook and stir for 5–7 minutes or until slightly thickened. Cool to room temperature, stirring occasionally.

Meanwhile, in a large bowl, beat cream cheese and confectioners' sugar until smooth. Beat in whipped topping until blended. Spread over crust. Combine peaches and pineapple juice. Arrange over cream cheese layer. Pour gelatin mixture over top. Cover and refrigerate overnight.

Hillcrest Inn & Carriage House

Peanut Butter Pie

Yield: 1 pie

"This recipe is a Chocolate City crowd pleaser."—Innkeeper

20 Oreo cookies, crumbled
2 Tbsp butter

Filling

1 8-oz. tub Cool Whip, thawed
1 8-oz. pkg. cream cheese, softened
½ cup sugar
1 Tbsp sea salt
1 cup peanut butter

Topping

1 12-oz. pkg. chocolate chips
¼ cup half & half

Preheat oven to 350°F. Microwave butter and cookies in small glass bowl for 1 minute. Mix well and press into springform pan. Bake for 10 minutes.

For the filling: Blend Cool Whip, cream cheese, sugar, salt and peanut butter together in mixing bowl. Spread over crust.

For the topping: Melt chocolate chips and warm half & half in microwave for 1 minute. Stir until smooth. Pour over filling when cool. Store in refrigerator.

Franklin Street Inn Pumpkin Streusel Bread Pudding

Yield: 12 servings

- 1 cup brown sugar
- ¼ cup flour
- 3 cups milk
- 1 tsp ground cinnamon
- 1 tsp vanilla
- ½ tsp ground nutmeg
- 3 eggs
- 1 15-oz. can pumpkin
- 6 cups cubed day-old French bread
- ½ cup currants or raisins

Streusel

- ⅓ cup flour
- ½ cup brown sugar
- ½ tsp ground cinnamon
- 3 Tbsp butter, softened
- ½ cup pecans, chopped

Bourbon Sauce

- 1 cup butter
- 1 cup confectioners' sugar
- 1 egg
- 2 Tbsp bourbon

Mix brown sugar, flour, milk, cinnamon, vanilla, ground nutmeg, eggs and pumpkin in a large bowl until well blended. Stir in bread cubes and currants/raisins. Let stand 10 minutes. Spoon into a greased 9x13-inch baking pan.

For the streusel: Mix flour, brown sugar, cinnamon, butter and pecans. Sprinkle streusel over bread. Refrigerate overnight.

Next morning, preheat oven to 350°F. Bake bread pudding for 40–50 minutes or until knife inserted in center comes out clean. Let stand 10 minutes.

For the bourbon sauce: Mix butter, sugar, egg and bourbon in a small pan. Heat and stir until sauce just reaches a boil. Remove immediately. Refrigerate or keep warm until ready to serve. Serve bread pudding hot with warm bourbon sauce.

Franklin Victorian B&B

Quick Apple Dumplings

Yield: 8 servings

"This is a wonderfully delicious recipe that is easier to make than you can imagine and it will bring more compliments than you ever thought possible. Friends will think you cooked for hours when you serve this one, and guests love it!"—Innkeeper

2 pkgs. regular crescent rolls
2 large apples, cut into 8 pieces and cored
1 cup white sugar
1 tsp cinnamon
1 stick butter, softened
1 8-oz. can (mini) Mountain Dew
whipped cream or vanilla ice cream
fresh mint, garnish

Preheat oven to 375°F. Roll 1 apple piece into each crescent roll. Place single file in a 9x13-inch glass cake pan. Crumble together white sugar, cinnamon and butter. Sprinkle mixture over apple and crescents rolls in pan. Pour Mountain Dew over the crescent rolls. Bake for about 40 minutes or until golden brown. Top with whipped cream or vanilla ice cream. Garnish with fresh mint.

Brayton B&B
Red Velvet Bread Pudding

Yield: 1 serving

"This recipe came to me when I was experimenting with a red velvet cake recipe and the cake stuck to the bottom of the cake pan. I had all this cake, but not in the form it should be. I started experimenting and came up with this little recipe."—Innkeeper

- 1 red velvet cake, broken into pieces, but not too fine
- 1 tsp or more of amaretto
- 1 whole egg
- 1 egg yolk
- ¼ cup half & half
- ⅛ tsp salt
- ½ tsp vanilla
- ¼ cup powdered sugar
- 3 Tbsp cream cheese

Preheat oven to 350°F. Mix cake pieces, amaretto, eggs, half & half, salt and vanilla together. Place in a soufflé cup. Mix the powdered sugar and cream cheese together. Fold the cream cheese mixture into the cake mixture, slowly and lightly. Bake for 30 minutes until puffed and pretty.

Variation: Instead of amaretto, use amaretto creamer with some cherry juice.

Hillcrest Inn & Carriage House

Rustic Fruit Tart

Yield: 1 pie

1 refrigerator pie pastry (or use your favorite recipe)
3 cups fruit (2 cups thinly sliced, peeled peaches, 1 cup blueberries)
1 cup mascarpone
½ cup sugar
1 Tbsp lemon juice
¼ tsp cinnamon
pinch of nutmeg

Preheat oven to 375°F. Warm crust to room temperature, then place on baking sheet. Mix fruit, mascarpone, sugar, lemon juice, cinnamon and nutmeg. Spoon onto crust. Fold up edges of crust, leaving center open. Bake for 30 minutes. Cool before serving.

Variations: Change the fruit to create seasonally appropriate options. Try strawberry-rhubarb, apples or pear-almond. Be creative and discover your own favorites. This tart is excellent when paired with cinnamon ice cream.

Garden Gate B&B

Scrumptious Chocolate Layer Bars

Yield: Makes 3 dozen

"This recipe is for chocolate lovers!
One bite will have you wanting more. "—Innkeeper

- 1 12-oz. pkg. semi-sweet chocolate chips (1½ cup)
- 1 8-oz. pkg. cream cheese
- 1 5.3-oz. can evaporated milk (2/3 cup)
- 1 cup walnuts, chopped
- 1 tsp almond extract, divided
- 3 cups flour
- 1½ cups sugar
- 1 tsp baking powder
- ½ tsp salt
- 1 cup softened butter or margarine
- 2 eggs
- ½ tsp almond extract

Preheat oven to 375°F. Combine chocolate chips, cream cheese and evaporated milk in a saucepan. Cook over low heat, stirring constantly until chips are melted and smooth. Remove from heat. Stir in 1 cup walnuts and ½ tsp almond extract. Blend well and set aside.

In a large mixing bowl, combine flour, sugar, baking powder, salt, butter, eggs and ½ tsp almond extract. Blend well. Press half of the mixture in 13x9-inch greased pan. Spread on chocolate sauce. Pour the remaining mixture over the filling. Bake for 35–40 minutes. Cool and cut into bars.

Inn on Hillwind
Special Chocolate Chip Cookies

Yield: 2½ dozen

"These scrumptious cookies have been enjoyed by our guests for many years. The previous owner of the inn generously passed on her signature recipe when we purchased the inn a few years ago."—Innkeeper

- 2¼ cups flour
- 1 tsp baking soda
- ½ tsp salt
- 1 cup (2 sticks) butter
- ¾ cup sugar
- ¾ cup brown sugar
- 2 eggs
- 2 tsp vanilla
- 1 cup Ghirardelli semi-sweet chocolate chips
- 1 cup Ghirardelli white chocolate chips
- 1 cup pecans or walnuts, chopped
- 2/3 cup dried cranberries

Preheat oven to 350°F. Mix flour, baking soda and salt and set aside. Cream butter and sugars. Add eggs and vanilla and mix well. Add dry mixture about 1/3 at a time to butter mixture, stirring after each addition. Stir in chips, nuts and dried cranberries. Drop by tablespoonful onto ungreased cookie sheet and bake for about 10–12 minutes.

Tips: To keep cookies from spreading too much while baking, keep butter and batter as cold as possible throughout the mixing process.

Victorian Rose B&B Steamed Cranberry Pudding

Yield: 8–12 servings

"This has been a family favorite for several generations. My B&B guests love this breakfast dessert."—Innkeeper

1⅓ cups flour
½ cup molasses
2 cups chopped cranberries
⅓ cup hot water
2 tsp baking soda
¼ tsp baking powder
½ tsp salt

Sauce

½ cup butter
1 cup sugar
¾ cup cream
1 Tbsp flour

Preheat oven to 350°F. Mix flour, molasses, cranberries, water, baking soda, baking powder and salt together and pour into a greased Bundt pan. Cover with foil and place pan in a larger cake pan with water. This causes the cake to steam. Bake for 1½ hours.

For the sauce: Stir butter, sugar, cream and flour together over medium heat until thickened. Pour over individual servings of steamed pudding.

Innkeeper Cookoff Recipes

Port Washington Inn

Door County Cherry Bread Pudding

Yield: 12 servings

"We first served this bread pudding for a small wedding brunch several years ago and after that it was added to our favorite breakfast recipes. Over and over, guests have raved about it, even some guests who claimed not to be big fans of bread pudding. This recipe has been a keeper!"—Innkeeper

- ¼ cup butter, melted
- 1 loaf of bread, cut into cubes
- 6 large eggs
- 3½ cups milk (2% or any, including some half & half, if desired)
- ½ cup Wisconsin maple syrup
- 1 cup dried Door County cherries
- raw sugar

Sauce

- frozen tart cherries, pitted
- frozen sweet cherries, pitted
- raw sugar

Preheat oven to 450°F. Melt ¼ cup butter in a jelly roll pan. Add the cubed bread to the pan. Place in oven and toast until nicely browned (watch carefully!). While bread cubes are toasting, use a blender to blend the eggs, milk and maple syrup. Place toasted bread cubes into a large bowl and pour the liquid from the blender over them, mixing well. Add this mixture to a previously well-buttered 9x13-inch baking pan. Add more milk (or half & half) so the level of liquid in the pan is approximately equal to the level of the bread. Sprinkle the dried cherries over the top, mixing them throughout the pan. Sprinkle lightly with raw sugar. Bake until the middle is firm and the top is nicely browned (approximately 1 hour).

(Continued next page)

Door County Cherry Bread Pudding *(Continued)*

For the sauce: Purée equal amounts of tart and sweet cherries, sweetened to taste with raw sugar. For a thicker sauce, leave cherries whole and lightly sweetened to create a sauce as they thaw.

Tip: We use two of our small loaves of homemade wheat bread. Make sure you have enough toasted bread cubes to fill a 9x13-inch pan, slightly heaped, as they will be absorbing some of the liquid.

WASHINGTON HOUSE INN

Cherry Pecan Scones with Maple Butter

Yield: 12 scones

"This is a guest favorite and, because it uses dried cherries, it can be made year-round."—Innkeeper

- 3½ cups flour
- ½ cup granulated sugar
- 1 Tbsp baking powder
- ¾ cup butter, softened
- ½ tsp salt (optional)
- 1 cup dried cherries
- 1 cup chopped salted pecans
- ¾ cup buttermilk

Sugar-Cinnamon Topping

- ¼ cup granulated sugar
- 1 tsp cinnamon

Maple Butter

- ½ cup softened butter
- 1 Tbsp maple syrup

Preheat oven to 400°F. Mix together flour, sugar and baking powder. Cut in softened butter until mixture resembles small pebbles. Add salt (optional). Toss in cherries and pecans. Add buttermilk and stir until moistened and a soft dough forms. Knead on a floured surface about 10 times. Roll out to ½-inch thick. Cut out scones into circles with biscuit cutter. Place scones on a lightly sprayed cookie sheet. Mix together sugar-cinnamon topping and sprinkle on scones. Bake for about 20 minutes or until lightly browned. While the scones are baking, blend butter and syrup until creamy. Serve scones with maple butter on the side.

Pedal'rs Inn

Cherry Cordial Panna Cotta

Yield: 6–8 servings

"Panna cotta is a guest favorite. This variation was inspired by a childhood delight—chocolate cherry cordials. This recipe can also be altered to accommodate dietary restrictions."—Innkeeper

- 1 cup tart cherries, pitted and in juice (save juice)
- 4 Tbsp Heering Cherry Liqueur
- 2 cups heavy cream
- 1/3 cup honey
- 1/8 tsp salt
- ½ cup cherry juice, plus 3 Tbsp
- ½ tsp vanilla
- 1 pkg. gelatin
- 4–6 oz. bitter-sweet chocolate

In a small bowl, place cherries in liqueur. Marinate in refrigerator for 1 hour. In a saucepan, combine cream, honey and salt. Drain and save liquid from cherries. Add additional cherry juice to make ½ cup of liquid. Stir into cream mixture. Heat over medium-high heat, stirring occasionally until steam appears. Do not boil. Add in vanilla. In a small ramekin, empty packet of gelatin. Stir in 3 tablespoons of cherry juice. Whisk gelatin into hot cream until dissolved. Pour into serving dishes and chill.

Chop chocolate in bits. Place in microwavable measuring cup. Heat at 30-second intervals until melted, stirring in between. Once thoroughly melted, pour into piping bag. On wax paper–covered tray, pipe out designs. Chill until hardened, about 20 minutes. Place chocolate decoration on top of panna cotta and serve.

Bowman's Oak Hill B&B

Wild Rice Cran-Apple Breakfast Bake

Yield: 4 generous or 8 small portions

"I was inspired to create this breakfast dish after WBBA came out with the 'secret ingredient.' Not having ever cooked with wild rice before, it stretched me a bit, but then that is good for me. When I read that it was actually not a rice but rather a cereal grain, I thought aha! I can do this."—Innkeeper

- 1½ cups cooked wild rice
- ¾ cup raw oatmeal
- 2 large red apples, unpeeled, thinly sliced
- ¾ cup dried cranberries
- ½ cup raisins
- ½ Tbsp cinnamon
- ½ cup chopped nuts (walnuts, pecans or a mixture)
- 2 cups milk
- ¼ cup brown sugar
- ¼ tsp salt
- Tbsp butter
- Low-fat vanilla yogurt, garnish
- pure Wisconsin maple syrup, garnish

Preheat oven to 350°F. In a large bowl, mix rice, oatmeal, sliced apples, cranberries, raisins, cinnamon and nuts. Combine milk, brown sugar, salt and butter in a microwavable bowl and heat until hot. Mix into rice and fruit mixture and place into buttered 2-quart casserole. Cover and bake for 30 minutes. Garnish with low-fat yogurt and drizzle with maple syrup.

Variation: For meat lovers, add a side of sausage with a whole-grain English muffin.

Sunnyfield Farm B&B

Wild Rice Pancake, Cranberry Delight

Yield: 8 servings

- ½ cup wild rice
- 2 cups whole-wheat flour
- 2 tsp baking soda
- ½ tsp baking powder
- 2 eggs
- 2 Tbsp honey
- 2½ cups buttermilk
- 2 Tbsp olive oil
- zest of one orange
- 1 cup minced dried cranberries, raisins or dried cherries

Chutney

- 1 cup water
- ¾ cup sugar
- ½ tsp cinnamon
- ¼ tsp ginger
- ¼ tsp allspice
- ⅛ tsp cloves
- ½ cup vinegar
- ½ cup dried cranberries or raisins
- 1 16-oz. pkg. cranberries (2 cups)
- 1 cup apples, peeled, cored and diced

Cran-Raspberry Syrup

- 1½ cups cran-raspberry juice
- 1½ cups sugar
- ¾ cup Karo syrup

Browned Sage Butter

- 5 Tbsp unsalted butter
- 15–18 sage leaves, broken into small pieces
- ¼ cup low-sodium chicken broth

(Continued next page)

Wild Rice Pancake, Cranberry Delight (*Continued*)

In a large saucepan, place ½ cup wild rice in 2 cups boiling water and cover. Cook for about 45–55 minutes, checking that the water doesn't cook dry. Place whole-wheat flour, baking soda and baking powder in a mixing bowl. Mix in eggs, honey, buttermilk and olive oil. Add 1¼ cups cooled wild rice. Add the orange zest. Add dried cranberries or raisins or dried cherries. Mix until moistened. Place about ¼ cup of batter on hot griddle. Turn when top bubbles. Continue until all the batter has been used.

For the chutney: In a pot, combine the water, sugar, cinnamon, ginger, allspice, cloves, vinegar, cranberries and apples. Bring to a boil and simmer for 10 minutes.

For the syrup: Combine cran-raspberry juice, sugar and Karo syrup. Bring to a boil for about 10 minutes.

For the sage butter: Heat butter on high heat in a frying pan. As soon as it gets hot, add the sage leaves and swirl to coat. Keep cooking until butter turns brown and sage leaves begin to turn brown. Immediately remove from heat.

To serve: Hollow out an orange half. Place two pancakes on plate. Fill the hollowed out orange with chutney. Fill a small pitcher with cran-raspberry syrup. Place pancakes on a plate and drizzle browned sage butter over pancakes.

Speckled Hen Inn
Chicken, Wild Rice and Apple Sausage

Yield: 8 servings

"This is a flavorful but very lean sausage that goes very well with eggs, potatoes and mushrooms for a hearty fall or winter breakfast or brunch. The recipe sounds complicated but it goes together very quickly. The sausage may be baked or sautéed."—Innkeeper

- 2 Tbsp olive oil
- 4 diced shallots
- 1 large tart cooking apple, peeled, cored and diced
- 1 medium onion, diced
- ¼ cup parsley leaves, chopped
- ½ lb. lean ground chicken breast
- 1 tsp salt
- ½ tsp ground white pepper
- ½ cup crushed ice
- 1 lb. chicken thigh meat cut into ¼-inch dice
- 1 cup cooked wild rice (measured after cooking)
- zest of 1 lemon, finely grated
- whole-berry cranberry sauce, garnish

Sauce

- ¼ cup mild Dijon mustard
- ¼ cup sour cream

Heat oil in a heavy sauté pan. Add shallots, apple, onion and parsley. Sauté, stirring frequently until golden brown. Remove from heat. Transfer to a bowl and chill. Place the ground chicken, salt and white pepper in the work bowl of a food processor fitted with a steel blade. Process for 30 seconds. With the machine running, add the ice a bit at a time. Process until combined. Transfer the ground chicken to a bowl and place in the freezer while preparing the other ingredients. Combine the diced chicken thigh meat with the wild rice and lemon peel. Stir in the chilled onion/apple mixture. Fold in the ground chicken mixture until all ingredients are equally distributed.

(Continued next page)

Chicken, Wild Rice and Apple Sausage (*Continued*)

At this point the mixture may be formed into patties and sautéed until browned and cooked through or formed into links by placing ½ cup of mixture onto a square of heavy-duty plastic wrap. Fold the wrap over the sausage and form the sausage link by rolling the plastic wrap and twisting the ends to form a 3-inch link. Continue with the remaining meat mixture. Refrigerate the formed links as they are completed. Poach the plastic-wrapped links in a pan of 160°F water for 12–15 minutes. Remove and drain. Remove the plastic wrap from the links. (The links may be prepared ahead to this point and refrigerated overnight or frozen.) Brown the links in a 350°F oven for 10–12 minutes or sauté in a bit of oil for 4–5 minutes.

For the sauce: Blend mustard and sour cream until smooth. Pipe a squiggle of mustard sauce in a decorative pattern onto a plate. Cut a sausage link into 3 diagonal pieces and arrange on the plate. Garnish with a spoonful of whole-berry cranberry sauce.

Speckled Hen Inn

Wisconsin Breakfast Panini

Yield: 4 servings

"This grilled breakfast sandwich is filled with the bounty of our state: baby Swiss cheese, applewood-smoked bacon, crisp red apple slices, and our homemade cranberry-cherry chutney. This recipe is easily scalable for any number of servings. You will need to use a panini press or heavy skillet to make this."—Innkeeper

8 slices country Italian bread
8 thin slices baby Swiss cheese
8 slices applewood-smoked bacon, cooked until crisp
1 large red crisp apple, cored and thinly sliced
melted butter for grilling
fresh herbs, garnish
apple slices, garnish

Cranberry-Cherry Chutney

1 cup water
1 cup sugar
12 oz. cranberries, fresh or frozen
½ cup cider vinegar
1 cup dried Door County cherries
1 tsp Penzeys Baking Spice
1 apple, peeled, cored and diced

(Continued next page)

Wisconsin Breakfast Panini (*Continued*)

Assemble the sandwiches by stacking the ingredients in the following order: 1 slice bread, 1 slice cheese, 2 slices bacon, apple slices, and another slice of cheese. Spread 1 tablespoon of chutney on the final slice of bread and place it, chutney-side down on the sandwich. Repeat the process for the other 3 sandwiches. Brush the outer side of the bread slices with melted butter. Place in the panini press and grill until the bread is golden brown and the cheese has melted. This may also be done in a heavy skillet by carefully flipping the sandwich to cook on both sides. Cut the sandwiches in half or quarters and serve warm with additional chutney if desired. Garnish with fresh herbs.

For the Chutney: Bring water and sugar to a boil in a medium saucepan. Add cranberries, vinegar, cherries, spice and apple and return to a boil. Reduce heat and simmer 15 minutes, until apple is tender and the cranberries have popped. Cool and refrigerate.

Tips: Panini is often served as a side dish with scrambled eggs with cream cheese and herbs. Garnish with fresh herbs and additional apple slices. It is also great in a breakfast-to-go bag for early-morning departures.

Old Rittenhouse Inn
Wisconsin Cranberry "Borscht" with Bison Strip Steak

Yield: 4 servings

"This entrée was inspired by the individuality of the three main flavors—cranberries, bison and beets—the warmth they create when combined and the color red."—Innkeeper

- 2¼ cups rich beef stock
- 1½ cups peeled red beets, cut into small wedges or large dice
- 3 Tbsp red wine vinegar
- kosher salt and freshly ground pepper, to taste
- 1 carrot, peeled and cut in large dice
- 1½ cups fresh cranberries
- 2 Tbsp sugar
- 1 cup finely shredded cabbage
- 4 Tbsp butter
- 1½ lbs. bison, NY strip loin, neatly trimmed
- kosher salt, to taste
- fresh ground white pepper, to taste
- 4 sprigs fresh thyme
- 2 Tbsp cold butter
- mashed potatoes
- crème fraîche, garnish
- fresh dill, garnish

(Continued next page)

Wisconsin Cranberry "Borscht" with Bison Strip Steak (*Continued*)

In a medium saucepan, bring the stock, beets, vinegar, and a pinch of salt to a boil. Simmer over medium heat until beets are tender, about 25 minutes. This recipe can be done a day in advance up to this point and brought back to a simmer at service time. This is also the perfect time to start preparing the bison. Add the carrots and simmer 5 minutes more. Add the cranberries, sugar and cabbage and simmer 3 minutes. While simmering, swirl in butter, taste and adjust with more sugar, salt and pepper.

Preheat oven to 350°F. Season the bison with salt and pepper. Heat a heavy, oven-proof frying pan until quite hot. Add the thyme and butter to the pan, scraping the brown bits into the butter. Place the steak on top of the thyme sprigs. Place the entire pan in the oven until the meat reaches desired doneness. Recommend rare to medium rare for best flavor and texture, about 10 minutes. Bison is very lean and will cook more quickly than beef. Let rest in a warm place 5 minutes before serving.

To serve: Remove the bison steak to a serving board and slice across the grain. Place a portion of mashed potatoes onto warmed plates. Carefully spoon the borscht onto the center of each plate and arrange the bison over the top, against the potatoes. Top with a dollop of crème fraîche and a sprinkle of fresh dill.

Westby House Inn & Restaurant Waffles with Cranberry Topping & Cinnamon Cream Syrup

Yield: 8 servings

"This combination of cranberries and waffles adds warmth to a fall breakfast. The thin cinnamon cream syrup puts a nice light finish to the meal."—Innkeeper

Topping

- 1 cup fresh or frozen cranberries
- 2 cups tart apples, pared and diced
- 1½ cups sugar
- 1/8 tsp cinnamon
- ¼ tsp nutmeg
- 1/8 tsp ground cloves
- ½ cup water, divided
- 2 Tbsp cornstarch
- ½ cup coarsely broken walnuts, garnish
- 1 cup whipping cream (optional)

Cinnamon Cream Syrup

- 2 cups brown sugar
- ½ cup light corn syrup
- ¼ cup water
- ¾ cup evaporated milk
- 1 tsp vanilla extract
- ½ tsp cinnamon

Make your favorite waffle recipe and bake on a waffle iron. Keep warm until served.

(Continued next page)

Waffles with Cranberry Topping & Cinnamon Cream Syrup (*Continued*)

For the topping: Combine the cranberries, apples, sugar, cinnamon, nutmeg, cloves and ¼ cup water in a medium saucepan. Heat, stirring occasionally, to boiling then cook 5 minutes. Mix the cornstarch into the remaining ¼ cup water to make a smooth slurry. Stir into the cranberry mixture. Cook, stirring constantly, until the mixture thickens and boils. Divide evenly over the waffles.

For the syrup: In a medium saucepan, combine the brown sugar, corn syrup and water. Bring the mixture to a boil and stir for 2 minutes to thicken. Remove from heat and stir in the milk, vanilla and cinnamon. To serve, ladle a small amount onto a serving plate and top with a waffle. Add the cranberry topping to the center of each waffle and ladle with additional syrup. Garnish with walnuts and fresh whipping cream.

Tip: This dish goes well with a side of lime-pepper seasoned bacon.

Special Dietary Recipes (gluten-free, vegan, etc.)

Cream Pitcher B&B

African Sweet Potato & Peanut Stew

Yield: 8 servings

1 Tbsp olive oil
1 medium yellow onion
1 medium green pepper (optional)
1 large garlic clove
1 Tbsp brown sugar
1 tsp grated ginger
½ tsp cinnamon
½ tsp cumin
¼ tsp cayenne
1½ lbs. sweet potatoes, peeled and cut into ½-inch cubes
1 15 oz. can tomato juice
1½ cups vegetable stock
salt
1 15-oz. can kidney (or red) beans
2 Tbsp smooth peanut butter
½ cup chopped dry roasted peanuts

Heat oil and sauté onion until soft. Add green pepper and garlic. Cover and cook until soft. Stir in sugar, ginger, cinnamon, cumin and cayenne. Cook for 30 seconds. Add sweet potatoes and stir to coat. Stir in tomato juice, vegetable stock and salt, to taste. Bring to a boil and reduce to a simmer until sweet potatoes are soft, about 30 minutes. After about 20 minutes, add the beans. Place the peanut butter in a small bowl and add ¼ cup broth to thin. Add to the stew pot. For a thicker stew, purée a cup or two of the stew and return it to the pot. Sprinkle with chopped peanuts before serving.

Dobranoc Inn
Cherry Pie Oats

Yield: 2 servings

- ½ cup oats, steel-cut
- 2 cups water
- ½ tsp salt
- ¼ tsp cinnamon
- 1 cup frozen cherries, unsweetened
- ½ tsp vanilla extract

Combine the oats, water, salt and cinnamon in a medium saucepan. Bring to a boil and reduce heat to very low. Cover and cook 25 minutes. While oats are cooking, remove cherries from freezer and cut each in half while frozen. Allow them to thaw a little until oats have cooked for 25 minutes. Stir in the cherries and vanilla extract. Cover and cook until oats are tender and thick, about 10–15 more minutes. Serve with your favorite sweetener.

Speckled Hen Inn

Coconut Basmati Rice Pudding

Yield: 8–10 servings

"This recipe was adapted from the original to be gluten and dairy free. It is sweet enough to be served as a dessert but not so sweet that it couldn't be served as a cereal-based entrée. Grilled pineapple is wonderful with this pudding."—Innkeeper

- 3 cups water
- 1 cup basmati rice
- 1 cup sugar, plus 2 Tbsp
- 2 large eggs
- 2 large egg yolks
- 3 Tbsp cornstarch
- 4 tsp vanilla extract
- 2½ cups unsweetened coconut milk
- 1 tsp salt
- 1 cup shredded coconut, toasted

Bring 3 cups water to a boil in a heavy, medium saucepan. Add the rice and reduce the heat to medium. Simmer uncovered until very tender, about 18 minutes. Drain if necessary.

Whisk ½ cup plus 1 tablespoon sugar, eggs, egg yolks, cornstarch and vanilla in a large bowl to combine. Bring coconut milk, remaining ½ cup plus 1 tablespoon sugar and salt to a boil in a heavy, medium saucepan. Pour over the egg-sugar mixture, whisking constantly. Strain the mixture back into the saucepan and bring to a boil over medium heat. Whisk gently until thickened. Remove from heat and fold in the cooked rice. Add all but ¼ cup of the toasted coconut.

Tips: To serve as a cereal course, keep and serve the pudding warm, topped with some of the remaining toasted coconut. To serve as a dessert, chill for at least 4 hours and serve with toasted coconut topping and perhaps some puréed tropical fruit.

Pedal'rs Inn B&B
Coconut Flour Pancakes

Yield: 4 servings

4	farm eggs, room temp
1–1¼	cups coconut milk
2	tsp pure vanilla extract
⅛	tsp Truvia (or 1 Tbsp honey)
½	cup coconut flour
1	tsp baking soda
½	tsp sea salt
½	tsp of xanthan gum
	coconut oil or gluten-free/dairy-free cooking spray
	butter, coconut butter, honey, syrup or fruit, garnish

Preheat griddle or nonstick pan over medium-low heat. In a small bowl, beat eggs to frothy stage. Stir in coconut milk, extract and sweetener, reserving ¼ milk. In a medium bowl, whisk coconut flour, baking soda, salt and gum together. Add egg/milk mixture into dry ingredients. Stir until flour is incorporated. If batter is too thick, add reserved coconut milk. Coat cooking surface with oil or spray. Ladle 3–4 tablespoons of batter onto pan for each pancake to make somewhat thick 2-inch pancakes. Cook for 3 minutes on each side until the bottom is brown. Flip and cook additional 3 minutes. Serve hot with butter, coconut butter, honey, syrup or fruit.

Brayton B&B

Dairy-Free Banana Bread Oatmeal

Yield: 1 serving

"I have a guest that visits us for a few days once a year. He cannot have any dairy products, including eggs. Every year, I try to come up with a few new recipes just for him that he can take home and make himself."—Innkeeper

- 1 cup water
- 1/8 tsp salt
- ¾ cup old-fashioned oatmeal
- 1 small banana (mashed)
- 2 Tbsp brown sugar
- ¼ tsp pumpkin pie spice
- 1½ Tbsp maple syrup
- almond milk (optional)

Bring water and salt to a rapid boil in a saucepan. Add oatmeal and bring to a boil. Add banana, brown sugar and pumpkin pie spice. Turn down heat to medium and cook for 5 minutes, stirring often. Remove pan from heat and stir in maple syrup. Cover and let sit for 3 minutes. Serve in a bowl with almond milk or on the side.

Lake Orchard Farm B&B

Eggs Florentine

Yield: 8 servings

"A delicious gluten-free option!"—Innkeeper

- 12 eggs
- ¼ cup butter, softened
- 1 lb. cottage cheese
- ½ lb. Swiss cheese, grated
- ½ lb. feta cheese, crumbled
- 1 pkg. frozen chopped spinach, thawed, drained, squeeze out all the water
- ½ tsp nutmeg
- 1 lb. bacon, crumbled

Preheat oven to 350°F. Grease a 9x13-inch casserole dish. Beat eggs slightly. Add butter and cheeses, mix well. Add spinach and nutmeg. Pour into casserole and bake 1 hour or until knife inserted in center comes out clean. Top with crumbled bacon during last 10 minutes of baking.

Lake Orchard Farm B&B Garbanzo Bean Chocolate Cake

Yield: 12 servings

"A delicious gluten-free option!"—Innkeeper

1½ cups semi-sweet chocolate chips
4 eggs
1 19-oz. can garbanzo beans, rinsed and drained
¾ cup white sugar
½ tsp baking powder
1 Tbsp powdered sugar

Preheat oven to 350°F. Grease a 9-inch round cake pan. Place chocolate chips into a microwavable bowl. Cook in microwave for 2 minutes, stirring every 20 seconds after the first minute, until chocolate is melted and smooth. Or, melt in a small sauce pot on the stove top. Combine the eggs and beans in the bowl of a food processor until smooth. Add the sugar and baking powder and pulse to blend. Pour in the melted chocolate and blend until smooth, scraping down the sides to make sure it is completely mixed. Transfer batter to the prepared cake pan. Bake 40 minutes or until knife inserted in the center comes out clean. Cool on a wire rack for 10–15 minutes. Dust with powdered sugar just before serving.

Pine Grove Park B&B Guest House

Gluten-Free Cherry Clafoutis with Almond Crème

Yield: 4 servings

- 8 oz. frozen or fresh pitted cherries
- 2/3 cup sugar, divided
- ½ tsp fresh lemon zest
- 4 egg yolks (save whites)
- 6 Tbsp gluten-free all-purpose flour
- 2 tsp vanilla extract
- 1 cup heavy cream
- ½ tsp salt

Almond Crème

- ½ cup sour cream
- ½ cup heavy cream
- ½ cup sugar
- ½ tsp almond extract

Preheat oven to 375°F. Mix cherries, 1/3 cup sugar and lemon zest in a bowl. Let stand. Blend remaining 1/3 cup sugar and egg yolks with an electric mixer until ribbon forms. Blend in flour, vanilla and cream.

In a separate bowl, whisk the egg whites and ½ teaspoon salt for about 30 seconds until foamy. Add the egg whites to the batter and blend with the electric mixer until incorporated. Butter a 10-inch round baking dish. Pour the cherry mixture in the bottom and spread around. Pour the batter over the top and bake for 35 minutes or until a toothpick comes out clean.

For the almond crème: In a food processor, blend the sour cream, heavy cream, sugar and almond extract until thickened. Add a dollop to each serving.

Port Washington Inn Gluten-Free Cornbread

Yield: 10-inch pie

"Several guests who are restricted to a gluten-free diet have happily taken this recipe home with them. Everyone who loves corn loves this cornbread!"—Innkeeper

- 2 Tbsp butter
- 10 oz. fresh, frozen, or canned corn
- 1¾ cups yellow cornmeal
- 1 tsp baking powder
- ½ tsp baking soda
- 1 tsp salt
- 2 eggs, beaten
- 2 cups buttermilk
- ¼ cup melted butter

Preheat oven to 350°F. Melt 2 tablespoons butter in a 10-inch deep pie plate. If using frozen corn, add corn and bake for 15 minutes, stirring once. If using fresh or drained canned corn, simply mix the corn with the melted butter in the pie plate. Combine cornmeal, baking powder, baking soda and salt in a mixing bowl. Combine beaten eggs and buttermilk. Fold into dry ingredients. Fold in ¼ cup melted butter to finish the batter. Add the batter to the buttered corn in the pie plate. Mix slightly to distribute the corn through the batter. Bake until nicely browned, about 1 hour, but check earlier.

Tips: Serve with honey butter (equal parts honey and butter whipped together), Wisconsin maple syrup and cranberry-orange sauce.

Oscar H Hanson House B&B

Pain au Chocolat

Yield: 8 pastries

"This is our Midwest version of a French classic, chocolate in puff pastry. Chocolate is a great morning starter. In fact, I've heard that we need a little bit of chocolate every day. Make it for people you love who are following a vegan, vegetarian, dairy-free or nut-free diet. It is also a fun family recipe for beginning chefs."—Innkeeper

1 sheet, puff pastry
1 Tbsp water
egg yolk
½ cup Enjoy Life chocolate chips

Preheat oven to 425°F. Line a large cookie sheet with parchment paper. Unfold pastry sheet and press seams together. Roll dough to a 16x12-inch rectangle and cut into eight 6x4-inch pieces. Mix water and egg yolk together in a small bowl and set aside. Place just less than 1 tablespoon of Enjoy Life chocolate chips at one end of each strip. Brush the other end with water. Loosely roll up each pastry. Place on the cookie sheet and brush with egg yolk and water mixture. Bake for 15–20 minutes until puffy and golden.

Oscar H. Hanson House B&B

Polenta Soufflé with Greens & Herbs

Yield: 9x13-inch pan

"I've tried other cornmeals. The white cornmeal, however, gives the best creamy texture and serves as a pearly white pillow for the greens and herbs. Serve this with a mixed fruit salad and bacon and a chocolate finish. This recipe is gluten free and vegetarian."—Innkeeper

Greens

½ lb. mixed greens such as spinach, stems removed
4 Tbsp unsalted butter, plus extra for pan
½ sweet Vidalia onion, chopped
1 clove garlic, crushed
¼ cup vegetable stock

Polenta

1½ cups whole milk
½ cup heavy cream
¾ cup white cornmeal
3 green (spring) onions, chopped, white and pale green parts only
1½ tsp fresh thyme leaves, stems removed
3 leaves fresh basil, chiffonade
salt and pepper to taste
½ cup Cheddar cheese

Soufflé

3 large eggs, separated
½ cup grated Parmesan cheese

Preheat oven to 350°F. Spray a 9x13-inch pan with nonstick cooking spray. Place parchment on the bottom and spray the parchment. Set aside.

(Continued next page)

Polenta Soufflé with Greens & Herbs *(Continued)*

For the greens: Stack 5 or 6 leaves of the greens on top of one another and roll up tightly. Cut on a diagonal into thin strips. Repeat with the remaining greens. In a large frying pan over medium heat, melt 4 tablespoons butter. Add the greens, onions and garlic and cook, stirring occasionally, until the greens are wilted, about 5–10 minutes. Add the broth. Reduce heat to medium-low. Cover partially and cook until the greens are tender, about 10–20 minutes. Remove from heat and let cool. Pour the greens into a sieve and drain well, pressing out any excess liquid. Recipe can be prepared up to this point the night before. Measure other ingredients for easy prep in the morning. Reheat greens in the microwave in the morning before adding to the grits mixture. Transfer the greens to a large bowl.

For the polenta: In a medium saucepan over medium heat, bring milk and cream to simmer. Slowly stir in the cornmeal, green onions, thyme and basil. Season with salt and pepper. Reduce heat to low, cover and cook stirring frequently until grits are soft and liquid is absorbed, about 20 minutes. (Note: the white cornmeal finishes cooking in less than 5 minutes.) Remove from heat and stir in the Cheddar cheese. Spoon hot grits into bowl with greens and stir well to combine.

For the soufflé: In a small bowl, lightly beat the egg yolks with a fork and quickly stir into the cornmeal mixture. In a large bowl, using an electric mixer on high speed, beat the egg whites until stiff. Stir ¼ of the beaten egg whites into the cornmeal mixture. Using a spatula, gently fold the remaining egg whites into the lightened cornmeal mixture. Pour into prepared pan. Sprinkle with Parmesan cheese. Bake until puffed and golden, about 40 minutes. Cut into portions and serve at once.

Tip: This dish tastes great reheated.

Crystal River Inn B&B

Radical Hash

Yield: 6–8 servings

"This dish was named by Robert, who is a physicist and loves to play with words. Because parsnips, sweet potatoes and onions are all root vegetables, he thought it would be fun to call it 'Radical Hash' since 'radical' means 'root.' It's a colorful dish and guests have fun guessing the vegetables."—Innkeeper

1 cup parsnip, diced small
1 cup sweet potato, diced small
oil, olive or olive/chili mixture
1 cup onion, chopped
1 cup zucchini, cut in ¼ and sliced
1–2 tsp Penzeys Fox Point Seasoning (or herb mix to taste)
black pepper
salt

Sauté parsnip and sweet potato in oil until slightly tender (al dente). Add onion and cook until translucent. Add zucchini and cook just enough for the zucchini to get al dente.

Season with Penzeys Fox Point Seasoning and black pepper. Toss and serve.

Tips: This dish scales up and down well and substitutions are fine. It's excellent with scrambled eggs. (Make a "loaf" of the scrambled eggs or make a rolled omelet. Cut an opening the long way on the eggs and place veggies in the cut.)

Oscar H. Hanson House B&B

Raw Brownie

Yield: 6x10-inch pan

"Everyone loves this brownie. I like this recipe because you can make it without ever turning on the oven. The mousse has the tastes and textures of a rich chocolate ganache. Very few will guess it's avocados that create the heavenly creamy frosting. This brownie can be served to individuals following a gluten-free, vegetarian, vegan or raw diet."—Innkeeper

- 1 cup walnuts
- 1 cup dates
- ¼ cup raw cacao powder

Brownie Mousse

- 2 avocados, large or 3 small, peeled and pits removed
- 1–6 Tbsp raw honey, depending on level of sweetness
- ¼ cup raw cacao powder
- 1 pinch of Himalayan salt
- 1 pinch of cinnamon
- 2 Tbsp coconut oil
- 1 tsp vanilla extract

Line a 6x10-inch pan with clear plastic wrap. For the brownie base: Grind the walnuts, dates and cacao powder in a food processor. Process until it forms a paste with granules, not smooth. The nuts should be visible. With the back of a large spoon, firmly press brownie base into prepared pan. Set the base aside. No need to clean to bowl of the food processor.

For the brownie mousse: Place avocadoes, 1 tablespoon honey, cacao powder, salt, cinnamon, coconut oil and vanilla in the food processor. Process until it forms a smooth paste. Taste and add honey until desired sweetness is reached. Spread the mousse over the brownie base. Cover with plastic wrap and freeze for at least 1 hour. Remove from freezer a few minutes before serving.

Oscar H. Hanson House B&B

Savory Quinoa Salad

Yield: 8 servings

"Is it a salad? Is it a meal? No, it's a breakfast entrée. Serve this warm or cold for those who are following a vegetarian, vegan, gluten-free or perhaps a raw diet. Quinoa is an ancient grain that some following a raw diet will consume cooked. Keep it vegan by using vegetable broth."—Innkeeper

- 1 cup uncooked quinoa, thoroughly rinsed
- 2–3 cups vegetable broth
- 1 cup fresh green beans, trimmed and cut into bite-size pieces
- 1 cup cherry tomatoes, halved
- ¼ cup small basil leaves
- 1 Tbsp chopped flat-leaf parsley
- 2 Tbsp cilantro sprigs
- 1 Tbsp snipped chives

Dressing

- 3 Tbsp olive oil (extra-virgin cold-pressed)
- 2 Tbsp lemon juice, fresh squeezed
- 1 clove garlic, peeled and crushed
- 1 tsp Dijon mustard
- ½ tsp Himalayan salt
- freshly ground black pepper, to taste

Rinse uncooked quinoa in cool water. Cook the grain in plenty of gently boiling vegetable broth for about 12–15 minutes or until softened. (Note: Organic quinoa may take a few minutes longer.) Place cooked quinoa into a fine sieve. Make several steam holes through the grain with a skewer, and let drain.

For the dressing: In a large bowl, whisk oil, lemon juice, garlic and mustard together with salt and plenty of black pepper. Add quinoa and toss to coat with dressing. Before serving, stir in green beans, tomatoes and herbs. Serve immediately.

Honeybee Inn B&B

Sailor Jack Vegan Muffins

Yield: 2½ dozen

- 2 cups sugar
- 2 Tbsp cinnamon
- 2¼ tsp salt
- 1½ tsp nutmeg
- 1 tsp allspice
- 1 tsp cloves
- 2½ cups water, divided
- ¾–1 cup raisins
- 2½ cups all-purpose flour
- 2½ cups cake flour
- 1 Tbsp baking soda
- 1½ tsp baking powder
- 1⅔ cups vegetable oil
- 3 Tbsp honey (optional)

Preheat oven to 375°F. Mix together in a large saucepan the sugar, cinnamon, salt, nutmeg, allspice and cloves. Add 2 cups of water and raisins. Bring mixture to a slow boil over low heat. Remove from heat and let stand overnight. (In the morning, it will look like thick slime.)

On the second day, mix together flours, baking soda and baking powder. Add oil, remaining ½ cup water and honey, if desired. Combine two mixtures and mix well. Grease muffin tins with shortening and dust with flour. Fill cups no more than ¾ full with batter. Bake until muffins test done, 20–25 minutes. Remove from pans while still hot and place on a cooling rack. Glaze with powdered sugar icing if desired.

Tips: Don't be too concerned about over mixing as with regular muffins. These are more like a cake. It takes time to stir the two mixtures together to get out the lumps.

Hamilton House B&B

Spanish Omelet

Yield: 8 servings

"This recipe was given to me by my mother who learned how to prepare it in a little shop in Spain. This is great when you have a house full of guests with various dietary restrictions. It is best prepared the night before. Europeans typically serve it a at room temperature, but here in the Midwest, I find it best to reheat and top with a little Parmesan cheese."—Innkeeper

- 2½ lbs. Yukon gold potatoes (or any), thinly sliced
- 1 onion
- salt to taste
- 4 eggs, well beaten
- vegetable oil, as needed
- salsa, garnish
- herbs, garnish
- Parmesan cheese, garnish

Cook potatoes and onion in large heavy skillet in plenty of oil until tender. Remove from heat. Cool in a large bowl. Add salt and eggs. Mix and return to well-oiled pan. Brown on first side until cooked through. Flip and brown second side. Garnish with salsa or herbs and Parmesan cheese.

Red Forest B&B
Tofu Asparagus Scramble

Yield: 2 servings

"After 22 years, I just had my first couple that requested a vegan breakfast. I thought, 'I can do this.' I went to vegan.com and looked at how they were using different ingredients to make a vegan breakfast. That morning I served an asparagus quiche to our other guests. I used all of the same vegetables and put them over a tofu scramble. The vegan guests loved it and were so pleased that I made the effort to accommodate their request."—Innkeeper

- 1 10-oz. block of tofu
- 1 cup frozen shredded hash brown potatoes
- 2 Tbsp diced onion
- 1 small tomato, seeded and chopped
- 1 cup chopped asparagus
- 1 cup chopped fresh mushrooms
- season salt
- salt
- pepper
- crushed red pepper
- dill weed
- butter flavored grape seed oil or olive oil

Rinse and drain tofu. Place on a paper towel to drain. Brown hash browns and onion in a little grape seed oil. Sauté tomatoes, asparagus and mushrooms in a separate pan with a little grape seed oil. Season to taste. In a medium sauté pan, heat about 2 tablespoons of grape seed oil. Flake and crumble tofu into pan. Add season salt, salt, pepper, crushed red pepper and dill weed to taste. Cook tofu until it starts to brown. (It will sort of look like scrambled eggs.) Serve tofu topped with hash browns and vegetables.

Tips: When serving vegans, we like the Sunny Millet Loaf from Natural Ovens Bakery in Manitowoc.

Dobranoc Inn

Uncle Mike's Baked Apple Oatmeal

Yield: 6 servings

- 2⅔ cups old-fashioned oats
- ½ cup dried cranberries
- 4 cups milk
- ⅓ cup packed brown sugar
- 2 Tbsp butter, melted
- 1 tsp ground cinnamon
- ¼ tsp salt
- 2 cups apples, chopped
- ½ cup walnuts, chopped

Preheat oven to 350°F. Mix oats, dried cranberries, milk, brown sugar, butter, cinnamon, salt and apples in a 2-quart casserole dish. Bake uncovered for 40–45 minutes or until most of the liquid is absorbed. Top with walnuts prior to serving.

ALPHABETICAL LISTING OF BED & BREAKFASTS

Recipe Index

A

B

C

D

E

F

G

H

I

Q

R

S